PATTERN
AND
PLACE

An introduction to the mathematics of geography

K. E. SELKIRK

School of Education,
University of Nottingham

CAMBRIDGE UNIVERSITY PRESS
Cambridge
London   New York   New Rochelle
Melbourne   Sydney

Published by the Press Syndicate of the University of Cambridge
The Pitt Building, Trumpington Street, Cambridge CB2 1RP
32 East 57th Street, New York, NY 10022, USA
296 Beaconsfield Parade, Middle Park, Melbourne 3206, Australia

First published 1982

Printed in Hong Kong by Wing King Tong

Library of Congress catalogue card number: 81-3847

British Library catologuing in publication data
Selkirk, K. E.
Pattern and place.
1. Geography - Mathematics
I. Title
510'.2491   G70.23
ISBN 0 521 28208 X

Contents

Preface

This is a book which relates the two fields of human endeavour which have always held the most interest for me. The necessities of the school curriculum forced me to abandon geography at the age of sixteen, and it was not until 1973 that the Schools Council Project: *The Mathematics Curriculum - A Critical Review* allowed me to take it up again in a formal way when I became leader of the subject-oriented group on geography and economics. I owe a debt to the other members of that group: Mr J.R.A. Cook, Mr D.S. Gibbons, Mr T.J. Heard, Mr B. Hughes, Mr P. Lowther and Mr D.R.F. Walker, as well as various groups of teachers whose names are unknown to me and who criticised our work. The outcome was chapters 6 and 7 of *Mathematics Across the Curriculum* edited by John Ling. To him and to the members of the central project team, especially Mr G.R.H. Boys and Mrs J.A. Gadsden, I am particularly grateful.

More recently, I have been grateful for help and encouragement received from members of the Geographical Association/Mathematical Association Joint Committee, especially Mr V. Tidswell for helpful suggestions. I must also thank Mr J. Baker of the Open University who offered help and encouragement, and Mr N. Grenyer and Professor H. Burkhardt who read the manuscript and made detailed criticisms. The responsibility for the content is, however, my own. I owe particular debts to Mr John Hersee of the School Mathematics Project for his encouragement and help in the publication of this book, to Mrs Angela Fullerton who typed the final manuscript, and to Mr Tony Seddon of the Cambridge University Press.

Finally I must thank my wife Jenny for her continual encouragement. Together with my three children and my brother-in-law she has had to endure my continual preoccupation with other things.

K.E. Selkirk,
Bunny,
Nottingham

Introduction

'Perhaps this age of specialists is in need of creative trespassers.'

Arthur Koestler, 1968, *The Sleepwalker*

0.1. Patterns

This book is about patterns in space which relate the two subjects of mathematics and geography. It is, as Koestler puts it, an act of 'creative trespassing' by a mathematician in the field of geography. This means that the approach is rather different from that adopted by many geographers, since the aim is mathematical rather than geographical cohesion. The hope is that by adopting this approach, geographers will understand more clearly the ways in which mathematics can throw light on the patterns they observe in the real world, while at the same time mathematicians can see how their own subject can be applied to geography without having to delve deeply into specialised geographical books.

0.2. Content of the book

There were three main criteria in the selection of material for this book. Firstly the mathematical level should not be substantially greater than that attained by someone who has completed a main school mathematics course up to the age of sixteen; in cases where the content is not likely to have been met on such a course then an explanation is given. Secondly the content should be relevant to the idea of pattern in space, thus excluding computing, as well as much arithmetic and most statistics. Finally the content should be of both mathematical and geographical interest so that some topics in geography are thereby excluded because of the obviously straightforward nature of their mathematics.

The book splits into two parts, the first entitled 'Concepts' and the second 'Models'. The division between them is to some extent arbitrary, but nevertheless indicates a shift in emphasis from the passive description of geographical ideas by mathematical concepts to the more active approach embodied in the ideas of a mathematical model.

0.3. Intended readership

There is always a danger that in stating the intended readership of a book, a wider audience will be excluded. There are sections of this book which will appeal to the economist, the historian, the sociologist, the chemist and the environmentalist. Indeed anyone to whom a map is more than just a means of finding one's way to a destination as painlessly as possible, will discover ideas of interest in the diagrams and wish to follow them up in the text.

However, the main target audience is, obviously, both geographers and mathematicians. Firstly teachers will find that their perspective of their own subject will be enriched by an understanding of how it relates to a second discipline, and will find ideas which can be developed with pupils from the age of nine or so right up to college and early undergraduate level. At the top end of the range the book can be read directly by students, especially by those at secondary school who intend to go on to higher education, or are already on such a course. At many levels there should be plenty of ideas which might initiate projects and investigations. Finally the book might serve as an example of inter-disciplinary work in both the environmental and educational areas, breaking down the barriers which tend to be erected between subject areas.

0.4. Using the book

Books should be read for enjoyment, remembering that ultimate enjoyment often entails hard work. This is not a course book, and many readers will not wish to read it in its entirety. While it is sensible to pick out the sections which are most interesting, a word of warning should be struck at this point. Many books about mathematics have a clear development, and dipping into later chapters can present problems. Part 1 has such a structure, and while some readers might find it easy going, they would still be wise to skim through it to pick up some of the ideas which are developed later. In part 2 many chapters or groups of chapters can be read independently, and the reader should turn to the chapter introductions for guidance.

Above all, this book is intended to be practical. If the reader is not inspired to follow up some of the ideas suggested for himself or herself in a new context, then it will have failed in its purpose. For this reason many of the practical examples have used readily available data from maps, gazetteers, road-books and atlases. For some exercises mathematical equipment will be needed, mainly compasses (as opposed to compass), protractors, rulers and patterned papers, particularly graph paper and paper with square and triangle patterns. Your friendly neighbourhood mathematics teacher may be able to help you with these.

Each reader will wish to carry out only a few of the exercises, and some are, indeed, more suitable for group than for individual work. Perhaps the most important point with most of the exercises is the interpretation of the results; there must be an attempt to link these to the real world. Mathematically inclined readers in particular will be tempted to overlook this point. While the book tries to set a good example here, space frequently prevents extended explanations of the examples. Many exercises will suggest further problems for investigation, and the reader should, if possible, follow these up, and thereby gain research experience of a humble, though none the less real, nature.

0.5. Fear of mathematics

A few words of comfort might be helpful to those who find the mere sight of a formula enough to 'turn them off'. Do not be afraid to skip passages which you cannot understand; even competent mathematicians have to learn to do this. If you find later you need to follow up the details, your very need will motivate your efforts to understand. If you still have difficulties, remember that mathematical understanding does not always come easily even to those practised in it; that a page of mathematics needs to be read with a pencil and paper handy; and that it will take much longer to read than a page of ordinary text. If often helps to follow through a numerical example in the text with one of your own using different figures. You can then sort out arithmetical difficulties which tend to impede understanding of the underlying concepts. An electronic calculator will take much of the sting out of the arithmetic and should be used wherever convenient. One with a square root facility is particularly useful, especially for readers who might wish to move on to study statistics at a later date.

Some chapters have a rather heavier mathematical content, notably 9, 21 and 30. Geographers should bear with these, omitting them if they wish; they are included partly for their particular interest to mathematicians.

Further reading

(General treatments at all levels, many including brief references to topics in later chapters)
Abler, Adams and Gould, 1972, pp. 3–148
Cole, 1969b
Cole and Beynon, 1968a, 1968b, 1972
Cole and King, 1968, pp. 1–97
Coulson, 1973
Daugherty, 1974, pp. 1–12
Fitzgerald, 1974, pp. 1–41
Haggett, 1972, pp. 1–19, 454–8
King, 1970
Ling, 1977, pp. 83–106
Mathematics for the Majority, 1974, pp. 8–51
Selkirk, 1976b
Sumner, 1978 (mathematically advanced)

PART 1
CONCEPTS

'Take away Number, Weight, Measure you exile
Iustice and reduce and haile-up from Hell the olde
and odious Chaos of Confusion.'

William Folkingham, 1610, *Feudigraphia*
(quoted in M. W. Beresford, 1971, *History on the Ground*)

1 Sets

1.1. Introduction

The idea of a set is sometimes described as pre-mathematical, and is nowadays frequently met by children as young as seven or eight years old. In this chapter we shall develop briefly only those ideas of sets which have a direct pay-off in geographical applications. One of the most useful gains from a study of set theory is that it encourages clear and careful definitions, and this precision of language will avoid many future problems. In the next chapter we shall investigate coordinate systems which develop out of set theory and provide one of the simplest and most obvious links between mathematics and geography.

1.2. Definitions

A set is a collection of distinguishable objects, for example the set of active volcanoes in South America, or the set of inhabited islands in Indonesia. It is necessary to have a criterion by which we know whether any object is included in such a set or not. In the above examples we need a clear definition of the word 'active', and to distinguish whether 'inhabited' includes seasonal habitation or not.

That such distinctions are not quibbles might appear clearer by taking a common example. A geographer doing work on the USA must be careful to say when he is working with the individual states whether he is referring to the set of all fifty states including Alaska and Hawaii or just to the forty-eight conterminous states. He will also need to note the status of the District of Columbia in which the capital Washington lies.

Those objects which belong to a set are called its *elements* or *members*. The safest way to define a set is to list its elements, and this is an alternative to a general definition. The set aspects of such definitions can be emphasised by writing them between braces. Thus we can give the set of prime factors of 10 as {2, 5} or as {prime factors of 10}. Since we must always be able to distinguish between the elements of a set, we cannot have the same element twice, and so {prime factors of 12} = {2, 3} and not {2, 2, 3}.

A set is usually denoted by a capital letter. It may well have an infinite number of elements, for example the set of points on a line. It is always a good idea when discussing sets to have a clear idea of the total collection of elements about which one is talking. This is usually known as the *universal set* and often denoted by $\&$. The universal set might be the set of pupils at a school or the set of European nations (though again one would have to be a little more precise about this for certain states, for example Turkey and San Marino). In this latter case one would write

$$\& = \{\text{European nations}\}$$

Out of this universal set we might wish to define certain other sets such as:

A = {Scandinavian nations}
B = {EEC nations}
C = {European nations with French as a national language}
  = {France, Belgium, Switzerland, Luxembourg}
D = {Benelux countries}
  = {Belgium, Netherlands, Luxembourg}

(At the time of writing there are ten members of the EEC, the original six together with Denmark, Eire, Greece and the UK.) Notice that for C and D the second definition resolves any difficulties about membership, for example the status of Monaco.

The elements of the set D are also elements of B, and this is written

$$D \subset B$$
$$\text{or } B \supset D$$

These statements may be read as 'All the Benelux countries are members of the EEC' or more briefly as 'D is contained by B', 'B contains D' or 'D is a *sub-set* of B'. All the sets A, B, C and D are sub-sets of $\&$ so that

$$A \subset \&, B \subset \& \text{ and so on.}$$

With the idea of a sub-set, classification becomes possible and the study of sets more meaningful.

1.3. Venn diagrams

Venn diagrams provide a convenient and simple way of visualising relationships between sets. Conventionally we regard the members of the universal set as points scattered about a rectangle. Members of any sets we wish to illustrate are drawn within ovals. Fig-

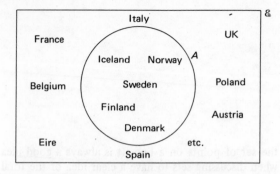

Figure 1.1. Venn diagram showing the set of Scandinavian nations A, as a sub-set of the set of European nations, &.

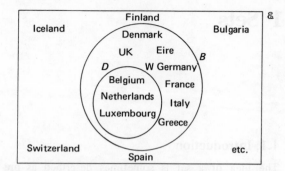

Figure 1.3. The set of Benelux countries, D, is a subset of the set of EEC nations, B, so that $B \cap D = D = $ {Belgium, Netherlands, Luxembourg}.

ure 1.1 shows the set of Scandinavian nations A as part of the universal set of European nations &, though not all the latter are named individually.

1.4. Three mathematical ideas

At this stage, mathematical interest in sets centres on three ideas. First all the members of the universal set which are not members of a given set form the *complement* of the given set. The complement of A is written A' or $\overline{A}$. In figure 1.1. the set A' is the set of all non-Scandinavian European nations and is represented by the points in the rectangle outside the oval curve.

The second, and for the purposes of this book most important, idea is that of the *intersection* of two sets. In figure 1.2 the intersection of the sets A and B from section 1.2 is illustrated by that part of the rectangle within both ovals, and this is written $A \cap B$. This set has only one member, namely Denmark. Readers should convince themselves that

$A \cap B = $ {Denmark}
$B \cap C = $ {France, Belgium, Luxembourg}

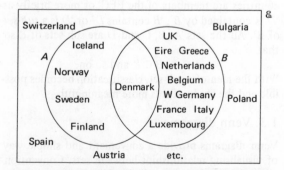

Figure 1.2. Denmark is the only element in the set of Scandinavian nations, A, which is also an element of the set of EEC nations, B, that is $A \cap B = $ {Denmark}.

and rather more complicated that
$B' \cap C = $ {Switzerland}
In figure 1.3, the set D is a subset of the set B, and this is illustrated by drawing one oval within the other. In this example
$B \cap D = $ {Belgium, Netherlands, Luxembourg}
In this special case it should be clear that $B \cap D = D$.

It sometimes happens that two sets have no members in common. In section 1.2 sets A and C have this property as well as A and D. Such sets are said to be *disjoint*, and their lack of 'overlap' can be emphasised by drawing the Venn diagram so that the ovals do not intersect as in figure 1.4.

The third idea, which is of somewhat less importance in this book, is that of the *union* of two sets. In figure 1.2 this is illustrated by that part of the rectangle in either one oval or the other, or both. This is written $A \cup B$, and
$A \cup B = $ {the EEC nations, Iceland, Norway, Sweden, Finland}
Note the conveniently abbreviated definition for this set.

Intersection will be met again in the next chapter, but while union is of less importance, the concept is nevertheless a useful one. For example the union of the set of sea-ports and the set of canal-ports in any country is of interest to the captain of a ship capable of both inland and sea voyages. The ideas of union

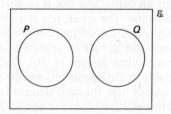

Figure 1.4. Venn diagram for two disjoint sets P and Q. There are no common elements.

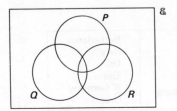

Figure 1.5. Venn diagram for three sets, *P*, *Q* and *R* showing all possible overlaps.

and intersection can be applied to three or more sets as illustrated in figure 1.5 with sets *P*, *Q* and *R*, and are capable of considerable mathematical development which we shall not require in this book.

1.5. Classification

Sometimes all the elements of a set can be assigned to one or other of two disjoint subsets. An obvious example is the set of all human beings which can be split into the set of all males and the set of all females, there being no other choice. Such a division is said to be *dichotomous*. Dichotomous divisions are the basis of many classification systems.

In some cases these systems are hierarchical, notably in biology where animals and plants are classified in increasingly detailed ways. Another example is in management structure. Such classifications are sometimes known as *keys*, and a particular element can be identified by a series of yes/no questions. This is equivalent to the binary coding dealt with in section 1.7 below.

1.6. Karnaugh maps

The Venn diagram has a number of disadvantages, particularly in the illustration of dichotomies. Firstly Venn diagrams are not easily drawn for more than three sets as in figure 1.5, and secondly they emphasise the inclusion-exclusion aspect at the expense of the idea of dichotomising a set into two parts. An alternative which seems little known to geographers is the Karnaugh map.

Instead of dividing the rectangle representing the universal set by ovals, the Karnaugh map achieves similar ends by drawing horizontal and vertical lines. Basic maps for two, three, four and five dichotomies are shown in figure 1.6, and these should make the idea clear. With more than five dichotomies, representation, while more awkward, can still be achieved. Figures 1.7 and 1.8 give examples of cross-classification with three and four sets of dichotomies respectively. Notice the common feature of this type of classification that different criteria tend to include or exclude the same nations.

Before leaving the topic of sets it is worth pointing out that there are a remarkable number of traps for the unwary in set theory, and it is not uncommon to see errors in published geographical texts. Geographers would be wise to seek advice when using more complicated examples.

1.7. Binary coding

Traditionally man, with ten fingers, has counted in tens. A more logical (though normally less useful) way of counting is in twos. This is usually called binary arithmetic and the counting numbers begin 1, 10, 11, 100, 101, 110, 111, 1000, the last of these being the number 8. Most school children today meet binary arithmetic at the age of eleven or twelve. Its great advantage is that there are only two possibilities for each digit which can be thought of as 'on' and 'off', or alternatively as 'yes' and 'no'. This is a highly convenient way of counting when electrical apparatus is being used and especially in computing. However it is unnecessary to understand binary arithmetic to use a

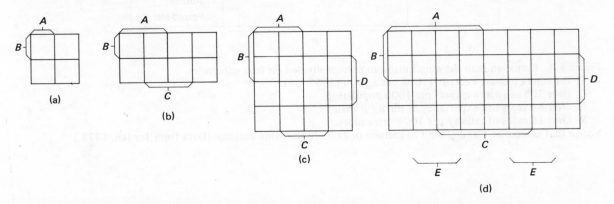

Figure 1.6. Blank Karnaugh maps for (a) two, (b) three, (c) four and (d) five dichotomous properties.

Concepts

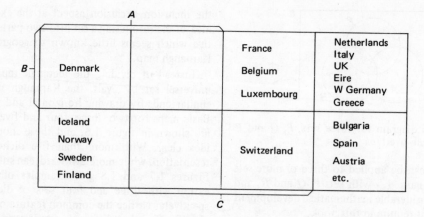

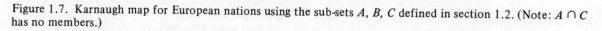

Figure 1.7. Karnaugh map for European nations using the sub-sets *A, B, C* defined in section 1.2. (Note: *A ∩ C* has no members.)

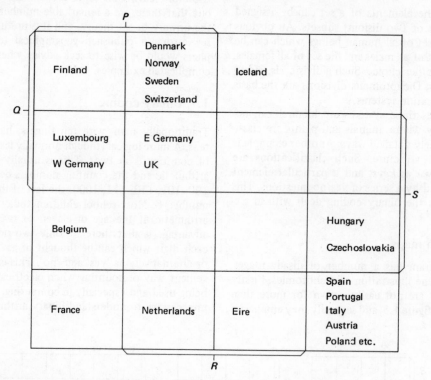

Figure 1.8. Karnaugh map showing European nations divided on four categories.
  P. Per capita income exceeds $1000 per annum (1965–66).
  Q. Over 300 daily newspapers per 1000 population.
  R. Over 68 years life expectancy at birth for males.
  S. Over 15 miles of railway per 100 square miles.
Notice that categories *P* and *Q* tend to include or exclude the same nations. (Data from Jordan, 1973.)

computer since the conversion is done automatically.

When a classification system is hierarchic and there are two choices at each division, a binary coding is a natural way of tracing a route through a system. For example each element of the cluster diagrams in chapter 20 can be identified in this manner. Starting at the right in figure 20.1 for example, and working leftwards, right and left turns at the junctions can be identified by 1 and 0 respectively. The process is rather like switching a railway wagon onto the various tracks in a marshalling yard, the ones and zeros identifying the positions of the switches. Readers who wish to pursue this topic further should consult almost any modern secondary school mathematics text.

Exercises

At the level of this chapter, sets form a basis of an attitude of thinking, and little further work should be necessary.

1. Using the definitions of section 1.2, draw Venn diagrams to illustrate (a) A and C (b) C and D where & is the universal set of European nations. Write down the elements of the sets $A \cup C, C \cup D, A \cap C, A \cap D, A' \cup C, A \cap C', C \cup D', C \cap D'$.
2. Using as universal set the nations of South America, write down the elements of the following sets:
   (a) {Spanish-speaking nations} = S
   (b) {nations with an Atlantic seaboard} = A
   (c) {former British colonies} = B
   Draw Venn diagrams to illustrate the relationship between S and A, A and B, S and B.
3. Think of some other geographical ideas which might be illustrated by Venn diagrams (Jordan, 1973, will give some ideas).
4. Give some more examples of hierarchical classifications (see, for example, Dudley, 1977).

Further reading

Abler, Adams and Gould, 1972, pp. 149-58
Bale, Graves and Walford, 1973, pp. 222-38
Cole, 1969b
Cole and King, 1968, pp. 30-46
Dudley, 1977, pp. 154-85
Haggett, Cliff and Frey, 1977, pp. 454-60
Jordan, 1973, pp. 81-100, 343-8
Sherlock and Brand, 1972

2 Coordinates

2.1. Introduction

Coordinate systems are of great importance in both mathematics and geography. In both subjects points must be located accurately in space, and a coordinate system enables this to be done. The number of co-ordinates (strictly the number of independent co-ordinates, see section 2.11) is the dimension of the space; one coordinate is needed to locate points on a line (not necessarily straight), two to locate points on a surface (not necessarily plane) and three in a volume. Mathematicians imagine higher dimensional spaces, but geographers will not require this. In this chapter we shall examine the commoner types of coordinate systems, concentrating particularly on the two-dimensional case which is of most interest to geographers.

It might seem odd to discuss coordinates before introducing the concept of distance, but the latter is not essential to a coordinate system, and we shall defer its study until chapter 3. Readers will however have an intuitive idea of distance which will be sufficient for this chapter.

2.2. Points on a line

A finite number of points on a line can be located by numbering them in order. Thus we might number the bus stops along a particular route or the bridges along a canal. The ordering is in fact merely a convenience, making it easy to locate particular points, and not an essential. When there is an ordering, we can even include a convention for inserting additional points, so that a new bridge between number 15 and number 16 might be labelled 15A. In a more sophisticated society it might be called 15.5. A variation of this linear numbering system occurs when we have a double line of points, as for example houses along a road which are numbered odd on one side and even on the other.

Any ordered numbering system must start somewhere. In most arbitrarily numbered systems, the first point is numbered one; later, when we introduce length we shall find it more convenient to number the starting point zero, and we shall call this point the *origin*. In introducing the idea of ordering a set of points, we have subtly enlarged upon the idea of a set and produced the important mathematical concept of an *ordered set*. In chapter 10 we shall examine the distribution of ordered sets of points more closely.

Arbitrary numbering systems, while simple and obvious, are somewhat uninteresting. They can be applied to finite numbers of points only, and do not respond easily to efforts to insert additional points between existing ones. As soon as we need to locate any individual point on a line we must use not just the counting numbers 1, 2, 3, ..., but also decimals such as 3.174. (There is no need to become involved here in the difference between rational and irrational numbers, because it has no practical effect upon what follows. We simply want an effective way of locating any point on a line to a reasonable degree of accuracy.)

One convenient way of doing this is to introduce the idea of a measuring stick. The work 'stick' is used loosely. The foot, the yard and the metre are familiar lengths where we can use a real measuring stick, but we can also imagine miles, kilometres, millimetres and even light-years being used as measuring sticks. The need is simply for some defined length which can be used as a standard. This need is a very primitive one; Thom, 1967, for example, has suggested that neolithic stone circles all over Britain were laid out with a standard measuring stick.

If we are to use a measuring stick, then we must have in addition a point from which we can start measuring. This point is the origin mentioned above. Because we can have negative numbers as well as positive ones, the origin does not need to be at the beginning of the line. In many geographical examples, however, the use of negative numbers is inconvenient, and the origin is placed at the end of the line (for an example see section 2.7). By using smaller measuring sticks, our basic stick can be divided into smaller and smaller units and we can measure the distance from the origin to any point on the line with sufficient accuracy. This can even be done along curved lines, though in this case we run into some difficulties to which we shall return in the next chapter.

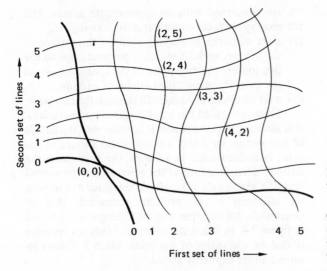

Figure 2.1. A coordinate system for points in a plane.

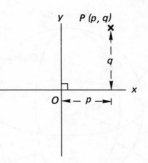

Figure 2.2. Rectangular Cartesian coordinates showing the point P with coordinates (p, q).

2.3. Points on a surface

The identification of points on a surface is more difficult. Anyone who has tried to find a house on a dark night on the type of modern housing estate with no clear road system will have experienced the difficulty of locating a finite number of points in an area. The problem can be solved by using two sets of lines. These need not be straight, but no two lines of one set must intersect, while any line from one set must intersect any line from the other. Figure 2.1 illustrates this, and points at the intersection of two lines may be located from the number of the line in each set. Several points on the surface are labelled on the figure, including the origin $(0, 0)$. Readers should be familiar with the use of two sets of numbers in this way to locate points such as $(2, 4)$, $(2, 5)$, $(3, 3)$ and $(4, 2)$ in the figure. We make a convention that one set of lines gives the first number and the other gives the second number, so that their order is important and the point $(2, 4)$ is not the same as the point $(4, 2)$.

Each point of intersection is now identified as the intersection of two sets of points, the word intersection carrying over from set theory. Unfortunately we can only locate points at intersections by this method, so clearly the idea needs tightening up.

2.4. Rectangular Cartesian coordinates in a plane

If the surface is a plane, then rectangular Cartesian coordinates are the simplest way of solving this problem. Each set is made up of equally spaced parallel lines and each line of one set is perpendicular to every line

of the other. Any point in the plane can then be located by taking one pair of lines in each set as an axis; these lines are usually labelled Ox and Oy respectively. The *coordinates* are then found by measuring perpendicular distances from Oy and Ox (note the order). The method of locating $P(p, q)$ is shown in figure 2.2, though p and q need not be positive as in that example, nor need they be whole numbers. Readers should not need to be reminded of the details.

It is a mathematical convention that Ox and Oy should be located so that the direction of turn from Ox to Oy is counter-clockwise and the angle between them is, of course, 90°. This raises a slight problem because it is different from the geographical convention for bearings, where angles are measured from north (usually placed at the top of the map in the direction of Oy) and in a clockwise direction. The contrasting methods are illustrated in figure 2.3. While negative numbers may appear in coordinates, geographers usually try to avoid them, and one way of doing this is given in section 2.7.

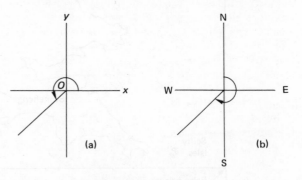

Figure 2.3. Mathematical and geographical conventions for measuring angle.
   (a) Mathematical – start from Ox, measure counter-clockwise.
   (b) Geographical – start from N, measure clockwise.

11

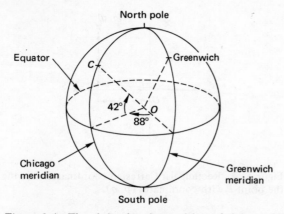

Figure 2.4. The globe showing position of Chicago (*C*) at 42° N, 88° W.

2.5. Locating points on curved surfaces: latitude and longitude

It· is impossible to draw two sets of parallel straight lines on a curved surface. Even where it is possible, as on the sphere, to draw two sets of curved lines, each at regular distances apart, it is usually inconvenient to use them for a coordinate system. In world geography

we are concerned with an approximate sphere, and the geographer takes coordinates by drawing:

(a) a set of circles of varying radii on the surface of the sphere, each of which is perpendicular to the line joining the two poles of the sphere known as the axis. These are called circles of *latitude*.

(b) a set of circles of equal radii through the two poles. These are called circles of *longitude* or *meridians*.

It is assumed that the reader is familiar with the details of this system by which a point on the surface of the earth is located using two angles, the first giving the latitude north or south of the equator and the second that of a semi-circle of longitude measured east or west by reference to an arbitrary meridian, that of Greenwich. An example, that of Chicago, is illustrated in figure 2.4. In this system the only distance involved is that of the radius of the earth which is always assumed, never explicitly stated.

2.6. Grid references

In the geography of more restricted areas, points are often given as grid references and readers will also be familiar with these. They are essentially the same as rectangular Cartesian coordinates, the origin *O* being

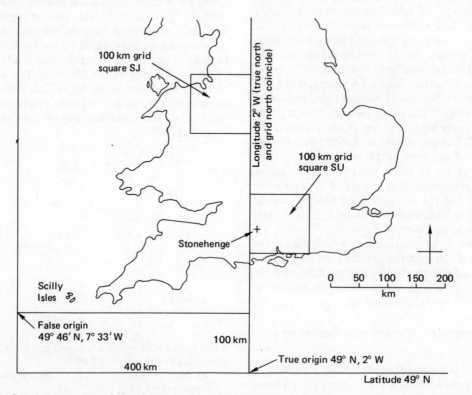

Figure 2.5. Southern portion of Great Britain showing false and true origins of the National Grid and the location of 100 km grid squares SJ and SU.

chosen so that negative values will not be required. The line *Ox* is directed towards the east and the line *Oy* approximately towards the north. Distances are measured eastwards and northwards, and these distances are often called the *easting* and the *northing* (corresponding to the lengths *p* and *q* respectively in figure 2.2). The two distances are measured in some convenient metric unit (on 1:50 000 maps this is usually units of 100 metres) and are run together without a comma and brackets as in mathematics. Thus the map reference 122422 for Stonehenge (figure 2.5) which is used in section 3.3 indicates a distance of 12 200 m eastwards and 42 200 m northwards from the origin of the conventional 100 km square in which Stonehenge lies. Grid references are thus very similar to coordinates, though they are of course only given to a certain degree of accuracy.

2.7. The British National Grid

The British National Grid is a typical example of how such a system may be developed. A difficulty is caused by the fact that the surface of the earth is approximately spherical rather than the plane used in rectangular Cartesian coordinates. Anyone who has tried to wrap up a football as a present will know that it is not possible to make a flat piece of paper lie on the surface of a sphere without stretching or creasing, so that approximation is necessary.

This is achieved by taking a line of longitude which runs north and south down the centre of the area of the map. In the case of Great Britain this is the line 2° W which runs approximately through Birmingham. A line of latitude, in this case the line 49° N, is then chosen for the other axis of the grid on the southern edge of the area to be covered. These lines are shown in figure 2.5 and their intersection, the point 2° W, 49° N, is the true origin of the British National Grid.

All other points are defined from these two lines, but involve a slight degree of approximation to account for the curvature of the earth, and this means that grid north and true north will differ slightly away from these two axes. The difference is most marked in the north west, in particular in the Hebrides, where it is as much as 4°, but it is minimised by starting from a north–south line in the centre of the map rather than at one edge.

Using this arrangement, all north–south measurements are positive, but some measurements will be westward from the 2° W meridian, and thus in a negative direction rather than eastwards and in a positive direction. To avoid this source of confusion, 400 km are added to all eastings. This is sufficient to ensure that all coordinates will be positive in the area. Further,

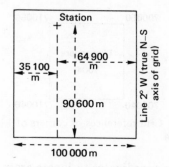

Figure 2.6. Location of Lime Street Station, Liverpool, in grid square SJ.

in order to ensure that all points on the mainland of Great Britain lie within a range of 1000 km north of the origin, 100 km is subtracted from all the northings. The effective origin of the Grid, known as the *false origin*, is thus 400 km west and 100 km north of the true origin and is approximately latitude 49° 46′ N, longitude 7° 33′ W. This is a point south-west of the Scilly Isles.

In section 2.6, conventional 100 km grid squares were mentioned. Great Britain covers a much larger area than 100 km × 100 km, so that the whole area covered by the National Grid is divided into 100 km squares. Each of these has two reference letters, and squares SJ and SU are shown in figure 2.5. Thus Stonehenge has a full grid reference SU/122422. Normally there is no possibility of confusion between places which are at least 100 km apart and the letters are omitted. Further details may be found on maps and in the Ordnance Survey literature, for example Harley, 1975.

Figure 2.6 illustrates the advantages of avoiding negative numbers. Lime Street Station, Liverpool, is 64 900 m westward from the true base-line of the grid. Given in coordinate form, it would have an *x*-coordinate of −649. In practice it is measured eastwards from the western edge of the 100 km square so that

$$1000 - 649 = 351$$

The full grid reference is thus SJ/351906. Some readers will recognise a similar arrangement in determining the logarithms of numbers less than one.

National grids are found in many other countries, especially in Western European countries and their former colonies. Most are very similar in lay-out, but one odd variation is that of Jamaica which uses feet instead of metres, leading to some awkward units. Such grids are usually found only on official government maps, though recently their use has spread to some tourist maps.

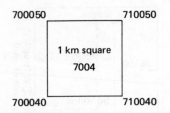

Figure 2.7. Grid references of corners of 1 km grid square 7004.

2.8. Using coordinates to locate areas

Grid references strictly refer only to points, but geographers and cartographers often use them to define a square area whose south-western corner is given by the grid reference. The reference 7004 would then be to the 1 km or 1000 m square whose corners have grid references 700040, 710040, 710050 and 700050. This is illustrated in figure 2.7.

The British Ordance Survey uses a similar system to index its 1:25 000 and 1:10 000 maps. For example the 1:25 000 map of Ponteland (Northumberland) is indexed NZ 07/17 and covers an area in the 100 km grid square NZ of 20 km from east to west and 10 km from north to south bounded by the points with grid references 000700, 200700, 200800 and 000800.

Simpler versions of this system are often used in popular maps and gazetteers, squares being indicated by a letter and a number, or by a capital and a lower-case letter.

2.9. Other ways of locating points in planes

Points in planes can be located in other ways, and these are particularly important in navigation and surveying, where angles are easier to determine than lengths. The most common alternative is by polar coordinates, illustrated in figure 2.8. An origin O and a fixed line Ox are needed. A point P is located by giving the distance r of P from O and the angle $xOP = \theta$, which, as pointed out in section 2.4, illustrated in figure 2.3, is measured counter-clockwise from Ox. (In some mathematical applications θ will be measured in

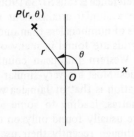

Figure 2.8. Polar coordinates.

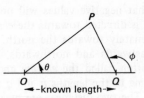

Figure 2.9. Bipolar coordinates.

radians rather than degrees, but this need not concern us.) A geographer is using the same system when locating a point by its distance and bearing from a known point (except for the annoying difference in conventions for measuring angle).

In bipolar coordinates, two points O and Q are fixed as in figure 2.9 and a point P is defined by two angles. This is effectively the method used by surveyors when working from a single carefully measured base-line and by navigators when working out their position from two known points. Provided the length OQ is known, every other point may be determined by measuring only angles. Bipolar coordinates are, however, relatively infrequent in mathematical use.

In all the above examples angles are always given between $0°$ and $360°$. If an angle falls outside this range, an appropriate multiple of $360°$ is subtracted, or if the angle is negative it is added. Thus $505°$ is given as $505° - 360° = 145°$. Similarly $-45°$ is given as $-45° + 360° = 315°$. This is an example of a special type of arithmetic, known in this case as arithmetic modulo 360.

A related problem which occurs in navigation and often causes surprising and unnecessary confusion is that of finding a *backbearing*, that is a bearing in the opposite direction to the one given. The usual rule is: if the bearing is greater than $180°$, subtract $180°$; if it is less than $180°$, add $180°$. Using modulo arithmetic this can now be modified to: add $180°$.

2.10. Locating points in three dimensions

The latitude and longitude system can be extended to incorporate a distance from the centre of the earth as well. We now have a system with three coordinates (a length and two angles) which can be used to locate any point in space, say an artificial satellite. More commonly we might use a slightly different system using the distance above sea-level.

Rectangular Cartesian coordinates may be extended to incorporate a third dimension as shown in figure 2.10. The addition of a third coordinate involves adding a third axis Oz to those in figure 2.2. There is a choice of two directions (up from the paper and down into the paper on figure 2.2), and the one conventionally

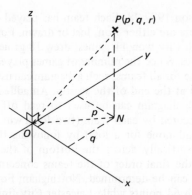

Figure 2.10. Rectangular Cartesian coordinates in three dimensions.

chosen is the upwards one which makes a right-hand set. This means that if the thumb, first finger and second finger of the right hand are held so that they are mutually at right angles to one another, then they can be pointed in the directions Ox, Oy, Oz respectively. The third coordinate of the point P is its perpendicular distance PN from the point N in the plane of Ox and Oy, and its first two coordinates are those of N. A geographical parallel would be that of giving a point by its grid reference and height above sea-level though in this case the units of the third coordinate might differ from the other two. We shall return to this in section 3.4.

2.11. Triangular graphs

(This section may be omitted at a first reading.)

An intriguing coordinate system is that of areal coordinates which are used in triangular graphs, or ternary diagrams as they are sometimes known. They are useful in geography for illustrating proportions of a whole which is divided into three pieces. For example soil consists of three main constituents, clay, sand and silt. These three constituents must add up to 100% of the total, so that a soil consisting of 50% clay, 20% sand and 30% silt might be described by three coordinates as $(50, 20, 30)$. Although there are apparently three independent coordinates here, this is not true in fact, since the percentage of clay is fixed by the other two constituents. This can be illustrated on a triangular coordinate system as shown in figure 2.11. The three corners of the triangle correspond to soils which are 100% clay, sand and silt respectively, and the sides opposite those points to soils which contain no clay, sand or silt respectively. The lines in between are labelled with the percentages of each particular component in 10% intervals. Notice the important fact that for any point the three coordinates add up to 100. The point S marks the point corresponding to a soil with 50% clay, 20% sand and 30% silt. With a little practice such a chart can give a rapid and clear idea of the constituent parts of a soil sample. This example is

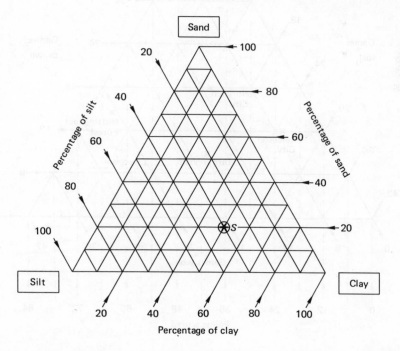

Figure 2.11. Areal coordinates used to describe soil types (the point S is the position of the example in the text).

15

used in Dinkele, Cotterell and Thorn, 1976a, pp.35-6, and other examples may be found in other books of that series.

Another example of such trichotomous data is given by the proportions of a population over sixty-five, between fifteen and sixty-five, and under fifteen years of age. This effectively isolates those proportions of a population which require different social provisions. In this case the corners of the triangle might represent the members of a senior citizens' club, the workers at a factory and the children in a school class with coordinates $(100,0,0)$, $(0,100,0)$ and $(0,0,100)$ respectively. A small portion of such a graph is illustrated in figure 20.8.

Areal coordinates need not sum to 100. An interesting example where the sum is 42 is given in figure 2.12. This shows the final results for some of the teams in the First Division of the English Football League for the season 1977-78. Each team has played 42 games, and these are either won, lost or drawn. For example Norwich City won 11 games, drew 18 games and lost 13 games. Since the number of games played must be the same for all teams, such a diagram can usually only be used at the end of the season. An added bonus is that the diagram can be used to read off the total points scored by each team (two for a win, one for a draw and none for a loss) by following the arrows drawn vertically across the bottom of the diagram. Hence the final order of the teams concerned in the League can be determined, Nottingham Forest came top with 64 points while Leicester City finished bottom with 22 points.

Unfortunately, after this was written, the points system was altered, and from the 1981-82 season this illustration can no longer be used for the English Football League.

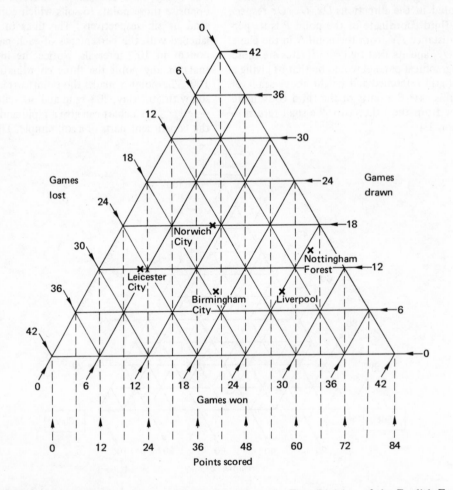

Figure 2.12. Triangular graph used to show positions of teams in the First Division of the English Football League at end of season 1977-78.

Exercises

1. (Mathematical) Find out how to convert rectangular Cartesian coordinates (p, q) to and from polar coordinates (r, θ) with the same origin and Ox line.

2. (Mathematical) What is the effect on the point (p, q) in rectangular Cartesian coordinates when the origin is moved to the point (a, b) without rotation?

3. One classification of scales of measurement is as follows:

    (a) Ratio scale: distances are measured from the starting point of the line. Phrases such as 'half the distance from the start', 'twice the distance from the start' have meaning.

    (b) Interval scale: distances are measured from some arbitrary point on the line, not the starting point, so that only line segments can be compared for length. (The most obvious example is temperature in degrees Celsius, which does not start at absolute zero. A temperature of 20 °C is not twice a temperature of 10 °C.)

    (c) Ordinal scale: the numbers are in order but distances are not correct, so that only relative ordering is possible.

    (d) Nominal scale: the numbers (or names) are assigned arbitrarily.

    Try to find examples from everyday life of these scales of measurement. (Some of your examples may sound trivial.) See also Hanwell and Newson, 1973, p.7.

4. Invent some other ways of defining points in three-dimensional space. (Cylindrical and spherical coordinates, which are not dealt with in this book, are developments of polar coordinates.)

5. Consider the problems of locating (i) an aircraft, (ii) an artificial satellite, (iii) a planet, (iv) a distant star.

6. Find out how surveyors carry out a triangulation survey. (See Birch, 1949, and Debenham, 1954, for example.)

7. Using the divisions of population outlined in section 2.11 plot the positions of some simple populations known to you on a triangular graph, for example your own and neighbouring households. Plot also the position of your parish, town, district or county if you can find details from the census reports.

8. Draw a diagram like figure 2.12 for some league you are interested in. (Remember all teams must have played the same number of games.)

Further reading

Abler, Adams and Gould, 1972, pp. 93–102
Birch, 1949, pp. 65–75
Cole and King, 1968, pp. 53–60, 79–85, 580–1
Davis, 1974, pp. 110–11
Dickinson, 1973, pp. 35–7
Dinkele, Cotterell and Thorn, 1976a, pp. 35–6
Dinkele, Cotterell and Thorn, 1976b, p. 21
Dinkele, Cotterell and Thorn, 1976c, p. 29
Haggett, 1972, pp. 82–91
Hammond and McCullagh, 1974, pp. 25–7
Hanwell and Newson, 1973, pp. 1–14, 91–3
Harley, 1975, pp. 17–29
Schools Council Geography Committee, 1979, pp. 21–7
Wilson and Kirkby, 1975, pp. 21–3

3 Distance

3.1. Introduction

In chapter 2 the use of a measuring stick was assumed in order to measure distances along axes for a co-ordinate system. In this chapter we shall extend the idea in the geographer's world. That the concept is more complicated than might appear at first sight is more apparent when we consider the ways in which we qualify the word distance in everyday speech: 'The distance via . . .', 'the distance along the road', 'the crow's flight distance', 'the airline distance'. These suggest respectively a choice of routes, a winding route, a straight line route, and a route made up of straight line segments. In the last two cases 'straight lines' are in fact portions of circles whose centre is at the centre of the earth; we call these *great-circles*. We shall, however ignore the difference this makes since it makes no effective alteration over quite large portions of the earth's surface.

3.2. Straight line distance

In figure 2.2 the point $P(p, q)$ is defined by a pair of rectangular Cartesian coordinates p and q. The distance OP from the origin to P can be found by Pythagoras' theorem:

$$OP^2 = p^2 + q^2$$

or

$$OP = \sqrt{(p^2 + q^2)}$$

In words the statement of the theorem is 'In any right-angled triangle the square of the length of the hypotenuse (the longest side) is equal to the sum of the squares of the lengths of the other two sides.'

For example the distance from the origin to $P(5, 12)$ is given by

$$OP^2 = 5^2 + 12^2 = 25 + 144 = 169 = 13^2$$

so that

$$OP = 13$$

Even if one or both of the coordinates is negative this still works.

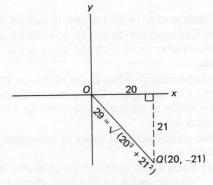

Figure 3.1. Distance from O to $Q(20, -21)$.

In figure 3.1 the distance from O to Q $(20, -21)$ is given by

$$OQ^2 = 20^2 + (-21)^2 = 400 + 441 = 841 = 29^2$$

so that

$$OQ = 29$$

This formula for distance is often generalised as in figure 3.2 to give the distance between any two points (x_1, y_1) and (x_2, y_2). The distances parallel to the two axes are $x_2 - x_1$ and $y_2 - y_1$ and the formula now becomes

$$d = \sqrt{\{(x_2 - x_1)^2 + (y_2 - y_1)^2\}}$$

This looks more formidable, but does precisely the same task. Essentially we begin by measuring the distances parallel to each of the axes. Since $x_2 - x_1$ is squared it makes no difference whether it is positive or negative, and it can equally well be written $x_1 - x_2$. Similarly for $y_2 - y_1$. Geometries for which this distance rule holds are called *Euclidean geometries*.

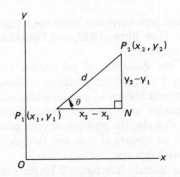

Figure 3.2. General formula for distance between two points P_1 and P_2, $d = \sqrt{\{(x_2 - x_1)^2 + (y_2 - y_1)^2\}}$

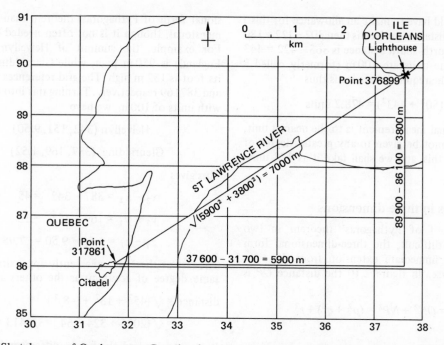

Figure 3.3. Sketch map of Quebec area, Canada, showing use of grid references to calculate distances.

3.3. Straight line distances on the map

We can use the method of section 3.2 to find distances on the map by using grid references. We first find the differences between the two eastings and between the two northings of the references and proceed as in section 3.2. Figure 3.3 shows how this may be done for a practical example, the calculation of the distance between the eastern point of Quebec citadel and the lighthouse at Ste Petronille on the Ile d'Orleans. This is taken from Quebec sheet 21 L/14 East Half. The two map references are 317861 and 376899 respectively. The east–west distance is

$$376 - 317 = 59 \text{ units}$$

and the north–south distance is

$$899 - 861 = 38 \text{ units}$$

The required distance is

$$\sqrt{(59^2 + 38^2)} = \sqrt{(3481 + 1444)} = \sqrt{4925}$$
$$= 70 \text{ units approximately}$$

Since the units are 100 metres, the distance is 7.0 km, and this can be checked on the actual map. (Notice that the zero is left after the decimal point as a reminder that the answer is accurate to 100 m.)

Of course we do not use this method normally, it is easier to use a ruler. If however we have only the references and no map, or, as more often happens, the

points lie on different maps, the method can be a useful one. For example in Britain, Stonehenge in Wiltshire has grid references SU/122422 while Uffington White Horse in Oxfordshire has reference SU/302865 and lies on a different 1:50 000 map. The location of 100 km square SU is shown in figure 2.5, and the two given points within that square in figure 3.4. (If the two points did not lie in the same 100 km

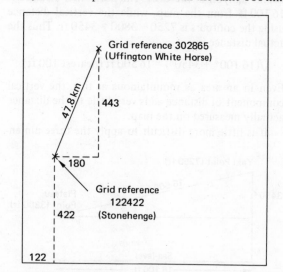

Figure 3.4. 100 km grid square SU showing positions of Stonehenge and Uffington White House.

19

square we would have to make an allowance for this.) The east–west distance involved is then $302 - 122 = 180$ units and the north–south distance is $865 - 422 = 443$ units. Again the units are 100 m (formerly called a hectometre). The required distance is thus

$$\sqrt{(180^2 + 443^2)} = 478.2 \text{ units}$$

Since the original measurement is to the nearest unit, the answer cannot be given to any greater degree of accuracy than this, and we shall take it as 478 units or 47.8 km.

3.4. Distances in three dimensions

While the proof of Pythagoras' theorem in two dimensions is difficult, the three-dimensional form follows as an immediate extension from the two-dimensional case. In figure 2.10 the distance OP is given by

$$OP^2 = ON^2 + NP^2 = (p^2 + q^2) + r^2$$

so that

$$OP = \sqrt{(p^2 + q^2 + r^2)}$$

and the general formula is

$$\sqrt{\{(x_2 - x_1)^2 + (y_2 - y_1)^2 + (z_2 - z_1)^2\}}$$

Usually when the distance between two points at different heights is required, it is easiest to measure the horizontal distance on the map. Figure 3.5 shows how the distance between Yaki Point and Plateau Point may be calculated from the 1:48 000 map of the Grand Canyon in the USA. The horizontal distance is 16 100 ft from the map, while the vertical distance using the contours is $7250 - 3800 = 3450$ ft. Thus the actual distance is

$$\sqrt{(16\,100^2 + 3450^2)} = 16\,500 \text{ ft (nearest 100 ft)}$$

Even in an area as mountainous as this, the vertical component of distance adds very little to the distance actually measured on the map.

It is little more difficult to apply the three-dimen-

sional form of Pythagoras' theorem than the two-dimensional, though it is not often needed in practice. For example, the summit of Helvellyn (Cumbria, England) is 950 m high, while Glenridding Bridge at its foot is 152 m high. The grid references are 342151 and 387169 respectively. Turning this into coordinates with units of 100 m, we have

$$\text{Helvellyn } (342, 151, 9.50)$$

$$\text{Glenridding } (387, 169, 1.52)$$

This gives

$$x_2 - x_1 = 387 - 342 = 45$$
$$y_2 - y_1 = 169 - 151 = 18$$
$$z_2 - z_1 = 1.52 - 9.50 = -7.98$$

The last of these is conveniently approximated to the same degree of accuracy as the others as -8. Thus

$$\text{distance} = \sqrt{\{45^2 + 18^2 + (-8)^2\}}$$
$$= \sqrt{\{2025 + 324 + 64\}} = \sqrt{2413} = 49.12$$

If we had ignored the height difference between the points, we would have had $(45^2 + 18^2) = 48.47$. Since our accuracy is to the nearest 100 m, these are 4900 m and 4800 m respectively, and the difference is only just detectable. Since we rarely wish to deal with slopes as steep as this, the effects of height can usually be ignored without appreciable error.

3.5. Distances along curved lines

While height can usually be ignored, the effect of measuring distances along curved lines is much more critical and we shall consider one geographical aspect of it in chapter 29. The initial problem can, however, be tackled here. The definition of the length of a curved line is difficult, and demands ideas of a limit which occur in calculus. We shall simply assume that a curved line has a length which is what we all 'think' it is and that this is roughly the sum of small lengths of straight line chords measured along the curved line. The shorter the chords, of course, the more accurate the measurement. This means that we can estimate the length of a curved line by using the edge of a sheet of paper as illustrated in figure 3.6.

An alternative method is to use a piece of cotton. This is intuitively more acceptable, but there are problems such as ragged ends, slippage, stretch and 'humping' of the cotton from the paper due to the twist of the cotton threads. Experience shows that in fact this method is less accurate. On the other hand, a wheeled map measurer is ideal for the task and should be used if available. If the correct map scale

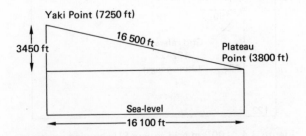

Figure 3.5. Pythagoras' theorem in a vertical plane.

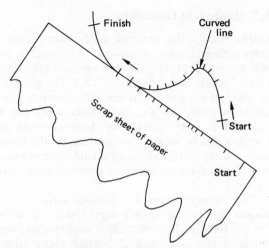

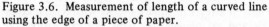

Figure 3.6. Measurement of length of a curved line using the edge of a piece of paper.

is not given on the dial of the measurer, the distance can always be run off against the scale given on the map itself.

To illustrate the effect of scale on the measurement of the length of a curved line, the length of the River Usk in the counties of Gwent and Powys (Wales) was measured between Crickhowell Bridge and Usk Bridge, Abergavenny on maps of four different scales. This stretch of river is not particularly sinuous, so that the results, given in table 3.1, are all the more striking. The results can be plotted against the representative fraction given as a decimal as in figure 3.7 or against its reciprocal as in figure 3.8.

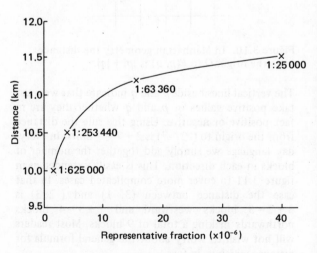

Figure 3.7. Distance measured along R. Usk plotted against representative fraction (in decimal form).

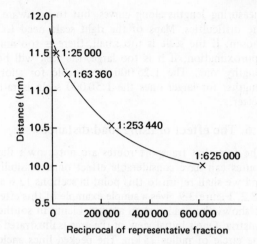

Figure 3.8. Distance measured along R. Usk plotted against reciprocal of representative fraction.

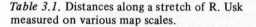

Map scale	Scale as decimal	Measured distance (km)
1:25 000	40×10^{-6}	11.49
1:63 360	15.7×10^{-6}	11.2
1:253 440	3.9×10^{-6}	10.5
1:625 000	1.6×10^{-6}	10

Table 3.1. Distances along a stretch of R. Usk measured on various map scales.

The measured distance must have a lower limit of 8.8 km which is the crow's flight distance between the two end points, but it is not at all clear that it must also have an upper limit, though this is in fact the case. We can begin to determine this upper limit by extrapolation of the curve in figure 3.8, shown dotted in the figure. This highly dubious procedure suggests that on a map of infinite scale, corresponding to the y-axis, the length might be measured as about 11.7 km. Whether this conclusion is justified or not, it is clear that small-scale maps do not just result in loss of accuracy in measurement, but produce a real reduction in the measured length because of loss of detail.

A similar but even more difficult problem is that of the length of a piece of coastline. There are many unanswerable questions; the state of the tide, the distance to measure up estuaries, and what size of convolution to ignore, headlands, rocks, pebbles or even grains of sand. A more advanced approach to this problem may be found in Haggett and Chorley, 1969, and Chorley, 1969. The moral is not to stop measuring lengths along curves, but to be aware of the difficulties. Maps of the right scale need to be chosen. If the scale is too small, there is too much approximation; if it is too large, the task will be a lengthy one. The 1:25 000 is suitable for shorter lengths, for larger ones the 1:50 000 scale is rather better.

3.6. The effect of using road distances

The fact that transport routes are not crow's flight routes can have considerable effect on accessibility, and we shall return to this point in sections 13.6 and 28.2. Figure 3.9 gives a simple example of this effect. It shows the road system around Lientz in southern Austria. One's initial view of the area is illustrated by the circle of radius 25 km. The pecked lines enclose all those points on roads which are 25 km and 50 km by road from Lientz, the figures at the road intersections showing the data used to draw these lines. We now have a very different view of the accessibility of the area round Lientz, the town of Luggau only 15 km south of Lientz is 53 km distant by road.

From this stem a number of geographical points including the importance of valleys and mountain passes and the asymmetry of the potential market area around Lientz. The pecked lines can, however, be misleading since they only refer to points on roads, and points off the roads will be even less accessible. The map could be further developed to illustrate time of travel to Lientz if we knew how fast we could travel along the various roads.

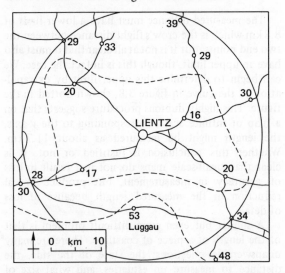

Figure 3.9. Road system around Lientz, Austria. The circle has a radius of 25 km, and the pecked lines enclose points within 25 km and 50 km road distance from Lientz.

3.7. Manhattan Geometry

Mathematically the patterns of distance around a town such as Lientz are difficult to investigate, and lack generality. Many cities, however, are planned in square blocks, especially in the USA. The geometry to which these give rise is not only interesting and simple in itself, but also has effects which can be discerned in many cities, even those which do not display a rigidly square street pattern. At the lowest level, a study of this geometry should increase awareness of the effects of transport networks upon travel distances.

The formulae given for distance earlier in this chapter assume that crow's flight travel is possible. For the traveller, however, this is rarely so. As a very simple special case we shall imagine a city with a pattern of streets in square blocks with regular crossroads and no one-way systems. We can easily take some intersection as the origin and the roads through it as Ox and Oy. On this road system, illustrated in figure 3.10, the distance between the origin and the intersection at the point $P(p, q)$ is given by

$$OP = |p| + |q|$$

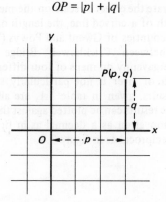

Figure 3.10. In Manhattan geometry the distance from the origin O to $P(p, q)$ is $|p| + |q|$.

The vertical lines beside p and q indicate that we must take positive values of p and q whether they are in fact positive or negative. Using this rule the distance from the origin to $(-2, -7)$ is $2 + 7 = 9$ units. In everyday language we simply add together the number of blocks in each direction. This is easily extended as in figure 3.11 to cover more complicated cases. In that case the distance between $(3, -1)$ and $(-2, 3)$ is $3 + 2 = 5$ blocks westward and $1 + 3 = 4$ blocks northwards making a total of 9 blocks. Most readers will not wish to worry about the general formula for distance which is, in fact

$$|x_2 - x_1| + |y_2 - y_1|$$

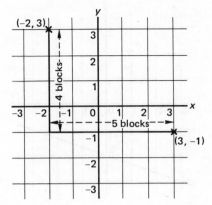

Figure 3.11. Distance between $(3, -1)$ and $(-2, 3)$ in Manhattan geometry.

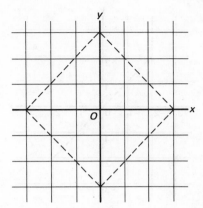

Figure 3.12. A 'circle' of radius 3 units in Manhattan geometry.

The geometry for which this formula for distance holds is called *Manhattan geometry*, and the distance rule is easier to apply than that for Euclidean geometry. One surprising result is that there is often more than one shortest route between two points; for example there are ten shortest routes between $(0, 0)$ and $(3, 2)$. We shall not, however, pursue this problem.

Notice that the formula for distance only applies to distances between intersections, since we can only use the lines of the grid. The distance between $(\frac{1}{2}, 0)$ and $(\frac{1}{2}, 1)$ is one unit by the formula, but two units on the ground. Mathematicians would prefer the formula to apply generally to all points whether intersections or not, but we must face the fact that mathematical convenience does not always fit in with the real world.

3.8. Some simple results in Manhattan geometry

(This section may be omitted at first reading.)

Many familiar results in 'normal' geometry assume odd forms in Manhattan geometry, and we give a few simple examples. Figure 3.12 shows the intersections within three blocks of the origin enclosed by a pecked line. This diamond-shaped area is the equivalent of a circle in Euclidean geometry and in a city might represent the acceptable distance of a house from a bus stop. Figure 3.13 shows how this might be developed into a pattern of bus services. A more economic pattern can be found for underground railways which are independent of the road system. This is illustrated in figure 3.14.

If two intersections lie on the same line it is quite easy to see the division line between their areas of influence. If they lie on different lines, the division

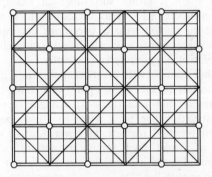

Figure 3.13 Bus stops (circles) and routes (double lines) in Manhattan-type city. Each stop has a three-block diamond-shaped catchment area. Note that only alternate routes interconnect. (Conjectural.)

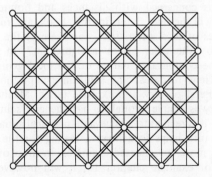

Figure 3.14. Underground stops (circles) and routes (double lines) in a Manhattan-type city. Each stop has a three-block diamond-shaped catchment area. (Conjectural.)

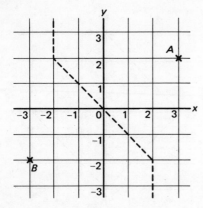

Figure 3.15. Mediator line of two points *A* and *B* in Manhattan geometry.

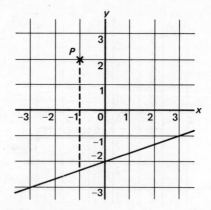

Figure 3.16. Perpendicular from a point *P* to a straight line in Manhattan geometry.

between them is rather surprising; an example is shown in figure 3.15. This division, which might represent the market areas of two shops, corresponds to the mediator or perpendicular bisector in Euclidean geometry, which is considered in chapter 13.

Another example with practical applications is that of the shortest distance from a point to a straight line. The example shown in figure 3.16 might represent the construction line of a sewer to a river outfall, where for practical reasons the sewer must lie along the line of a road. Such results are not difficult to prove, but demand clear thinking; the reader who wishes to pursue the idea further is recommended to read Krause, 1975.

3.9. Local geometry

Manhattan geometry is a particular and particularly interesting example of a local geometry. The road system around Lientz in figure 3.9 is another. Many problems concerned with distances and boundaries which will be met later in this book are further examples of local geometries, for example the areas served by the pillar boxes in figure 13.7. In some cases the complicated nature of the local geometry is sufficient to defeat any solution except those in very general or very approximate terms. Manhattan geometry is simple enough to have general solutions and yet it is related to a believable practical situation. This in turn helps to achieve a feeling for the situation in more complicated examples. In most of this book, for example chapter 14, it will however be necessary to use Euclidean geometry as an even cruder approximation to the real world. In some cases as in section 14.3 we can indicate how departures from Euclidean geometry will affect our results.

The contrast between figures 3.9 and 3.12 indicates a central problem in applying mathematical results to geographical situations, and it is an important task of this book to connect the two. The mathematical solution has a simplicity and regularity which can give the geographer greater insight into the less regular workings of the real world, highlighting both the regularities and departures from regularity; while the practical situations such as that of the area round Lientz can encourage the mathematician to seek for solutions which have a greater generality and impact on the real world.

Exercises

1. Produce your own version of figure 3.9 for a centre in a mountainous area of your own choice.
2. Use grid references to work out crow's flight distances between two points. Check your results by measurement if possible. (A calculator with a square root facility is helpful.)
3. (Mathematical) At what gradient does the inclusion of height make 1% and 10% differences to distances measured on the map? (See Chapter 5.)
4. Repeat the exercise of figures 3.7 and 3.8 for a stretch of river or mountain road of your own choosing.
5. (Mathematical) In Manhattan geometry investigate:
   (a) when the distance formula breaks down if the chosen points do not lie on the intersections and travel is along 'roads' only.
   (b) the mediator lines of two points, developing a general rule.
   (c) the shortest route from a point to a straight line, developing a general rule.
   (d) the number of shortest routes between two given points, developing a general rule.
   (e) whether the mediators of three points meet in a single point as in Euclidean geometry.
6. Repeat question 5(b) to (e) for some other regular patterns, e.g. equilateral triangles, regular hexagons, right-angled isosceles triangles, 2 x 1 rectangles, and rhombuses with 60° and 120° angles.

Further reading

Chorley, 1969, pp. 419–30
Cole and King, 1968, pp. 51–60
Debenham, 1954, pp. 31–43
Dinkele, Cotterell and Thorn, 1976a, pp. 19–20
Haggett and Chorley, 1969, pp. 66–70
Krause, 1975

4 Area and density

4.1. Introduction

Much of geography is the study of a two-dimensional surface, the surface of the earth. Since from time to time various areas need to be compared, it is necessary to be able to measure area. Area is an example of a compound unit which involves multiplying a length by a length. If the area happens to be a rectangle, then it may be calculated by multiplying the length and breadth of that rectangle. Notice, however, that the units of each measurement must be the same: if length and breadth are both measured in metres, then the area will be measured in square metres; if in feet, the area will be in square feet, and so on.

This idea can be extended to cover triangles and more complicated figures provided that they are bounded by straight lines. By use of calculus and other devices beyond the scope of this book it becomes possible to calculate the areas of shapes bounded by circular arcs and by other curves whose equations are known. Unfortunately most areas in geography are not like this but are bounded by streams, ridges, roads and other lines whose shape is anything but mathematically defined. It is therefore necessary to devise practical methods of estimating irregular areas.

4.2. Geometrical boundaries in geography

Examples of geometrical boundaries in geography do occur. Usually they are straight lines between two defined points, or along lines of latitude or longitude as, for example, part of the boundary between Namibia (SW Africa) and Botswana. Such boundaries are typical of the era of efficient surveying methods and particularly European colonial development. A more unusual example of a geometrical boundary is given by a large portion of the parish boundary of Glossop, Derbyshire, which is an arc of a circle of radius one mile. Geometrical boundaries are often highly inconvenient; one such anomaly is the north-west corner of the state of Arizona which is virtually cut off from the rest of the state by the Grand Canyon.

Areas such as the state of Wyoming which have completely geometrical boundaries are quite rare. While such areas can be calculated mathematically, the calculations are completely outside the scope of this book.

4.3. Units of area

It was pointed out in section 4.1 that area is measured in units of length squared. This is abbreviated by writing the square sign (^{2}) after the unit of length. It is as well to remember that since there are 1000 m in 1 km, there are $1000^2 = 1\,000\,000\,\text{m}^2$ in $1\,\text{km}^2$. The same principle applies to all area units. The metric unit of area is 100 m x 100 m = 1 hectare (ha). We thus have

$$10\,000\,\text{m}^2 = 1\,\text{ha}$$
$$100\,\text{ha} = 1\,\text{km}^2$$

Those who are not familiar with imperial units of area may like to be reminded that 4840 square yards equals 1 acre and 640 acres equals 1 square mile. A convenient conversion factor is that 2.47 acres is approximately 1 hectare. If 1:25 000 maps are used, 1 square inch is almost exactly equivalent to 100 acres (99.639 in fact).

4.4. Upper and lower bounds for the area of an irregular shape

The example of the length of coastline mentioned in section 3.5 suggests that there may be no upper limit to the length of a line, it just depends on the detail we are prepared to measure. It is easy to show, however, that every area has both an upper and a lower limit, and these tend to the same limit as accuracy improves. In figure 4.1 the irregular area can be surrounded by a rectangle 4 units by 5 units giving an upper limit of 20 square units. Removing unwanted squares reduces this to 15 square units. Increasing the fineness of the mesh gives an upper bound of 50 quarter squares, that is $12\frac{1}{2}$ square units.

Inside the area, a similar process shows 21 entire quarter squares giving a lower bound to the area of $5\frac{1}{4}$ square units. By using finer and finer meshes, these values can be made as near as we like to one another, though it is clear that the process will be long and tedious. We therefore seek a more rapid, if mathematically less rigorous, process.

In what follows we shall ignore problems of the earth's curvature and of the increase in area caused by undulations in the ground. They are difficult to allow for, and their practical effect is often small.

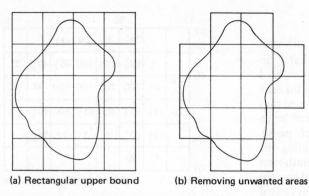

(a) Rectangular upper bound   (b) Removing unwanted areas   (c) Using a finer mesh

Figure 4.1. Making an upper bound to the area of an irregular shape.

4.5. Measuring area by counting squares

One practical way of measuring areas is to adapt the square counting method. This can be done by averaging the upper and lower bounds. Thus in figure 4.1(c) we might estimate the area to be

$$\tfrac{1}{2}(12\tfrac{1}{2} + 5\tfrac{1}{4}) = 8\tfrac{7}{8} \text{ square units}$$

This is an equivalent process to counting whole squares inside the area and allowing half for each square through which the boundary passes. There are 21 whole squares and 29 part squares, each of area $\tfrac{1}{4}$ square unit giving

$$\{21 + (\tfrac{1}{2} \times 29)\} \times \tfrac{1}{4} = 8\tfrac{7}{8} \text{ square units}$$

The assumption is that the part squares nearly cancel one another out in pairs. This is nearly true, but can cause errors as pointed out in section 4.6.

As an illustration of a practical problem, we shall take an area whose size can be verified independently; the moderately large English parish of St Briavels,

Gloucestershire. The whole of this parish is on the Ordnance Survey 1:25 000 sheet (First Series) SO50 and 1:50 000 sheet (First Series) 162. (Parish boundaries are being omitted from Second Series sheets which are currently appearing. The parish also appears on the 1:25 000 Outdoor Leisure Map 'Wye Valley and Forest of Dean'.) The boundaries of this and surrounding parishes are shown in outline, together with 1 km grid lines, in figure 4.2. Each grid square in the figure represents an area of 100 hectares, and the official area of the parish can easily be ascertained, for example from the 1971 census returns, where it is given as 1933 hectares.

Examination of figure 4.2 shows that the parish covers 7 whole grid squares and parts of 28 others. Thus an estimate of the area is

$$700 + (\tfrac{1}{2} \times 2800) = 2100 \text{ ha}$$

For such a large mesh, this is not a bad estimate, but we shall examine how it can be improved.

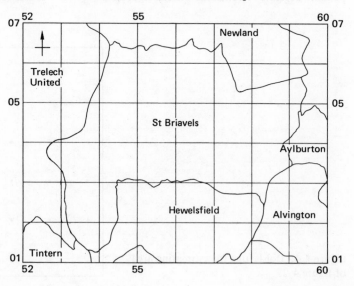

Figure 4.2. St Briavels and surrounding parishes showing 1 km grid squares.

4.6. The problem of shared squares

Consider the square in figure 4.2 whose south-west corner has grid reference 540060. This is shared between the three parishes of St Briavels, Newland and Trelech United. If it counts as half a square for each parish, it will altogether be counted $1\frac{1}{2}$ times, and thus the area will be over-estimated. This bias can be removed by counting this square as $\frac{1}{3}$ to each parish. In the figure there are 6 such squares (including one which has grid reference 540010 for its south-west corner), and a seventh square which is shared by four parishes. Thus the estimate of the area must be revised to

$$7 + (\tfrac{1}{2} \times 21) + (\tfrac{1}{3} \times 6) + (\tfrac{1}{4} \times 1) \text{ km}^2 = 1975 \text{ ha}$$

This over-estimates the actual area by approximately 2%, a reasonably accurate estimate for such a coarse grid.

4.7. Increasing accuracy

The calculations above can be made directly from the 1:50 000 map, though it is helpful to pencil in the parish boundaries before starting. Accuracy may be increased by using a 1:25 000 map. A piece of tracing paper can then be prepared with a square of size 40 mm x 40 mm subdivided into 4 mm x 4 mm squares. This is placed over each 1 km grid square on the map and the area worked out in whole and part squares as in section 4.6. Each small square is equivalent to an area of one hectare. It is convenient to note down the areas as in figure 4.3. The result, allowing for 7 squares where boundaries meet as in section 4.6, is 1937 ha. This is an error of 0.2% and may well be close to the possible degree of error in the official figures.

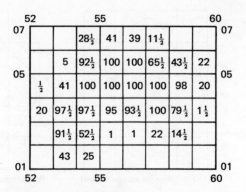

Figure 4.3. Estimated number of hectares in each km grid square of figure 4.2.

4.8. Measuring area by a dot lattice

The method of section 4.7 is tedious to perform accurately, and there is sometimes ambiguity at the edges of the squares. These problems can be avoided by the use of a dot lattice to estimate area. Each dot can be imagined as the centre of a square which we include if the centre lies within the area to be measured. The square mesh need not then be drawn, and we are left with a square array of dots. If the map has a grid on it, then the dots may conveniently be taken as the intersections of the grid lines. Alternatively the dots may be drawn on tracing paper, using a pattern like that in figure 4.4, where the dots are a distance apart equivalent to 1 km.

This method of estimating area is suggested in at least one school text (School Mathematics Project, 1965, pp.154–6, written for more able eleven year old children) though rather cursorily and with a rather coarse lattice. With a finer lattice, however, it rapidly

Figure 4.4. Dot lattice for estimating area of figure 4.2.

becomes apparent that it is an efficient way of estimating areas quickly. In the St Briavel's map, for example, there are 19 intersections of grid lines within the parish boundary, giving a first estimate of area as 1900 ha in only a few seconds.

The position of the lattice is, of course, arbitrary, and if the grid of figure 4.4 is placed over the map of figure 4.2 the number of points over the area can be varied between 16 and 22 by moving it about (though the extremes are quite hard to achieve). These values give some idea of the possible range of error with the method. A closer mesh lattice will reduce the percentage error considerably; in the St Briavels example, a half-kilometre lattice on the 1:25 000 map gives 75 dots with 3 more on the boundary. If the latter are counted as half this gives an estimated area of $1912\frac{1}{2}$ ha. This is an error of about 1%, which can be reduced further by using a still closer lattice.

4.9. Density

We need to know areas to make valid comparisons. It is of little use comparing the populations of Britain and Canada for many purposes because the population of Canada is spread over a far wider area than that of Great Britain. The fact that Britain has twice the population of Canada becomes even more surprising when this is taken into account. The measure we need to make true comparisons such as this is density. Here it is important to notice that the geographical use of density is rather different to the physical use of the word. In physics we are using mass as a basis rather than number of persons, but more importantly in physics density refers to a mass in a given volume. In geography density usually refers, however, to area, and this point can be emphasised when necessary by calling it *areal density*. Thus we talk of population in numbers of persons per square kilometre, and wheat yield in tonnes per hectare.

Density is one step further than area in the development of compound units; this trend towards the use of more complicated compound units is characteristic of all quantitative sciences. There is, however, little

mathematical development of the concept and a simple example should suffice.

The population of Nigeria in 1971 was about 66 000 000 and its area 925 000 km^2. Thus the population density was

$$\frac{66\,000\,000}{925\,000} = 71 \text{ persons km}^{-2}$$

(note the use of km^{-2} for 'per km^2', the minus sign indicating division by km^2). This fact is of little interest except for purposes of comparison; when one discovers that at the same time the population density of the Niger Republic immediately to the north of Nigeria was 3 persons km^{-2}, one begins to ask geographical questions.

It is unwise to give figures such as these to too great a degree of accuracy, partly because they are inevitably several years out of date, but more importantly because the population figures of developing countries are unlikely to be very accurate.

There are two points about density over which care should be taken. Firstly quantities which are themselves ratios should not be expressed in terms of densities. While it might be reasonable to give the number of cases of bovine tuberculosis per square kilometre, it would not be correct to work out the proportion of cows suffering from bovine tuberculosis per square kilometre since this quantity, which is a proportion, is not related to an area. The second point is a geographical one. This is that areal density is a concept which cannot be completely realised in real terms. The density of population may be worked out over the unit of a parish, but most of the population in the parish will actually be clustered around the village centre or centres, and many areas of the parish may have a local density of zero. Thus, while a good population density map should be calculated over reasonably small units of area, these units should not be too small, or the overall effect will be to produce a map which is too difficult to interpret. For methods of drawing such maps a book on the drawing of geographical diagrams such as Dickinson, 1973, or Monkhouse and Wilkinson, 1976, should be consulted.

Concepts

Exercises

1. Estimate the area of a suitable town or parish both by the square and by the dot methods. Use a 1:25 000 map if possible, and use at least two sizes of dot lattice to give yourself an idea of the accuracy of each. Check your answers by looking up the official figures.
2. Use the point lattice method (using grid square intersections at $\frac{1}{2}$ km intervals) to estimate roughly the areas of ten to twenty parishes which you know from the 1:50 000 map. Check the accuracy of your measurements by looking up the official figures.
3. Calculate population densities for the parishes in question 2 and account, if possible, for the variations in these.
4. Attempt to classify the parishes of question 3 by population density. Such classifications as 'suburban development', 'small industrial development', 'undeveloped', 'market town' might be appropriate,
5. Find some more examples of inconvenient geometrical boundaries in geography.

Further reading

Davis, 1974, pp. 65–83
Dickinson, 1973, pp. 37–67
Monkhouse and Wilkinson, 1971, pp. 73–80
School Mathematics Project, 1965, pp. 154–6

5 Gradient and profiles

5.1. The third dimension

In much of this book the geographer's world will be thought of as two-dimensional. But apart from the problem of mapping the surface of a sphere onto a plane sheet of paper, there is also the problem of allowing for the unevenness of the surface of the earth. The illustration of this is one of the central problems in drawing any relief map.

The ability to visualise the third dimension in map reading is a valuable skill which can only be acquired by practice, and efforts to assist it have gone to the extent of printing maps on moulded plastic, exaggerating the height dimension considerably. Layer colouring, hill shading and hachuring are simpler methods of obtaining the same result. By far the commonest method, however, is the use of contour lines which represent on the map points on the ground of equal height above sea-level.

Similar skills are also valuable to the mathematician and to the artist, engineer and architect. Since models are expensive to make and difficult to store, any technique which aids the visualisation of a three-dimensional object from a two-dimensional drawing is useful. One such technique is the cross-section, or profile, which we shall examine in this chapter.

We have observed in section 3.4 how comparatively small the height dimension is compared with the horizontal dimensions in most practical situations. It is nevertheless important because the earth's gravitational field means that work has to be done when climbing, and potential energy is released when descending. This not only has profound effects on communications, but also affects climate and provides a source of hydroelectric power.

5.2. The measurement of gradient in mathematics

In chapter 4 we saw how two lengths multiplied together produced an area. If we divide the lengths we have a quantity which is a ratio and has no physical dimension. Consequently the units in which we measure the lengths are immaterial provided they are the same; the results are always just a number. When a vertical length is divided by a horizontal length then their ratio gives the gradient of the sloping line which has those two lengths as components. In figure 3.2, the *gradient* of the line P_1P_2 is defined mathematically to be

$$\frac{y_2 - y_1}{x_2 - x_1}$$

which is the same as

$$\frac{y_1 - y_2}{x_1 - x_2}$$

When the line goes from bottom left of the graph to top right, this quantity produces a positive ('uphill') gradient; when it goes from top left to bottom right it produces a negative ('downhill') gradient.

The gradient is closely related to the angle θ which the sloping line makes with the horizontal as shown in figure 3.1. The gradient is also the *tangent* of the angle θ, abbreviated to tan θ. (This use of the word tangent should not be confused with the related, but different, use of the word to describe a line touching a circle.) Thus we have

$$\tan \theta = \frac{y_2 - y_1}{x_2 - x_1}$$

Taking the example from the Grand Canyon in figure 3.5, the average gradient between Plateau Point and Yaki Point is the vertical height difference (3450 ft) divided by the horizontal distance (16 100 ft). This is

$$\frac{3450}{16\,100} = 0.214$$

Instead of giving this gradient, we can find the angle whose tangent is 0.214 from published tangent tables, which gives 12.1°. The quantities 0.214 and 12.1° are different but related concepts. The reader who is used to metric units might be concerned about the use of feet in this example. However the equivalent lengths in metres are 1050 m and 4910 m, and the corresponding calculation gives the same result.

5.3. The measurement of gradient in practical situations

Unfortunately in practical uses, gradient is written down in a variety of ways. Sometimes the number 0.214 is written as a percentage thus: 21.4%. This is a popular way of giving gradient on the continent of Europe, and has recently begun to appear on British road signs. It can be misleading, since we tend to *think* of a gradient of 100% as a vertical line, while in reality it means a distance of 1 unit up for 1 unit along, that is a slope of 45°. This percentage figure is sometimes given as 21.4 cm per m or 214 m per km (the latter seems to be a Scandinavian usage) which is clearer and gives a sensible measurement of the idea.

The British tradition is to give gradients in the form 1 in n. Thus in our example we have to solve the equation

$$\frac{1}{n} = \frac{3450}{16\,100} = 0.214$$

which means that

$$n = \frac{1}{0.214} = 4.67$$

Thus the gradient is 1 in 4.67. This is usually rounded to the nearest whole number, which involves the sacrifice of a considerable degree of accuracy when gradients are steep. The reader may care to check by measurement on figure 3.5 that the gradient of the line is about 1 unit up for $4\frac{2}{3}$ units across, and that the angle is about 12°.

5.4. The sine-tangent problem

A further complication is illustrated in figure 5.1. It is much easier for a surveyor working on the ground to measure the distance along the slope rather than the horizontal distance. We then have the sine of the

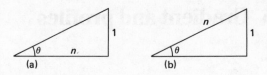

Figure 5.1. Tangent (a) and sine (b).

angle θ rather than its tangent, and the value of n is somewhat larger than that measured along the horizontal for the same slope. When a map is used to measure gradient the reverse is the case; it is easier to measure the horizontal distance. Fortunately the errors caused by this difference are small, indeed it is because of their small size that the ambiguity has arisen. Up to angles of 8° or so (that is gradients of 0.14 or 1 in 7), the error is as little as one part in 100.

5.5. Plotting a profile

The simplest form of profile is one based on a straight line transect of a piece of country. There are two main reasons for doing this, firstly to highlight the topography of the area, and secondly to determine the intervisibility of two points. When studying topography, care needs to be taken to use meaningful lines; the most useful are those which cut across the grain of the structure and so identify the ridges and valleys. For intervisibility profiles, only the higher points will need to be plotted, and allowance may have to be made for buildings and trees.

Figure 5.2 shows a typical profile taken from a 1:62 500 scale map of Copperopolis, California. The profile runs across the grain of the country in Calaveras County (which will be familiar as the home of Mark Twain's Jumping Frog). The production of a profile of this sort can be accomplished very easily. First pencil a line on the map along which the profile is to be drawn, then draw a frame of the same length with

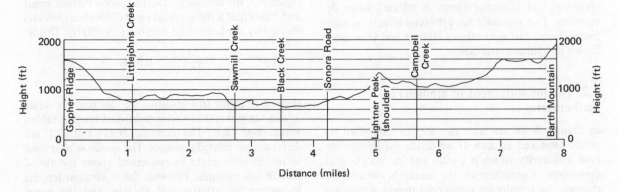

Figure 5.2. Profile across part of Calaveras County, California (vertical exaggeration about 1:4.2).

a series of horizontal lines for heights at suitable intervals on a piece of paper. Lay the edge of a piece of scrap paper along the line of the profile on the map, and mark off the points where the edge cuts contours and labelling sufficient to avoid confusion. (Where slopes are uniform and contours reasonably close, intermediate ones may be omitted.) The results can then be transferred to the frame at the correct heights by laying the edge of the scrap paper along a suitable height line for each section of the profile. Finally the points are joined up into a continuous curve. An example of a practical use for such a profile occurs in Kent and Moore, 1974.

5.6. Scale factor and vertical exaggeration

In a number of places we have talked about 1:50 000 and other scale maps. This quantity is, of course, the ratio of the distance on the map to the distance on the ground and can be thought of as a fraction, $\frac{1}{50\,000}$. Since it is a ratio of two lengths, it is, like gradient, a dimensionless quantity. In mathematics it is often called a *scale factor*. Common map scales are 1:100 000, 1:50 000 and 1:25 000 which are 1 cm to 1 km, 2 cm to 1 km and 4 cm to 1 km, respectively.

The use of non-metric units in nations with British or American traditions had led to some odd-looking map scales, such as 1:63 360, 1:126 720, 1:253 440 and 1:633 600; respectively 1 inch to 1, 2, 4 and 10 miles. These have often been later metricated to 1:62 500, 1:125 000, 1:250 000 and 1:625 000.

In most profiles it is necessary to emphasise the height dimension by enlarging the vertical scale compared with the horizontal. The size of this exaggeration is known as the *vertical exaggeration*. If this is not done, the slopes do not stand out sufficiently well. For example in the original drawing for figure 5.2, the horizontal scale was 1:62 500, since the profile distances were taken from the map directly, and this was the map scale. The vertical scale was drawn to a scale of 1:15 000, so the vertical exaggeration is

$$62\,500 \div 15\,000 = 4.2 \text{ approximately}$$

This figure can also be obtained by measurements on the scales of the profile.

In areas of low relief, vertical exaggeration will need to be greater than this, but care should be taken when comparing two profiles to ensure that the scales on both axes are the same. The exaggeration should

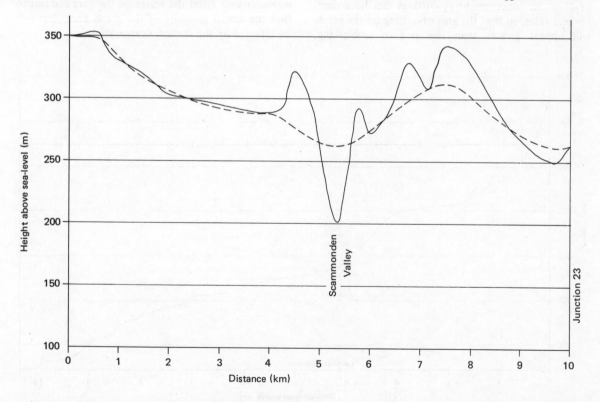

Figure 5.3. Profile of part of M62, Yorkshire, England (vertical exaggeration 1:25). The pecked line shows the estimated level of the westbound (southern) carriageway.

not be too great; for normal use that of figure 5.3 is too large, and 1 to 8 or 1 to 10 is more reasonable.

5.7. Profile along a transport route

Interesting cross-sections can also be attempted for transport routes; canals, roads and railways. Scale is a problem since 1:50 000 maps have to be used very accurately to obtain a good result, but larger scales need large sheets of paper. Figure 5.3 shows a profile of the M62 motorway in Yorkshire for 10 km west of junction 23, taken from the 1:50 000 map. The very high vertical exaggeration of 1:25 has been used. The method of plotting is a combination of the methods used in sections 3.5 and 5.5, using the edge of a piece of paper and moving it about. Ground level is estimated from the contours on the southern side of the motorway, and the level of the road estimated from cutting and embankment symbols. The embankment across the Scammonden Valley is also used as a dam to impound a reservoir.

One of the objects of the transport engineer is to equalise cutting and embankment volumes, and this can be checked by measuring the areas between the two graphs above and below the pecked line. In practice, in rocky country, cuttings can have near-vertical sides, so that the area of cutting on the graph will appear greater than the area of embanking,

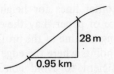

Figure 5.4. Extract from figure 5.3, showing calculation of gradient.

although the volumes are equal. The ideas of gradient of a curve and area under a curve provide the basis of differential and integral calculus, but we shall not pursue them in this book.

Profiles can be used (rather inexactly) to estimate gradients of transport routes. For example figure 5.4 shows an enlarged portion of figure 5.3 between the $5\frac{1}{2}$ and $7\frac{1}{2}$ km points. A stretch of 0.95 km with constant gradient rises about 28 m, so that the estimated gradient is

$$28 \div 950 = 0.029$$

This is equivalent to 2.9% or 1 in 34. When estimating gradients from profiles it is important to take the measurements from the scales on the axes and not to find the actual gradient of the graph since that will be affected by the vertical exaggeration.

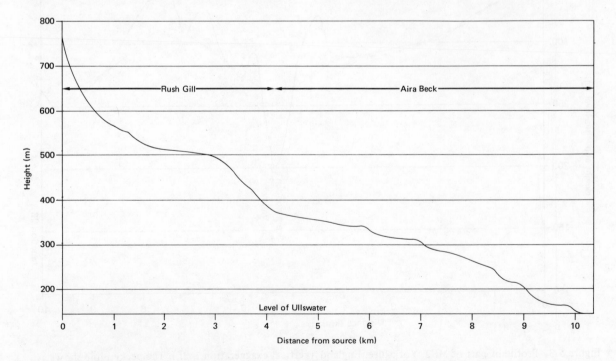

Figure 5.5. Gradient profile of Rush Gill – Aira Beck, Cumbria, England (vertical exaggeration 1:8).

5.8. River profiles

A common geographical use of profiles is along the course of a stream or river. These are better taken from the 1:25 000 scale. Figure 5.5 shows one taken from a map of this scale of a stream called Rush Gill and, lower down, Aira Beck in Cumbria, England. It rises on Stybarrow Dod (grid reference 345191) and enters Ullswater just below the well-known waterfall Aira Force. (The basin of this stream is shown in figure 5.8.) Measurements along the stream are too short to use a map measurer efficiently and are very tedious using a paper edge because of the meanders. Nor can direct plotting onto the profile be done because of the need for scale-reduction. A further problem is that contours, while given in metres, are at 50 ft intervals on this map, giving an awkward interval. The resulting profile is anything but smooth, and the geographer will wish to explain it in terms of the geological structure and history of the area (see for example Sparks, 1972).

5.9. Plotting gradient against distance

(Sections 5.9 to 5.11 may be omitted at a first reading.)

Instead of plotting distance along a stream against height, we may plot it against gradient. For example in figure 5.5 the distance between 533.4 m and 518.2 m contours is 50 ft or 15.2 m, while the distance along the stream is 1.64 − 1.36 = 0.28 km, or 280 m. Thus the average gradient on this section is

$$15.2 \div 280 = 0.054$$

This is between 1.36 and 1.64 km from the source, and the average gradient is then plotted against the mid-point of this at

$$\tfrac{1}{2}(1.36 + 1.64) = 1.50 \text{ km}$$

on the graph. The complete graph is shown on figure 5.6. Because of its irregular nature, no attempt has been made to smooth the graph.

Strictly the gradients in figure 5.6 are negative, but this is usually ignored since there can be no confusion. The first 0.5 km is probably very inaccurate, but below this the steeper sections of the stream profile stand out clearly as peaks, and figures 5.5 and 5.6 should be carefully compared. An interesting point is that waterfalls such as Aira Force (about 9 km from the source) should appear as points of infinite gradient. The scale of the map is, however, too small to allow this to emerge.

5.10. Logarithmic profiles

Another way of achieving a clear picture of a river profile can be obtained by plotting the logarithms of the heights rather than the heights themselves as given in figure 5.5. The modified diagram is shown in figure 5.7, the individual points being plotted as crosses. In such diagrams the points usually lie approximately on a straight line and this is drawn in figure 5.7. Departures from the straight line trend now become more

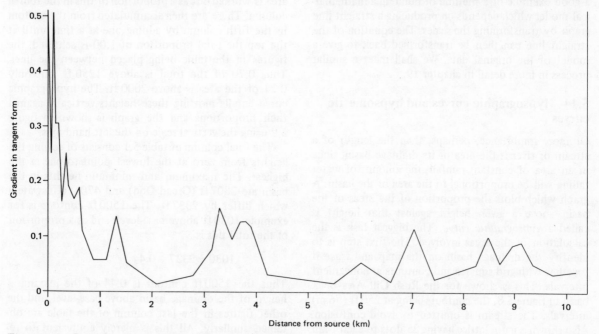

Figure 5.6. Gradient plot for Rush Gill – Aira Beck.

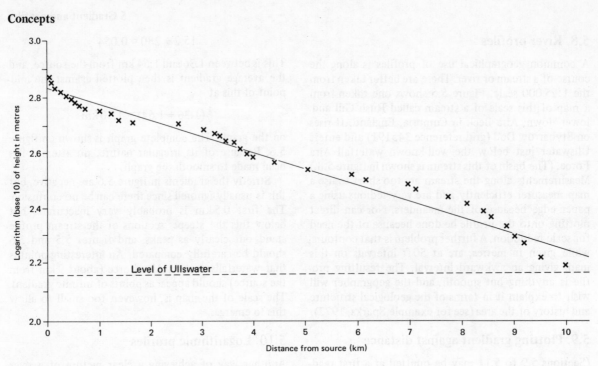

Figure 5.7. Logarithmic profile along Rush Gill – Aira Beck.

apparent. The trend line is called a line of regression and can be determined accurately by statistical methods (see for example Gregory, 1975, or Hammond and McCullagh, 1974). The logarithmic transformation is a good example of a method of building a mathematical model which depends on producing a straight line graph by transforming the scales. The equation of the straight line can then be transformed back to give a model of the original data. We shall meet a similar process in more detail in chapter 19.

5.11. Hypsographic curves and hypsometric curves

Of more importance, perhaps, than the length of a stream or river is the area of its drainage basin, since in an area of constant rainfall, the amount of water falling will be proportional to the area of the basin. A graph which plots the proportion of the areas of the basin above a given height against that height is called a *hypsographic curve*. The biggest task is the calculation of the areas involved. The first step is to identify the drainage basin on the map and trace it together with grid squares and contours at convenient intervals. This is shown for the Rush Gill–Aira Beck basin in figure 5.8, the contours being at 250 ft (76 m) intervals. The stream is omitted to avoid confusion. Also shown is a dot lattice having 25 dots to each 1 km grid square, so that each dot is the centre of an area

of 4 hectares. This is used to determine the area between each set of contour lines, the results being given in the first three columns of table 5.1.

The total area of the basin is 13.64 km², and each area is worked out as a proportion of this in the fourth column. These are then accumulated from the bottom in the fifth column by adding one at a time until at the top the total proportion of 1.00 is achieved, the figures in the table being placed between the lines. Thus 0.70 of the total is above 1250 ft, but only 0.24 of the area is above 2000 ft. The hypsographic curve entails plotting these heights vertically against their proportions and the graph is shown in figure 5.9 using the vertical scale on the left-hand axis.

The final column of table 5.1 consists of scaling the heights from zero at the lowest point to one at the highest. The maximum and minimum heights in the basin are 2807 ft (Gread Dod) and 470 ft (Ullswater) which differ by 2337 ft. The 1500 ft contour is for example 1030 ft above base-level, and as a proportion of the total this is

$$1030 \div 2337 = 0.44$$

Thus the 1500 ft contour is 0.44 of the maximum height of the drainage basin above base-level, and the other figures in the last column of the table are obtained similarly. All this is merely equivalent to re-numbering the vertical axis of figure 5.9 from zero to

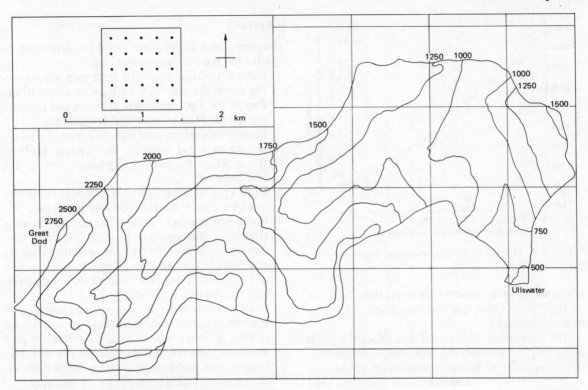

Figure 5.8. Basin of Rush Gill – Aira Beck showing contours every 250 ft.
Inset Dot lattice for calculating areas.

Height (ft)	Dots	Area (km²)	Proportional area	Proportional cumulative area	Proportion of maximum height difference of basin
				1.00	0.00
470–500	1	0.04	0.003		
				1.00	0.01
500–750	7	0.28	0.021		
				0.98	0.12
750–1000	36	1.44	0.106		
				0.87	0.23
1000–1250	60	2.40	0.176		
				0.70	0.33
1250–1500	57	2.28	0.167		
				0.53	0.44
1500–1750	50	2.00	0.147		
				0.38	0.55
1750–2000	49	1.96	0.144		
				0.24	0.65
2000–2250	36	1.44	0.106		
				0.13	0.76
2250–2500	27	1.08	0.079		
				0.05	0.87
2500–2750	17	0.68	0.050		
				0.00	0.98
2750–2807	1	0.04	0.003		
				0.00	1.00
Total	341	13.64	–	–	–

Table 5.1. Calculation for
construction of hypsometric
graph of Rush Gill-Aira Beck

Concepts

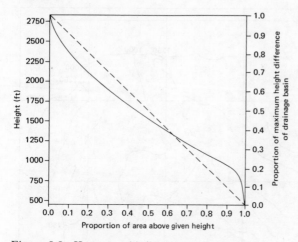

Figure 5.9. Hypsographic/hypsometric curve for Rush Gill – Aira Beck.

one as shown in the vertical scale on the right-hand side of the figure. Using this scale the graph is called a *hypsometric graph*.

The proportion of the total area under the graph in figure 5.9 is called the *hypsometric integral*. In this example it is almost exactly equal to the area under the straight pecked line which is half the total area. The hypsometric integral for this basin is therefore about 0.5. This suggests that the stream has eroded about half the possible material in the basin, and that the area has neither high plateaux nor low-lying plains. A more extensive account of the above ideas may be found in McCullagh, 1978. Examples of somewhat similar ideas may be found in Holt and Marjoram, 1973, and in Bale, 1976, dealing with population study and industrial diversification respectively.

Exercises

(Exercises such as these are useful for developing an eye for the third dimension in a map.)

1. Using a 1:50 000 or similar scale map, draw a profile across the grain of the terrain for about 10 km. Repeat for a perpendicular direction and compare the results. State your vertical exaggeration.
2. Choose some steep road hills on a map of a mountainous area and calculate their average gradient. If you know the maximum gradient, how do the two compare?
3. Draw a profile along a suitable stretch of motorway in a hilly area. Use a 1:25 000 map if you can.
4. Plan a new stretch of railway line across undulating territory, remembering that embankment and cutting rarely exceeds 10–15 m, and that viaducts and tunnels are expensive. Keep gradients as low as possible and estimate your maximum gradient. (A 1:50 000 map is suitable.)
5. Draw a profile along an unimproved main road. If you can find a road whose line has been determined at two different periods (e.g. part Roman, part mediaeval), use this and compare the two sections.
6. Draw a river profile such as that in figure 5.5 for a stream about 10 km long. Use a 1:25 000 map.
7. Draw a similar profile for a longer stream (for example, the River Coquet in Northumberland) to a smaller scale using a 1:50 000 map.
8. Carry out a hypsometric survey of a drainage basin covering an area of 10–20 km² using a 1:25 000 map. Repeat the exercise for a river which you think will provide a differently shaped graph.

Further reading

Bale, 1976, pp. 163–8
Guest, 1975, pp. 14–15, 30–1, 34–5
Hammond and McCullagh, 1974, pp. 63–9
Holt and Marjoram, 1973, pp. 228–31
Kent and Moore, 1974
McCullagh, 1978, pp. 21–34
Mathematics for the Majority, 1974, pp. 24–8
Monkhouse and Wilkinson, 1971, pp. 118–54
Sparks, 1972, pp. 94–119

6 Time, speed and rate

6.1. Time

The three basic units of physical science are length, mass and time. Geography is concerned largely with the first, hardly at all with the second, and with time to a limited extent. Time is important in geography in two ways, firstly in its historical dimension and secondly with ideas of rate of change, and especially with speed. The field of historical geography is an important but specialist one, and we shall only touch on it in this chapter before turning briefly to ideas of speed and rate.

6.2. The time-series graph

Time-series graphs are common and have an extensive statistical literature; here we merely give two introductory examples as a reminder of the idea and to serve to point out a few basic ideas about graphs. Readers wishing to follow these ideas further should consult statistical texts such as Gregory, 1975, or Hammond and McCullagh, 1974.

Regular census figures in developed countries provide interesting time-series. In Britain, for example, these began in 1801, though the accuracy of the earlier ones is somewhat questionable. Boundary changes make interpretation difficult at times, but many rural parishes have remained unchanged throughout the census period.

Figure 6.1 shows the populations of three adjacent villages in south Nottinghamshire; all are well nucleated, the majority of the population living near the village centres. They show a period of growth, decline and re-growth, but they also show contrasts. While Bunny and Bradmore remained under a single landowner their sizes remained identical, but after this period Bunny acquired some ribbon development. Costock, which was not an estate village followed a similar pattern to the other two for most of the nineteenth century but twenty years later. Here is fruitful material for the local historian.

Figure 6.2 is given in two forms. It shows a time-series, taken from figures in the British Annual Abstract

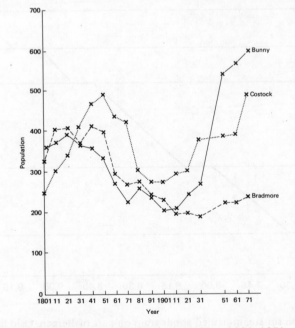

Figure 6.1. Populations of three parishes in south Nottinghamshire, 1801–1971.

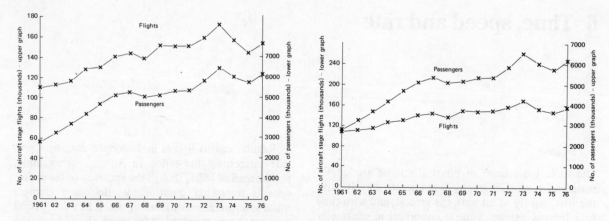

Figure 6.2. Alternative illustrations showing British internal air flights and passenger numbers for 1961–1976.

of Statistics, for airline passenger flights and passenger numbers, the scales for these being to the left and right of the graphs respectively. The two graphs give quite different impressions without any of the commoner tricks used in such cases. The first graph suggests that the numbers of flights and passengers are going up in unison, while the second that the numbers of passengers are going up more swiftly than the numbers of flights. The only differences between the two sets of graphs are the different scales used on the vertical axes. Many similar problems of graphical and statistical interpretation may be found in Huff, 1973, and Reichmann, 1961.

6.3. Speed

Speed is largely of interest to geographers in the field of communications, although wind speeds and river flow rates are also of importance. Figure 6.3 shows a type of distance-time graph which may be familiar to readers. Such graphs are actually used in planning railway timetables. Note that horizontal portions of the graph indicate time spent at stations, and that a train travelling in the opposite direction would be represented by a downward sloping line. (It is almost a universal convention to plot time horizontally on graphs.)

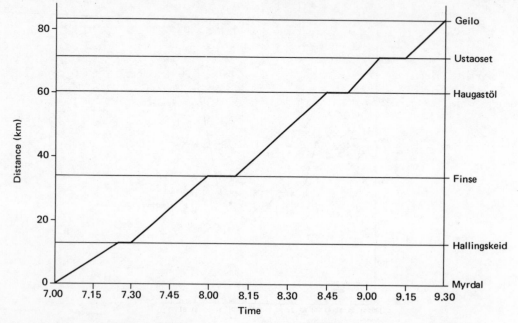

Figure 6.3. Distance-time graph for steam-hauled goods train on part of Bergen–Oslo line, Norway, summer 1961.

In the figure the section from Myrdal to Hallingskeid is covered in 25 min for the 13 km. This is a speed of 13/25 km per minute or 31 km per hour. The quantity 13/25 is also the gradient of the graph, illustrating the point that the gradient of a distance-time graph gives the speed; the steeper the graph, the faster the train. Thus on the downhill stretch from Haugastöl to Ustaoset, the speed scheduled is 54 km per hour. In fact the graph is not a straight line but a continuous curve, and the speed is then given by the gradient of the tangent to the curve; the graph merely gives a suitably simplified representation of reality.

The historical change in speed is particularly easy to investigate for railways by using old timetables. In Britain these are known as *Bradshaw's Guides* and those for 1887, 1910 and 1938 have been reprinted. It is an interesting exercise to plot the fastest train speeds for various journeys on a time-series graph, when various points emerge, for example the importance of electrification, and the failure to increase the speed of many cross-country journeys appreciably for the last century. An alternative and striking illustration of this is given in figure 25.5.

6.4. Rate

When we divide a quantity by a time we obtain a rate. Thus speed is the rate of change of distance. In all the graphs in this short chapter, the gradients correspond to rates. In figure 6.3 the gradients are in fact speed, in figure 6.1 the gradients are rate of increase in population, or, where negative, rate of decrease of population, and in figure 6.2 we have rate of increase of aircraft flights and of passenger numbers.

Rates of increase can be averaged over a period to provide a meaningful figure for comparison. In figure 6.2, for example, the average rate of increase of passengers over the fifteen year period was 220 000 per year. It would be unwise, however, to do this with more wildly fluctuating graphs such as those in figure 6.1; even in figure 6.2 the figure conceals an actual decrease over the last three years of the period.

Exercises

(The range of statistics suitable for plotting in graphs is enormous and the reader should have no difficulty in locating suitable figures.)

1. Using a diary, draw a graph showing lighting up time throughout the year (remember to allow for summer time). Calculate the rate of change of lighting-up time in minutes per week at three different times in the year by drawing tangents to the graph.
2. Using the mean monthly temperatures for a given location, draw a graph giving temperatures throughout the year. Calculate the rate of change of temperature in degrees per month in mid-April and mid-September by drawing tangents to the graph.
3. Find out about moving averages from a book such as Gregory, 1975, or Hammond and McCullagh, 1974. Plot some moving averages, e.g. five decade moving averages for figure 6.1 or five year moving averages for figure 6.3.
4. Find out how train speeds have altered on several contrasting routes, graphing the years 1887, 1910, 1938 and the present day.

Further reading

Briggs, 1974, pp. 45–51
Cole and King, 1968, pp. 404–22
Everson and Fitzgerald, 1969, pp. 112–21
Gregory, 1975, pp. 235–7
Hammond and McCullagh, 1974, pp. 70–88
Huff, 1973
Reichmann, 1961
Tidswell, 1976, pp. 256–9
Walker, 1973b, pp. 8–30
Wilson, 1973b, pp. 52–9

7 Vectors

7.1. Introduction

Many of the quantities which are used in science have not only magnitude, but direction. This is particularly true in physics where such quantities as force, momentum, velocity, acceleration, electrical potential and electrical current all have an associated direction as well as a size. Sometimes the direction is implicit; electrical current usually flows along a wire and we assume this without being told, needing only to know in which direction along the wire it flows. Sometimes it must be made explicit; to know the velocity of a rocket we must know both its speed and its direction, and indeed we also need to have some frame of reference or coordinate system to which we can relate this velocity.

Such quantities are called *vectors*. A vector quantity is strictly one which has magnitude and direction and combines according to the vector law of addition. Since every quantity we shall meet in this chapter which satisfies the first two criteria may be assumed to satisfy the third, we need not worry too much about the import of the third one.

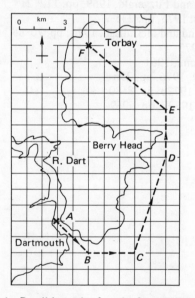

Figure 7.1. Possible path of yacht from Dartmouth to Torbay.

It may be because the idea of a vector is more powerful in three dimensions than two that geographers have made relatively little use of the idea, but the concept is worth some study. Because of this lack of use, some of this chapter is original in content, and therefore tentative in tone, but it also makes a good introduction to the following chapter. Most children learn about vectors in modern mathematics courses at about the age of twelve or thirteen, and it is therefore helpful to consider possible geographical uses of the concept.

7.2. Vectors in navigation problems

A common way of introducing vectors is by navigation problems as in figure 7.1 where a yacht is sailing from Dartmouth to Torbay along the course indicated. Navigators do not usually use a grid and normally work in nautical miles, but in this example we shall use the National Grid and work in kilometres. The route begins with the section **AB**, which may be defined as 2 km easting and −2 km northing (that is 2 km 'southing'). This is conventionally written

$$\begin{pmatrix} 2 \\ -2 \end{pmatrix}$$

While the coordinates (2, −2) refer to a specific point defined with reference to an origin, the vector refers to a movement of a particular length and direction which might be anywhere on the map. We are now in a position to write down the five vectors **AB**, **BC**, **CD**, **DE** and **EF** and to add them up by adding the *components* (that is eastings and northings) separately:

$$\begin{pmatrix} 2 \\ -2 \end{pmatrix} + \begin{pmatrix} 3 \\ 0 \end{pmatrix} + \begin{pmatrix} 2 \\ 6 \end{pmatrix} + \begin{pmatrix} 0 \\ 3 \end{pmatrix} + \begin{pmatrix} -5 \\ 4 \end{pmatrix} = \begin{pmatrix} 2 \\ 11 \end{pmatrix}$$

The final vector **AF** shows a total movement of 2 km east and 11 km north of the starting point.

7.3. Defining a vector by magnitude and direction

In practice navigators would give the vector **AB** in figure 7.1 as 2.8 km on a bearing of 135°. While this is convenient in many ways, it is much more difficult

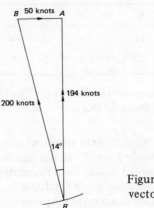

to calculate the overall result using this method. We shall assume the reader has met the simple trigonometry required to change from one form of giving a vector to the other, and merely give brief examples to refresh the memory (readers who wish may omit the details). For the vector **CD** in figure 7.1, the magnitude is 6.3 km, and the direction is 18° east of north. Then

x-component (easting) = 6.3 sin 18°
= 6.3 × 0.31 = 2.0 km

y-component (northing) = 6.3 cos 18°
= 6.3 × 0.95 = 6.0 km

The values of sin 18° and cos 18° are obtained from tables. In other examples, the reader may have to take negative signs into account.

The reverse procedure has already been met in essence. For **EF** the magnitude is, for example,

$$\sqrt{(5^2 + 4^2)} = \sqrt{41} = 6.4 \text{ km}$$

the same process as in section 3.2. The angle θ which **EF** makes with the horizontal is then given as in section 5.2 by

$$\tan \theta = \tfrac{4}{5}$$

so that using tables, $\theta = 39°$. The geographical bearing of the vector **EF** is thus 270° + 39° = 309°. When vectors are given in magnitude–bearing form, they must be converted to component form before adding them. The alternative procedure of accurate scale drawing is possible, but there is a grave danger of serious cumulative errors in more complicated drawings.

7.4. Velocities as vectors

(This section may be omitted at a first reading.)

All vector quantities may be added in the way described in sections 7.2 and 7.3. We give a lone example using velocities as an example. An aeroplane has to fly due north from Rome to Venice. The wind has a velocity of 50 knots from the west. (Winds are exceptional in that the direction they come from rather than where they are going is always given. A knot is a speed of one nautical mile per hour.) If the aircraft's air-speed is 200 knots, what is the effective speed relative to the ground, and on what course should the pilot steer?

The velocity diagram is shown in figure 7.2. The velocity of the aeroplane through the air is represented by **RB** which is drawn to scale and the velocity of the wind by **BA** which is again drawn on the same scale. The resulting velocity, represented by **RA** must be due north. The figure is most easily drawn by beginning

Figure 7.2. Example of using vectors to add velocities.

with AB and AR, and locating B. (R cannot be located since we do not know the velocity **RA**. However, we do know **BA**.) A pair of compasses is used to mark off an arc centre B, radius BR which will be four times the wind speed. The answer can then be obtained by measurement on the figure (or by calculation). The pilot needs to steer on a bearing of 346° (14° west of north), and the ground speed will be 194 knots. Since the distance from Rome to Venice is about 212 nautical miles, the time will be (212/194) = 1.09 hours or about 1 hr 6 min.

7.5. Prevailing wind

We can associate another magnitude with wind, the percentage frequency with which it blows from one of the eight cardinal points of the compass. Table 7.1 gives data for two stations from observations taken over a period of forty years. Such data are often illustrated by wind-roses such as those in figure 7.3, where the lengths of the eight arms are proportional to the percentage frequencies given in table 7.1.

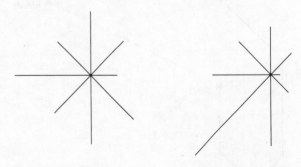

(a) Lerwick, Shetland   (b) Belvoir Castle, Leics.

Figure 7.3. Wind-roses showing relative frequencies of winds at two stations in Great Britain.

Direction	N	NE	E	SE	S	SW	W	NW	Calm
Lerwick (Shetland Isles)	14	10	6	13	14	11	16	10	6
Belvoir castle (Leics.)	10	6	2	5	15	24	13	10	15

Table 7.1. Percentage frequencies of winds for two stations in Britain. (Data from Bilham, 1938.)

A question which we might wish to ask about such data is 'What is the prevailing wind?' In the case of Belvoir Castle, this is fairly obviously from the south-west, and the direction with the greatest relative frequency could be taken as the direction of the prevailing wind. But for Lerwick four different directions have almost equal percentages, and only two of these are from adjacent directions. In this case the need for some more accurate definition becomes apparent.

One way of attempting a solution to this problem is to treat each arm of the wind-rose as a separate vector, each one of which points towards the centre of the rose. This is done for Belvoir Castle in figure 7.4, starting with the north wind and working clockwise round the rose, making each vector proportional in length to the corresponding arm of the rose. The resultant vector (pecked in the diagram) gives the bearing of the prevailing wind as 242°, that is between south-west and west. Figure 7.4 is difficult to draw accurately, and the solution by calculation using the method of section 7.3 is recommended for those who can manage it.

. The magnitude of the resultant vector has some meaning, but the temptation to associate it with velocity should be avoided. In some sense it is a measure of the dominance of the prevailing wind. The lengths of the resultant are 31 units at Belvoir Castle and 9 units at Lerwick, indicating that the direction of the prevailing wind is much more marked at the former station.

This technique appears to have been little used, but one might speculate on the patterns which would arise if sufficient data were available. It suffers from the disadvantage that it takes no account of wind speed. It might also be used to study the movement of sand dunes, the spread of wind-borne seeds and the effects of atmospheric pollution. A similar technique has been used to study tidal movements, and Sparks, 1972, gives an example which includes a weighting for the magnitude of the wind.

7.6. Road systems as vectors

The roads leading out of a town are vectors in a rough and ready sense, and we can treat them as vectors to examine the road system. Since roads are not straight lines, some arbitrary way must be found of fixing their exact bearing. There are ways of deciding which roads are radial roads (leading out of the town) and orbital roads (going around it) and we shall look at this again in section 21.8, but for the time being we will allow common sense to decide which roads lead radially away from the town centre.

We can fix the directions of radial roads by drawing a circle around the town centre with a fixed radius. Where the radial road cuts this circle will arbitrarily determine the direction of this road by its bearing from the town centre. Since in most developed countries towns are 15–25 km apart except in heavily industrialised areas, about half this distance is a suitable radius, and thus we shall fix an arbitrary radius at the convenient distance of 10 km

Figure 7.5 illustrates this for Shrewsbury, England, which has nine main roads leading from it (Department of the Environment 'A' class roads). Straight lines are drawn from the town centre to the points where the roads cut the 10 km circle, and the bearings of these lines are recorded in table 7.2. Each road is then regarded as a vector of unit length and the components worked out from the sines and cosines of

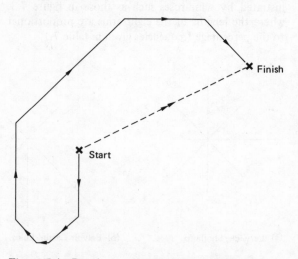

Figure 7.4. Resultant wind direction at Belvoir Castle, Leics.

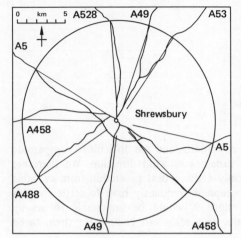

Figure 7.5. Main road system for 10 km around Shrewsbury.

Road	Destination	Grid-bearing	x-component	y-component
A49	Whitchurch	21°	0.36	0.93
A53	Market Drayton	36°	0.59	0.81
A5	Telford	106°	0.96	−0.28
A458	Much Wenlock	135°	0.71	−0.71
A49	Church Stretton	187°	−0.12	−0.99
A488	Bishop's Castle	235°	−0.82	−0.57
A458	Welshpool	269°	−1.00	0.02
A5	Llangollen	301°	−0.86	0.52
A528	Ellesmere	359°	−0.02	1.00
	Total		−0.20	0.69

Table 7.2. Calculation of resultant road vector for Shrewsbury, England.

appropriate angles found from the bearings. The components are added as in the table, and the magnitude and direction of the resultant calculated as in section 7.3 giving a vector of magnitude 0.72 with bearing 344°. This direction seems to reflect the paucity of routes in the hilly areas to the south of the town.

This system takes no account of the importance of the individual roads, giving them all equal weights. A more sophisticated calculation could be based on the actual traffic flows along the roads as measured in a sampling experiment. These flows could then be multiplied by the individual components for each road. Alternatively a points system could be given according to the assumed importance of each road in the system, for example: motorway, 16 points; primary road, 8 points; other main road, 4 points; secondary road, 2 points; minor road, 1 point. In these systems, however, the magnitude of the resultant vector would be very hard to interpret.

Even with the simple system outlined for Shrewsbury above, the magnitude means little except to compare the amount of bias in the road systems for several towns. For inland towns it is usually low, and in some cases, for example Orange on the River Rhone in France, the radius of the circle can make some difference. We shall return to these ideas in the next chapter. A further use of vectors is implicit in section 17.7, where they can be used in the determination of the most favourable point for locating an industry.

Exercises

1. Make a study (as a group exercise) of prevailing winds over the British Isles.
2. Study the transport systems of a group of related towns for any bias in either the road or rail systems. For example use the towns along the Welsh Border from Chester to Hereford, the towns of the Rhone Valley, towns along either side of an international boundary such as the USA and Canada.
3. Analyse rail services around a town using the number of trains per weekday as the magnitude of each vector. Does the result show any special bias towards the capital city or local large town?
4. The figures on a dartboard are an example of a vector system such as those examined here. An interesting project is to design a dartboard in which the bias is a low as possible. (See also Selkirk, 1976a, and Cook, 1977.)

Further reading

Bilham, 1938, pp. 42-72
Cole and King, 1968, pp. 417–19 and 596–600
Cook, 1977
Guest, 1975, pp. 90–3
Selkirk, 1976a
Sparks, 1972, pp. 255–6

8 Quantification

8.1. Introduction

In sections 7.5 and 7.6 we saw how a mathematical concept might suggest useful tools for measuring geographical ideas. In this chapter we shall reverse the process and develop mathematical tools for handling geographical concepts. To do this we shall choose some unfamiliar but simple (and therefore rather unimportant) concepts and the ideas will be tentative in tone. However, as we shall see in chapter 9, geographers have frequently had difficulties themselves in their search for ways of measuring new concepts.

The first step in the path to quantification of a new concept is frequently comparison. For example Brasilia is more central than Rio de Janeiro as capital of Brazil, Italy has a better developed road system than Greece and Bolivia is more mountainous than Paraguay. In this chapter we shall show how comparisons such as these can be refined to produce numerical measurements of the basic ideas.

8.2. Hilliness of a road

The first example stems from a simple real life situation in which the author was involved some years ago. The members of a cycling club in Oxford used two different roads for time-trials over a distance of 25 miles. Each course was for 12½ miles out and home along a main road outside the city; one was on the Brackley road (A43) and one on the Faringdon road (A415). Naturally the question arose as to which was the more difficult course.

This is a complex question which can be split up into simpler questions. Such factors as quality of road surface, shelter from the wind, amount of other traffic on the road and the psychological attitudes of the riders might be considered. However, perhaps the most important question is the degree of hilliness of each course, and this is the aspect we shall deal with here.

A typical scientific reaction to a problem such as this would be to carry out a controlled experiment and analyse the times of the riders over the two courses. However, such experiments are expensive and time consuming, and it is difficult to compensate for such variables as wind direction. We therefore attempt only a theoretical prediction from available data. Geographers frequently have to settle for this approach since it would be impossible to set up experiments on a scale vast enough for them to be valid.

Figure 8.1 gives sketch maps with contours and spot heights for the two courses, taken from Ordnance Survey 1:50 000 maps 152 and 164. Heights are given in metres, though the contours are in fact at 50 ft intervals. The reader should stop at this point and try to decide which course looks the more difficult.

The Brackley course rises 64 m from 61 m to 125 m, while the Faringdon course falls 5 m from 126 m to 121 m. At first sight the former involves more climbing. Closer examination shows that the Faringdon course has a low point at about 76 m, which involves additional climbing. A more detailed examination of heights by adding all differences between consecutive points of known height (since they have to be climbed in one direction or the other) gives for the Brackley course

$$2 + 1 + 7 + 15 + 10 + 3 + 20 + 4 + 9 + 2 + 3 = 76 \text{ m}$$

A similar calculation for the Faringdon course gives 125 m. This confirms the author's experience that the Faringdon course is harder, though it should be noticed that there are more spot heights and contour lines on that road which make it easier to include minor variations in its profile.

8.3. Developing a measure of hilliness

There are three ways of developing the idea of measuring hilliness. The first is generalisation, that is making the idea more widely applicable. The hilliness of different lengths of road might need to be compared, and to do this we adapt the idea of gradient. Thus the Brackley road has 76 m of height change in 20 km ($12\frac{1}{2}$ miles). Its hilliness might therefore be defined as 3.8 m per km. This is merely another way of saying that its average gradient (including both up and down grades) is 0.0038. It would, however, be unsuitable to use this measure for a canal, where the actual total

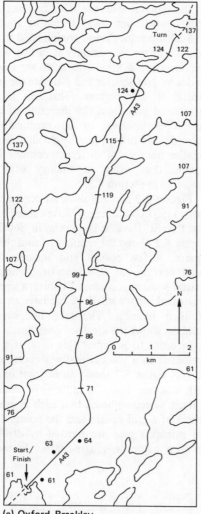

(a) Oxford–Brackley

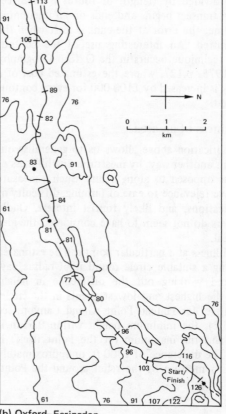

(b) Oxford–Faringdon

Figure 8.1. Comparison of hilliness of two roads near Oxford.

height change would be more important.

The second development is to increase accuracy by using a larger scale map or carrying out an original survey. However, a third development, that of simplification, can often yield more useful ideas. The obvious extreme simplification of using only the two end points is, as we saw in section 8.2, too drastic. A more reasonable simplification is to count the number of times each road crosses a contour line. This is six for the Brackley course and nine for the Faringdon course. This is a very crude measure in an area of only slightly undulating relief; it would be very much improved if 1:25 000 maps with contours at 5 m intervals were available. On the scale used here a road may rise and fall a small amount and cross the same contour several times, or cross no contour. In an

area of high relief, this measure is much more accurate.

For example, on a 1:50 000 map of Morocco with 10 m contour interval, two sections of the Marrakech to Fès road can be compared in a matter of moments:

| Moussa – Beni Mellal | $11\frac{1}{2}$ km | 12 contours |
| Beni Mellal – Aich | 13 km | 3 contours |

The advantage of simple measures is that they encourage measurement; the disadvantage of the hypsometric survey in section 5.11 is the time spent measuring areas. Unfortunately the most mathematically correct measures are often the hardest to use, as we shall see in the next chapter.

Howling and Hunter, 1975, have proposed

contour counting as a measure of relief except that they use it for a straight line transect, dividing the number of contour intervals by the length of route, which is effectively the technique above. Their suggestion that this is equal to (number of contour lines + 1) divided by (length of route) is incorrect unless the transect begins and ends on an uncounted contour line; the error at the ends is least when the +1 is omitted. An interesting use of the contour counting technique occurs in the Oxford Geography Project, 1975, p.127, where the estimated cost of a motorway is increased by £100 000 for every contour line crossed.

8.4. Hilliness of an area

The simplification above allows us to generalise our measure in another way, by measuring the hilliness of an area as opposed to along a line. Such a measure would have relevance to ease of farming, difficulty of communications, and likely tourist interest. Oddly geographers do not seem to have considered the idea a great deal.

The hilliness at a particular point can be estimated by drawing a suitable circle round it of radius, say, 0.5 km and working out the difference in height between the highest and lowest points in the circle. For example, for Plateau Point, Grand Canyon (see section 5.2), the minimum height within 0.5 km is 2475 ft and the maximum (at the Point itself) is 3775 ft. The difference of 1300 ft, or approximately 400 m, is a measure of the relief around the Point.

In the Canyon area, the relief can be three times this while only 2 km away it can be as little as 50 ft.

Such a measure is too complicated to use for many points and we can simplify it in two ways. Firstly if the map has a kilometre grid, we can replace the circles by grid squares and estimate the hilliness at the centre of each square. This can introduce some directional bias from the direction of the grid lines, but it is unlikely to be practically significant. Secondly we can replace height difference by counting the number of different contour lines in each square, thus using an analogy with the process suggested in section 8.3.

Figures 8.2 and 8.3 show an example of this taken from 1:50 000 Ordnance Survey sheet 159 and covering the St David's Peninsula in south-west Wales. Figure 8.2 shows the number of contours in each grid square. A few coastal grid squares which contain small portions of cliff have been eliminated. Other coastal squares contain, of course, a smaller land area than usual and we will therefore have an underestimate of their hilliness. The solid line surrounding the numbers shows the idealised coastline.

In order to interpret this data, it is necessary to present it in a more visually acceptable manner. To do this figure 8.3 shows an *isogram* or *isopleth* map with 'contour' lines for hilliness of values $2\frac{1}{2}$ and $4\frac{1}{2}$. It must be remembered that each figure refers to the centre of a grid square and the points through which the isopleths pass are plotted by dividing the lines between adjacent square-centres in suitable ratios.

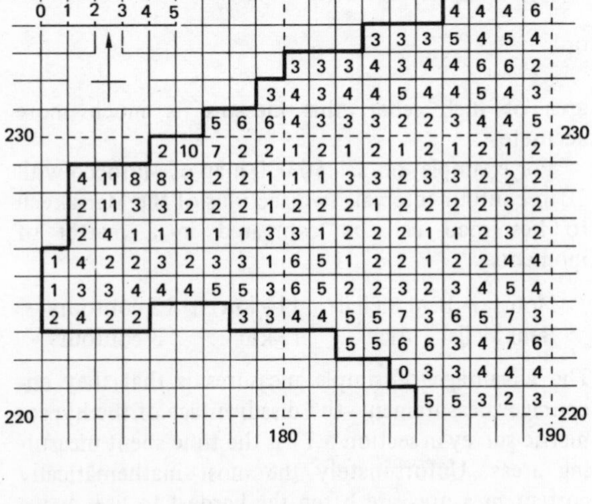

Figure 8.2. Number of contour lines in each 1 km grid square – St David's area, Wales.

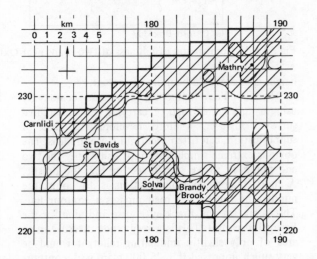

Figure 8.3. Lines of equal hilliness drawn from data of figure 8.2, using isograms of values $2\frac{1}{2}$ and $4\frac{1}{2}$.

Thus if adjacent values are 4 and 5, the $4\frac{1}{2}$ isopleth passes mid-way between them; if adjacent values are 4 and 7, then the $4\frac{1}{2}$ isopleth divides them in the ratio 1:5. This process is known as *interpolation*. With a little practice it may be carried out quite quickly and accurately.

In figure 8.3 the area of low relief on the peneplain in the centre of the picture is not unexpected. More surprising is that the coastal area, in spite of its cliffs, only emerges as an area of medium hilliness. The very hilly areas are caused by two other features, the igneous outcrops around the hill Carnlidi in the north-west, and the steep sided valleys of Brandy Brook and at Solva and Mathry. These impede communications across the south of the peninsula, and correlate well with areas of woodland on the 1:50 000 map, where the ground is too steep to cultivate and protected from the prevailing south-westerly wind.

A map such as that above takes about one hour to draw; this is not an excessive time. If isograms are too complicated, then the squares themselves may be shaded, and this is an even easier process. We shall meet a similar technique in chapter 18 when we examine density of road networks.

8.5. Directional bias

Usually concepts lead to the need for, and development of, a measuring device. In the last chapter, the converse happened when the existence of vectors suggested the consideration of the road system leading from a town as a set of vectors. In the case of Shrewsbury (section 7.6), the nine main roads produced a resultant vector with magnitude 0.72 and direction 344°. This idea is developed for four towns on the Welsh Border of England in table 8.1, two major centres (Shrewsbury and Hereford) and two centres of slightly less importance (Ludlow and Leominster).

Shrewsbury and Ludlow have a resultant vector of the same magnitude, 0.72. However, Ludlow, with its poorly developed road system, is less likely to have a vector of such large magnitude. In order to compare the towns on the same basis, we must allow for the differing number of routes for each town. We do this by defining the directional bias coefficient B as follows:

$$B = \frac{\text{magnitude of the resultant vector}}{\text{sum of magnitudes of individual vectors}}$$

In our examples, we have taken the magnitudes of individual vectors as one in every case, but this

Town	'A' class roads	Resultant vector Magnitude	Direction	B	
Shrewsbury	9	0.72	344°	$0.72 \div 9$	= 0.08
Ludlow	5	0.72	163°	$0.72 \div 5$	= 0.14
Leominster	8	0.38	171°	$0.38 \div 8$	= 0.05
Hereford	10	1.32	333°	$1.32 \div 10$	= 0.13

Table 8.1. Calculation of the directional bias coefficient B for four towns.

definition will cover cases where we wish to give different values to the vectors according to their importance. The value of B cannot be less than zero, nor can it be more than one, so that the range of values which B can take is very convenient. Shrewsbury, for example has a value of B equal to $0.72 \div 9 = 0.08$.

It can now be seen that none of the four towns has a large bias – one would not expect this for well-developed inland route centres. The most biassed towns are Ludlow with its poorly developed road system, and Hereford with its lack of main roads to the south-east. If the direction of the bias is examined there is a tendency for it to lie in the direction of easiest communication, or away from the direction of hardest communication. An extended examination of further towns along the Welsh Border produces no tendency for routes to lie away from or towards that border, and this conclusion is not altered by giving magnitudes to the roads according to their importance.

8.6. Understanding what a measure describes

In developing a coefficient to measure an idea we are trying to reduce what may be an ill-thought-out and loosely defined concept to a single number. One problem is that the number might not describe precisely what we think it does. In order to understand what the number does describe, we must apply it; and there are two ways in which we can do this. One way has been dealt with above, that is by trying out the idea in specific geographical contexts. The other way of trying it out is by inventing simple hypothetical cases and seeing what results they give. This is a more mathematical approach, and curiously it is easier because the labour of computation is usually simplified.

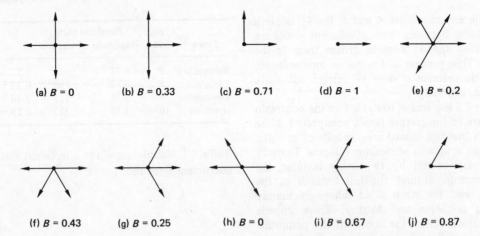

(a) $B = 0$ (b) $B = 0.33$ (c) $B = 0.71$ (d) $B = 1$ (e) $B = 0.2$

(f) $B = 0.43$ (g) $B = 0.25$ (h) $B = 0$ (i) $B = 0.67$ (j) $B = 0.87$

Figure 8.4. Values of the directional bias coefficient B for some simple systems based on angles in multiples of $90°$ or $60°$.

Figure 8.4 shows some examples of simple hypothetical systems which can easily be analysed, and by examining them, something can be learned about the way in which the quantity B works. Symmetrical systems such as (a) and (h) show no bias; the roads balance out. It is as well to notice (h) carefully, because in one sense that system certainly shows bias, but in two opposite directions. Thus symmetrical bias will not be revealed by the coefficient. Examples (b), (f) and (i) show cases which would be typical of sea-side towns. The lowest non-zero value is (e) which has 0.2 with one road missing from a symmetrical six road layout. Even this is high compared with the values in table 8.1. Example (j) may be compared with St David's in figure 8.3, where for the main road system $B = 0.92$, the angle between the two roads there being $45°$.

Case (h) leads us to consider further ways of describing bias, which can be developed from the angles between adjacent roads (in this case $120°$, $60°$, $120°$ and $60°$) compared with the ideal of $90°$ between each pair for a four road system. Readers might care to consider ways of developing this.

8.7. Eccentricity

As a final example of measuring a concept we consider the idea of developing an index of eccentricity. In chapter 12 we shall examine how centres can be located, and here we shall try to assess how far a particular point is from being the centre of a given area. The idea is of such obvious importance that it is rather surprising that little use has been made of it. What properties should a coefficient of eccentricity possess? It is convenient if there is a limited range of values from zero to one; and for an area the shape of

a circle we would like the centre to have eccentricity zero, and a point on the circumference to have eccentricity one. This is easily achieved by dividing the distance of the point from the centre of the circle, L, by its radius, R. Thus the eccentricity, E, may be defined by $E = L/R$, where (provided the point is within or on the edge of the circle) $0 \leq E \leq 1$. Values of E greater than one will be achieved when the point is outside the circle, which can usefully emphasise an atypical situation such as that of the county hall of Northumberland, England, which lies outside the county boundary. We have still to fix the circle, a point we will examine more closely in chapter 12, but it is most convenient here to draw the smallest possible circle around the area we are considering. This is illustrated in figure 8.5, and provides the chief difficulty of the process since it must be done by guesswork. The circle is called the *circumcircle* of the area, and the centre the *circumcentre*.

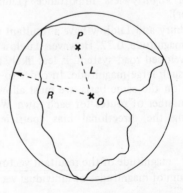

Figure 8.5. Eccentricity of a point P in an irregular shape $(E = L/R)$.

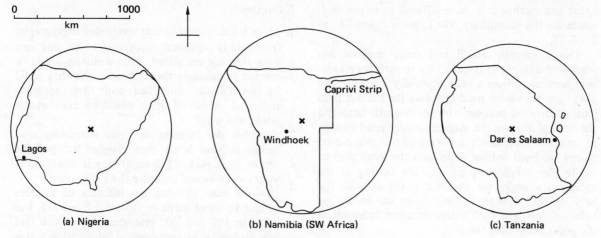

Figure 8.6. Circumcentres (×) and capitals of three African countries.

Table 8.2. Calculation of eccentricity of capital city for three African nations.

Country	Capital	L (km)	R (km)	E = L/R
Nigeria	Lagos	700	780	0.90
Namibia	Windhoek	220	830	0.27
Namibia (without Caprivi strip)	Windhoek	140	760	0.18
Tanzania	Dar-es-Salaam	430	770	0.56

Figure 8.6 shows examples of three African countries and the relevant calculations are given in table 8.2. There is, in fact, no need to calculate the distances in kilometres; the measurements can be taken directly from the map, whatever the scale, since E has no units. The table shows a good range of values from 0.18 to 0.90, so that E discriminates well between different situations. The high value of Lagos in Nigeria is typical in nations which have developed as a hinterland from a coastal port; some countries in this situation, such as Brazil, have subsequently moved their capitals. Namibia illustrates one danger of using the circumcircle; the removal of the narrow Caprivi strip (an anachronism from colonial days) makes a vast difference to the value of E. We shall return to this point in chapters 9 and 12.

8.8. An alternative measure of eccentricity

Another and at first sight rather crude method of measuring eccentricity is illustrated for Tanzania in figure 8.7. This method is affected slightly by the map projection, but we shall ignore this. A pair of east-west parallel lines is drawn which just enclose

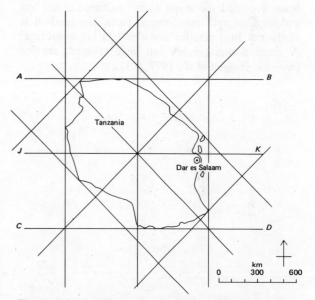

Figure 8.7. An alternative method of calculating the eccentricity of a point in a region (Tanzania).

the area to north and south. These lines are labelled AB and CD in the figure, and JK is drawn mid-way between them. We then measure the distance, S, of AB (or CD) from JK and the distance, M, of the point under investigation from JK. From these we calculate $F_1 = M/S = 0.10$ in much the same way as we found E in the last section.

This process is repeated for NE-SW lines ($F_2 = 0.50$), north-south lines ($F_3 = 0.81$) and NW-SE lines ($F_4 = 0.59$) and finally we average this giving

$$F = \tfrac{1}{4}(0.10 + 0.50 + 0.81 + 0.59) = 0.50$$

Concepts

Using this method it is more difficult to obtain high values for the eccentricity. For Lagos in figure 8.6 (a) $F = 0.61$.

This apparently rough and ready measure has several advantages. It is quite easy to perform reasonably accurately from a map, especially if a ruler and a 45° set square are used to locate the parallel lines (the differences between the north–south lines and the vertical edges of the map are usually small enough to ignore). Alternatively a tracing of the area can be placed on lined writing paper and the lines used to locate the parallels by placing the tracing at the appropriate angles for the four positions with the help of the set square. Once again the index lies between zero and one, except in some cases where the point lies outside the area.

The method can be refined by using more than four sets of lines, although this alters the value of F but little; the ultimate would be an infinite set of lines. Provided the shape to be measured is not too awkward or split into several parts, the method is easily put into practice and this is a big advantage. A more accurate index can be developed, see for example, Haggett et al., 1977, p.312.

Exercises

1. Make a list of some indices mentioned in geography (particularly economic geography) and find out how they are calculated. What statistics would be needed to calculate them? Discuss how they could be generalised, simplified and their accuracy increased. Which of these would be most worthwhile, and why?
2. Compare the hilliness of some alternative road routes in your home area. Suggest two possible routes for a 40 km (25 mile) bicycle time-trial in your local area and compare their hilliness.
3. Draw a map showing the hilliness of an area similar to those maps in figures 8.2 and 8.3. Use between 100 and 200 grid squares. Can you find any geological or geographical information which will explain your results?
4. Continue your investigation of bias in questions 2 and 3 of chapter 7.
5. 'Aspect' is important in farming. This means the lie of the land, northern slopes of a valley catch more sunlight than southern slopes (in the northern hemisphere). Aspect has two components, direction and amount of slope. How could you incorporate these into a vector description of aspect? Can you discover any relationship between aspect and land use? (See, for example land-use maps such as that in the Oxford Geography Project, 1975, facing page 110).
6. Use an index of eccentricity to investigate the centrality of the capitals of South American nations, or of local government centres in your area, to the areas they serve. Comment on any recent boundary changes, for example those in Great Britain.

Further reading

Haggett, Cliff and Frey, 1977, p. 312
Howling and Hunter, 1975

9 The shape of areas

9.1. Introduction

In this chapter the theme of quantification is continued by examining the measurement of a concept which a number of geographers have tried to pin down over recent years. This is the elusive idea of the shape of an area. It is no part of the contention of this chapter that this concept is of earth shattering importance to all geographers. Rather it is of interest to a minority of researchers in particular branches of geography. It is, however, useful as a vehicle to show how a particular idea has been tackled in practice by geographers, to illustrate a number of pitfalls in the process of quantification, and to provide excellent examples of algebraic formulae in use.

It is not surprising that geographers have found shape difficult to quantify, since the idea lacks clarity from the start. This accounts for the variety of approaches. The main concept in geographers' minds seems to be summed up in the word 'compactness'; and this idea is of value not only in economic and political geography, but also in physical geography. Readers who are troubled by the algebraic formulae in this chapter can easily omit it, although it will probably be worth the effort to understand their use since this is inevitable in many applications of mathematics to the sciences.

9.2. Form ratio

The earliest examination of shape by a geographer seems to have been an investigation of drainage basin characteristics by Horton in 1932. He measured the area of the shape, A, and the length of the line, L, joining the area's two most distant points. Thus for the Rush Gill–Aira Beck basin considered in section 5.11, $A = 13.64$ km^2 and $L = 7.4$ km as illustrated in figure 9.2.

Since A has the units of length squared, and L of length, the quantity A/L will also have units of length, and will therefore vary with the size of the figure. This is illustrated in figure 9.1 which shows two rectangles of the same shape, the second being twice the size of the first. Notice that when lengths are doubled, areas are quadrupled; this important point is often

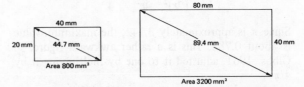

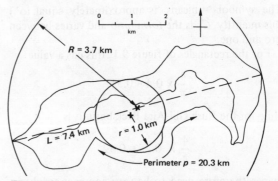

Figure 9.1. Areas and lengths on two similar figures drawn to scale.

Figure 9.2. Rush Gill – Aira Beck basin (figure 5.8) showing constants used in calculation of various shape ratios.

forgotten. The quantity A/L also changes from

$$800 \div 44.7 = 17.9 \text{ mm}$$

to

$$3200 \div 89.4 = 35.8 \text{ mm}$$

Thus A/L depends on the size of the figure and is not a measure of its shape. The easiest way to overcome this problem is to use the square of the length, giving the ratio A/L^2. For both halves of figure 9.1 this gives the value 0.4; in the first half, for example,

$$A/L^2 = 800 \div 44.7^2 = 800 \div 2000 = 0.4$$

This is, in fact, Horton's ratio and its value for the Rush Gill – Aira Beck example is

$$13.64 \div 7.4^2 = 13.64 \div 54.76 = 0.25$$

It is useful to know the maximum and minimum values of such a ratio. For a long, narrow shape, the area may be almost zero and L may be as large as we like. Thus A/L^2 has a minimum value of zero. The most compact figure of all is the circle where L is equal to the diameter. If r is the radius of the circle, two well-known formulae are

$$A = \pi r^2$$

and

$$L = 2r$$

Hence

$$\frac{A}{L^2} = \frac{\pi r^2}{(2r)^2} = \frac{\pi r^2}{4r^2} = \frac{\pi}{4}$$

Since π is approximately 3.142, the maximum value is about 0.788. This is a rather awkward figure, so Gibbs, 1961, adjusted it to one by multiplying it by $4/\pi$:

$$C_1 = \frac{4A}{\pi L^2} \approx 1.27\left(\frac{A}{L^2}\right)$$

(The symbol $\approx$ means 'is approximately equal to'.) This quantity, C_1 is the *form ratio* and varies between zero and one.

For the rectangles of figure 9.1, this has a value

$$\frac{4}{\pi} \times 0.4 = 0.51,$$

while for the Rush Gill-Aira Beck basin it is

$$\frac{4}{\pi} \times 0.25 = 0.32$$

Shapes therefore need to be very compact to obtain values of the form ratio above 0.5. Further examples of the form ratio are given for four eastern European countries in table 9.1 under the heading C_1. Two of these are illustrated in figure 9.3 where the reader should take care to avoid confusing L with the diameter of the circumscribing circle.

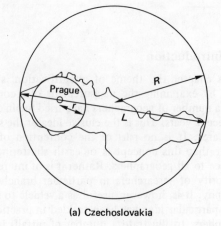

(a) Czechoslovakia

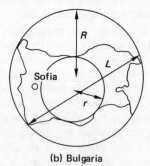

(b) Bulgaria

Figure 9.3. Calculation of shape ratios for two east European countries.

	Czechoslovakia	Austria	Bulgaria	Romania
A	128 000 km^2	83 600 km^2	111 000 km^2	239 500 km^2
L	765 km	595 km	520 km	740 km
R	385 km	300 km	275 km	370 km
r	108 km	120 km	126 km	223 km
p	2210 km	1870 km	1800 km	2440 km
C_1 (form ratio)	0.28	0.30	0.52	0.56
C_2 (circularity ratio)	0.33	0.30	0.43	0.50
C_3 (compactness ratio a)	0.28	0.30	0.47	0.56
C_4 (radius ratio)	0.28	0.40	0.46	0.60
C_5 (compactness ratio b)	0.711	–	–	0.969

Table 9.1. Constants and shape ratios for four countries in east Europe (see text for details).

9.3. Variations on the form ratio

Schumm, 1956, who also worked with drainage basins, used the *elongation ratio* which is separately quoted in several books. Schumm's ratio is, however, merely the square root of the form ratio, C_1, which means that it still has the same limits zero and one, but that its value is larger than the form ratio, since finding the square root of a number less than one increases its size. Other books use the same title for a different ratio which is L divided by a length perpendicular to L.

Haggett, Cliff and Frey, 1977, p. 309, also define the *ellipticity ratio*, which is merely the reciprocal of the form ratio, that is $\pi L^2/4A$. Its values vary from infinity to one, the latter being the value for a circle.

9.4. Circularity ratio

Ideas of shape can be approached in a different fashion by looking at the perimeter (p). Clearly, the longer the perimeter of a shape compared with its area, then the more convoluted is that shape. Miller, 1953, used this idea, again in the study of drainage basins. The same stages in the development can be worked through as in section 9.2. Since p is a length, it must be squared, giving an initial trial ratio of A/p^2. Once again this has a minimum value zero, and the maximum value will occur with the most compact shape – the circle. Here $A = \pi r^2$ and $p = 2\pi r$. This gives the maximum value of the ratio as

$$\frac{A}{p^2} = \frac{\pi r^2}{4\pi^2 r^2} = \frac{1}{4\pi} \approx 0.08$$

In order to make the maximum value one, we multiply by 4π, and define the *circularity ratio*, which we shall denote by C_2, as

$$C_2 = \frac{4\pi A}{p^2} \approx \frac{12.6A}{p^2}$$

We shall return to a further discussion of this ratio later, but an immediately obvious difficulty is the problem of measuring boundary length which was considered in chapter 3.

The boundary problem, however, raises no difficulties in the shapes of figure 9.1. In the first shape

$$C_2 = \frac{4\pi \times 800}{120^2} = 0.70$$

and the reader can check that the second shape gives the same value. For figure 9.2, the perimeter is difficult to determine exactly but may be estimated as 20.3 km, which gives $C_2 = 0.42$, indicating a fairly compact drainage basin. Further examples may be found in table 9.1.

9.5. Compactness ratio

The compactness ratio, C_3, is a slightly modified version of a coefficient suggested by J.P. Cole in 1964 in the study of political divisions and quoted in Blair and Biss, 1967. Since in many applications the most crucial points in an area are those furthest from the centre, we work out the circumradius R of the shape. This is the radius of the smallest circle surrounding the shape and is worked out by trial and error using a pair of compasses as in section 8.7. Using the same procedure as in sections 9.2 and 9.4, this gives

$$C_3 = \frac{A}{\pi R^2} \approx 0.32 \frac{A}{R^2}$$

Since, as pointed out in section 9.2, L is often very close in value to $2R$, C_1 and C_3 often produce similar values. Figure 9.2 presents an example of this case, since there $R = 3.7$ km giving $C_3 = 0.32$ as for C_1. Table 9.1 gives further examples.

9.6. Radius ratio

This avoids the need to find the area of the shape and is thus useful when the area is not readily available as in the study of drainage basins. As well as finding the circumradius, R, we can also find the *inradius, r*, which is the radius of the largest circle which will fit inside the shape, called the *incircle*. The radius ratio is defined by

$$C_4 = r/R$$

This has a pleasing simplicity. For figure 9.1, $C_4 = 20 \div 44.7 = 0.45$, while for figure 9.2, $C_4 = 1.0 \div 3.7 = 0.27$. Other examples may be found in table 9.1.

9.7. Criticism of coefficients C_1, C_2, C_3, C_4

One difficulty with the coefficients has already been noted, that is the problem of measuring p when calculating the circularity ratio. For example the values of p given in table 9.1 were taken from a 1:10 000 000 map, and cannot possibly be accurate. The other measurements will be to a higher standard of accuracy.

Another drawback in calculating the same ratio, C_2, is that in table 9.1 it is the only measure on which Czechoslovakia is less compact than Austria, and this suggests that it measures a somewhat different concept to the other ratios. Figure 9.4 gives a more telling example and also underlines the point made in section 8.6 about the value of considering simple mathematical examples as well as more complicated geographical ones. That figure shows three equal areas,

Concepts

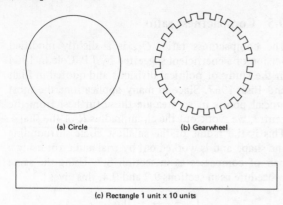

(a) Circle   (b) Gearwheel

(c) Rectangle 1 unit x 10 units

Figure 9.4. Three shapes of equal areas.

a circle, a gearwheel, and a rectangle whose sides are in the ratio 1 to 10. Few would doubt that the rectangle is by far the least compact of these shapes. However, assuming the radius of the circle to be one unit, its perimeter is 2π units. The perimeter of the gearwheel has been arranged to be 4π units, just twice as long. Because in the formula for C_2 the quantity p is squared, for the gearwheel $C_2 = 0.25$ since the area is unchanged. For the rectangle, the length is 5.60 units and the breadth 0.56 units giving the same area of 3.14 units and a perimeter of 12.32 units. This gives $C_2 = 0.26$, a value 'more compact' than the gearwheel.

In fact C_2 does not measure shape so much as a concept which might be called 'boundary convenience'. Since the more accurately we measure the perimeter, the more convoluted the boundary will appear, increasing accuracy will only serve to reduce C_2 further. In view of the difficulty of determining the catchment area of a river basin accurately, C_2 would appear to be particularly unsuited for use in this situation. It might be more appropriate to use it in political geography where the length of the boundary may be related to the amount of interaction with other nations, and to the difficulty of defending or policing the frontier.

All the other measures are open to the objection that they depend on a few special points (two when measuring L, three each fixing the circles when measuring R and r). C_1 is easiest to use if the area is known, since it then only requires a ruler. For certain shapes, the correct circumcircle is difficult to fix accurately which reduces the usefulness of C_3 and C_4. If the area is not known, C_4 is the most useful and requires the largest number of special points, that is six.

Geographers deserve some criticism for the cavalier way they have treated these formulae. Not infre-

quently they are quoted incorrectly, and in one case an already incorrect formula has been quoted with a further error. This is a timely warning against using formulae without understanding of their purpose. Even where complete understanding of the derivation is unlikely, a few simple trial exercises such as those in figures 9.1 and 9.4 will often avoid serious errors.

The measurement of shape has also been applied to particles of rock in physical geography, though here the shape of volumes rather than areas is considered, and the techniques are for the specialist. The reader should consult the references to Hanwell and Newson, 1973, and Cole and King, 1968, at the end of the chapter.

9.8. Compactness ratio

(This section may be omitted at a first reading.)
Blair and Bliss, 1967, proposed another compactness ratio which is completely different from C_3. This is

$$C_5 = \frac{A}{\sqrt{\{2\pi \int_A x^2 \, dA\}}}$$

where x is the distance of a typical point of the shape from the centroid (see section 12.12), and the integration is over the whole area. While this formula will be well outside the mathematical understanding of most readers, a few may recognise its relationship to the radius of gyration of a thin lamina.

Blair and Biss point out that C_5 tends to be larger than the other ratios, but still lies between zero and one. Two examples of their calculations are given in table 9.1, and in their paper they list values for fifty national territories. Of these, none is as compact as the square ($C_5 = 0.977$), but nearly half are more compact than an equilateral triangle ($C_5 = 0.909$). It has the important property that every point in the area is given equal prominence. Offshore islands have only a minimal effect, and 'holes' (e.g. omitting Lesotho from South Africa) cause no problems. Unfortunately its complexity rules it out for everyday use.

9.9. Average contact number

(This section may be omitted if desired.)
Haggett, Cliff and Frey, 1977, pp. 57–60, relate the use of C_1 in examining the shapes of a hundred Brazilian counties. Figure 9.5 shows the three most elementary ways in which regular shapes can pack together, and the triangles, squares and hexagons have values of C_1 equal to 0.42, 0.64 and 0.83 respectively. It might be expected that for counties not on the

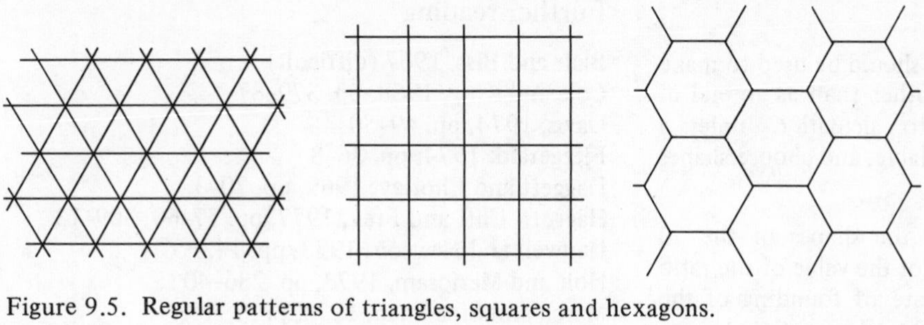

Figure 9.5. Regular patterns of triangles, squares and hexagons.

border of a territory, values of C_1 would cluster around these numbers. The distribution of values of C_1 in this example gives some evidence that this might be the case.

Following this lead they then categorise each county by the number of other counties it touches. In figure 9.5, for example, each triangle touches three other triangles, each square touches four others and each hexagon touches six others. Thus we can categorise the packing of the counties by calculating their 'average contact number'; if this is three the packing is triangular and so on.

This idea can be shown to be unsound by using Euler's formula which is familiar in many modern mathematics courses. This states that

$$v + r = e + 2$$

where in any planar map,

v is the number of vertices (junctions) under consideration,

r is the number of regions,

e is the number of edges which join the vertices and separate the regions.

We shall meet this formula again in section 26.4. It is convenient for the following argument to introduce the idea of a half-edge, so that $h = 2e$. Since each edge joins two vertices we can assign a half-edge to each vertex; and since each edge separates two regions we can assign a half-edge to each region. Thus in a regular hexagonal system, each vertex has three half-edges and each hexagon six half-edges.

Consider an irregular map of regions. It is rare for more than three regions to meet in a point. It usually happens only when regions are arbitrarily assigned as in the western USA (Utah, Colorado, Arizona and New Mexico). In England there is a Four Counties Inn (Staffordshire, Leicestershire, Derbyshire and Warwickshire) and a four counties stone (Gloucestershire, Warwickshire, Worcestershire and

Oxfordshire), but in both cases these relate to earlier boundaries which have since been changed. Thus we may assume that every vertex has three half-edges:

$$v = \tfrac{1}{3} h$$

and hence from Euler's formula

$$r + \tfrac{1}{3} h = \tfrac{1}{2} h + 2$$

This gives

$$r = \tfrac{1}{6} h + 2$$

$$\Rightarrow \qquad \frac{h}{r} = 6 - \frac{12}{r}$$

(The symbol $\Rightarrow$ may be read as 'hence'.)

The contact number for a region is the number of half-edges around it, so that the average contact number is the total number of half-edges, h, divided by the number of regions, that is h/r which is given above. For the current counties of England and Wales, for example, there are 22 which have no coastline, and these have 130 edges giving an average contact number of $130/22 = 5\tfrac{10}{11}$. The formula gives $5\tfrac{5}{11}$; the discrepancy is due to the fact that the formula ignores the counties round the edge of the region which also have 'contacts'. The conclusion must be that unless there are many cases where more than three regions meet in a point, the average contact number will always be rather less than 6, and that as the number of regions increases, its value will become closer and closer to this limit.

Concepts

Exercises

Exercises involving the ratios should be used to make comparisons between areas rather than as an end in themselves. Do not attempt to calculate C_2 unless a wheeled map measurer is available, and choose shapes whose areas are known.

1. Use one ratio to analyse the shapes of the 50 states of the U.S.A. and plot the value of the ratio on a graph against the date of founding of the state. Account for any trends and exceptional cases.
2. Select areas of Britain (or another country) where the topography has
   (i) a marked linear trend,
   (ii) no obvious trend.
   Analyse the shapes of parishes in each area and account for any findings.
3. Devise an index of hilliness either by using the ideas of chapter 8 or using (area of shape) ÷ (height range)^2, and compare its value for some areas with the values of one of the shape ratios.
4. (Mathematical) Calculate the values of C_1, C_2, C_3, and C_4 for the pentominoes (there are twelve different pentominoes, each consisting of five squares placed together edgewise).
5. Consider whether the compactness of a country might be related to:

   (a) historical loss or gain of territory,
   (b) evolved boundaries (as in W Europe) compared with externally imposed boundaries (as in Africa),
   (c) a federal system of government.

6. Analyse the compactness of the pre-1974 and post-1974 counties of England and Wales and compare them. Is there any difference between metropolitan and non-metropolitan counties in the post-1974 scheme?
7. (Mathematical) Show that $C_3 \leqslant C_1$.

Further reading

Blair and Biss, 1967 (difficult)
Cole and King, 1968, pp. 379–87
Davis, 1974, pp. 49–50
Fitzgerald, 1974, pp. 36–8
Haggett and Chorley, 1969, pp. 70–3
Haggett, Cliff and Frey, 1977, pp. 57–60, 309–13
Hanwell and Newson, 1973, pp. 143–5
Holt and Marjoram, 1973, pp. 236–40
March and Steadman, 1974, pp. 191–3
Meyer and Huggett, 1979, pp. 116–21
Selkirk, 1976b
Tidswell, 1976, pp. 273–5
Wilson, 1973b, pp. 10–14

10 Points on lines

10.1. Distributions of points

In this chapter and the next we examine distributions of points, firstly along lines and secondly in planes. This is as close as this book comes to the study of statistics since the ideas in these chapters are essentially statistical. Geographers have been much more interested in areal distributions than linear distributions, but the latter idea also has value and makes an easy introduction to the more complicated areal case.

10.2. Randomness

Before embarking on the central task of this chapter, it will be useful to study the idea of randomness to which we shall return in more detail in chapter 22. One difficulty about randomness is that while we all have some intuition about what the word means, it is almost impossible to define in any exact sense. We shall not attempt any formal definition, but instead try to reinforce our intuitive understanding.

If we toss a fair cubic die, most people would agree that the numbers 1 to 6 are equally likely to turn up, that is that the die is a random generator of the six digits. In reality, the tossing of a die is not random but a complicated mechanical process which is too difficult to analyse; if it could be analysed, then the result could be predicted. In other words, there is no such thing as a random number or a random result. What a random result really means is that the knowledge required to predict the result is so detailed that it is inaccessible to us.

In practical situations, the process is often reversed. We have a result and wish to know if it is in fact random (in the sense used above). There is not just one alternative to randomness, but two. Distributions can either be clustered, as rooks' nests are distributed in rookeries, or they can be regularly spaced, as is quite likely to occur with robins' nests. Either of these deviations from randomness will, of course, raise questions about the forces causing them.

One important question which we shall hardly attempt to answer is how big the deviations from randomness need to be before we can safely assume some non-random process is operating. This is a most important question, both for geographers and for statisticians, but unfortunately requires an understanding of confidence limits, which are outside the scope of this book. Anyone who wishes to use the ideas in this chapter or the next will need to pursue this idea in more advanced texts and articles (for example many of those quoted in the further reading section). Briefly, for a small number of points, deviations from randomness must be quite large to be meaningful, while for a large number of points, deviations can be much smaller.

So that we can demonstrate the idea of randomness in a non-practical situation, we shall need to generate some random digits from 0 to 9. Again we shall return to this in more detail in chapter 22, but random number tables are readily available in statistical texts and books of statistical tables. Start anywhere in the tables and work through the numbers systematically, either horizontally or vertically. If random number tables are not available, use a telephone directory. Find a page of private subscribers and read off the next to last digit of each number, reading down the page in turn.

10.3. The nearest neighbour statistics

Suppose we have a line of length L with n points distributed along it. Between the points are $n-1$ spaces. If two of the n points are end points of the line, the average distance between spaces is $L/(n-1)$. If the points are irregularly distributed, some points will have a smaller distance than this between them. If for each point we measure the distance of its nearest neighbour, then the average distance of this must be less than $L/(n-1)$; and it is possible to show that if the n points are randomly distributed anywhere on the line (not necessarily at the end points) then the average distance of the nearest neighbour is in fact $L/2(n-1)$.

We can now calculate the average distance of the nearest neighbour and compare it with the value expected in the random situation giving

$$S = \frac{\text{average observed distance of nearest neighbour}}{\substack{\text{average distance of nearest neighbour} \\ \text{in the random situation}}}$$

$$= \frac{\text{average observed distance of nearest neighbour}}{L/2(n-1)}$$

When the points are, in fact, distributed randomly, then observed and predicted values will be approximately equal, and a value of S about equal to one will be obtained.

If the observed points tend to lie together in clusters, then the observed distances will be small, and S will be appreciably smaller than one. The more marked the clustering, the smaller will be the value of S, and if, for example, the points occur in coincident pairs, we could have S equal to zero.

On the other hand, if the points are evenly distributed, the observed distances will be larger and the value of S will be greater than one. For a completely even distribution, with one point at each end of the line, then

$$S = \frac{L/(n-1)}{L/2(n-1)} = 2$$

Thus $0 \leqslant S \leqslant 2$, that is S has a range from zero to two rather than from zero to one as in most indices. This is convenient because of the special significance of the value one which indicates randomness.

10.4. A mathematical example

Imagine a line 1000 units long and then pick random numbers to represent points on the line. The digits are chosen in threes from the random number tables to give numbers from 000 to 999. They are then sorted into numerical order and illustrated in figure 10.1, which gives three examples, two with sets of ten points and one with all twenty points together. Table 10.1 illustrates the calculation of S for the first set of random numbers, and the average nearest neighbour distance is

$$518 \div 10 = 51.8$$

The expected value is

$$L/2(n-1) = 1000 \div 2(10-1) = 55.56$$

giving

$$S = 51.8 \div 55.56 = 0.93$$

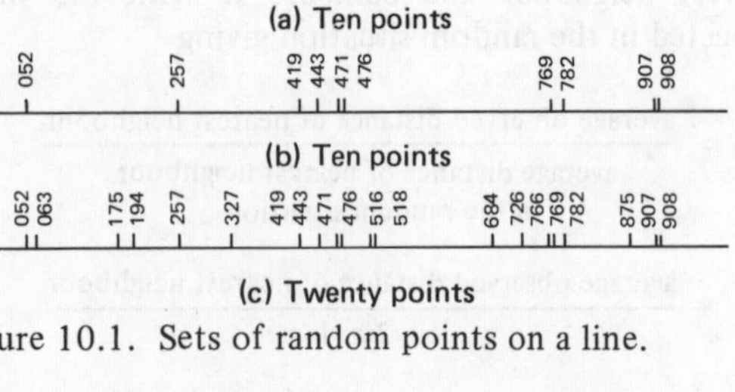

Figure 10.1. Sets of random points on a line.

This value is rather less than one suggesting a slightly clustered distribution, but the difference from one is too small to confirm this. The reader may check that, for the examples (b) and (c) in figure 10.1, $S = 0.82$ and $S = 0.74$ respectively. While we would in general expect randomly chosen points to give $S = 1$, it so happens that in the genuinely random cases chosen here the points indicate slight clustering which is in fact spurious. Once again, the value of 'playing' with an index to obtain a feeling for it is illustrated.

Random no.	Nearest neighbour	Distance
063	175	112
175	194	19
194	175	19
327	194	133
516	518	2
518	516	2
684	726	42
726	766	40
766	726	40
875	766	109
Total		518

Table 10.1. Calculation of nearest neighbour statistics for ten random points on a line 1000 units long.

10.5. A practical example

This example uses an idea suggested by Dacey, 1960, and extracts data from the 1:625 000 route planning map of Great Britain. The end points of the line are chosen without reference to the points used in the calculations; this is a condition for the correct use of the statistic S. We define a river mouth as the point where a river system with at least one named river on the map enters the sea. The end points of this examination of river mouths are the point where the English-Scottish border meets the North Sea, and Gore Point near Hunstanton in Norfolk. These are illustrated in figure 10.2. The careful definition of river mouths is necessary to cope with situations like that where the River Pont, which is named, is a tributary of the River Blyth, which is unnamed on the map. This definition also has the advantage of excluding minor river systems. There is no need to convert the distances measured on the map to kilometres, we can retain the arbitrary units used in the figure which are in fact the distances on the map measured in millimetres. The distances measured are crow's flight

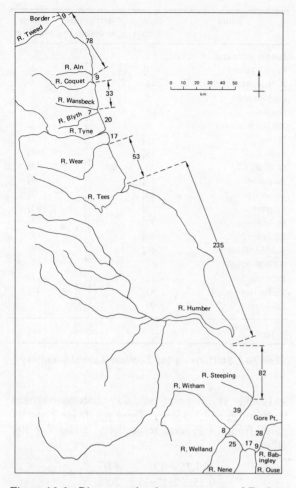

Figure 10.2. River mouths along east coast of England (distances in arbitrary units).

River	Intermediate distance	Nearest neighbour distance
(Scottish border)	9	
Tweed		78
Aln	78	9
Coquet	9	9
Wansbeck	33	7
Blyth (named as Pont)	7	7
Tyne	20	17
Wear	17	17
Tees	53	53
Humber	235	82
Steeping	82	39
Witham	39	8
Welland	8	8
Nene	25	17
Ouse	17	9
Babingley	9	
(Gore Point)	28	
Total	669	369

Table 10.2. Crow's flight distances (arbitrary units) between river mouths on part of the east coast of England.

distances between river mouths which are easier to measure than coastline distances and might be more relevant in some cases, for example in the creation of drainage boards. The calculation is shown in table 10.2.

The average observed distance is $369 \div 15 = 24.60$, while the average expected distance is

$$669 \div 2(15-1) = 23.89$$

Hence

$$S = 24.60 \div 23.89 = 1.03$$

Intuitively it might have been assumed from figure 10.2 that there is strong clustering in the north (R. Aln - R. Wear) and the south (R. Witham - R. Babingley). In fact the value of S indicates a random distribution.

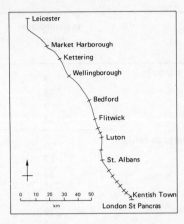

Figure 10.3. Railway stations between London and Leicester.

Station	Distance (miles)	Intermediate distance)	Nearest neighbour
London St Pancras	0		
Kentish Town	$1\frac{1}{2}$	$1\frac{1}{2}$	$2\frac{1}{2}$
W. Hampstead Midland	4	$2\frac{1}{2}$	1
Cricklewood	5	1	1
Hendon	7	2	2
Mill Hill Broadway	$9\frac{1}{4}$	$2\frac{1}{4}$	$2\frac{1}{4}$
Elstree	$12\frac{1}{2}$	$3\frac{1}{4}$	$2\frac{3}{4}$
Radlett	$15\frac{1}{4}$	$2\frac{3}{4}$	$2\frac{3}{4}$
St Albans City	20	$4\frac{3}{4}$	$4\frac{3}{4}$
Harpenden	$24\frac{3}{4}$	$4\frac{3}{4}$	$4\frac{3}{4}$
Luton	$30\frac{1}{4}$	$5\frac{1}{2}$	$2\frac{1}{2}$
Leagrave	$32\frac{3}{4}$	$2\frac{1}{2}$	$2\frac{1}{2}$
Harlington	$37\frac{1}{4}$	$4\frac{1}{2}$	3
Flitwick	$40\frac{1}{4}$	3	3
Bedford Miland Rd	$49\frac{3}{4}$	$9\frac{1}{2}$	$9\frac{1}{2}$
Wellingborough	65	$15\frac{1}{4}$	7
Kettering	72	7	7
Market Harborough	83	11	11
Leicester	99	16	
Total		99	$69\frac{1}{4}$

Table 10.3. Stations on the London–Leicester railway line.

10.6. An example dealing with the problem of end points

In many examples the end points are not independently chosen, but are members of the set of points chosen on the line. Pinder and Witherick, 1975, suggest that these points simply be ignored. We illustrate the adjustment by an example showing the stations on the London–Leicester railway line, illustrated in figure 10.3, the distances in miles being taken from the railway timetable. This gives, using the seventeen stations which are not end points,

$$S = \frac{66.25 \div 17}{99 \div 2(17-1)} = \frac{4.07}{3.09} = 1.32$$

The inclusion of all nineteen stations gives

$$S = \frac{85.75 \div 19}{99 \div 2(19-1)} = \frac{4.51}{2.75} = 1.64$$

However neither method reduces the situation to correspond as closely as possible to the one where the end points of the line are not in the chosen list of points. We need to imagine an infinite line with points scattered up and down it at random. Then if we take a sample length of this line, its end point will lie in general between two of our random points. Thus it makes sense to choose estimated end points *between* two of the chosen points, and the best estimate we can make is halfway between. This change will mean ignoring the two end points (in our example St Pancras and Leicester stations) for the purpose of calculating our average observed distance, which will be 4.07 miles as before. However in calculating the length of the line L, we start at a point mid-way between St Pancras and Kentish Town,

and end at a point mid-way between Market Harborough and Leicester. These points are $\frac{3}{4}$ and 91 miles from St Pancras respectively, giving $L = 90\frac{1}{4}$ miles. Then

$$S = \frac{69.25 \div 17}{90.25 \div 2(17-1)} = \frac{4.07}{2.82} = 1.44$$

It is recommended that this procedure should be adopted rather than either of the first two.

The result indicates some degree of regularity as one would expect. An examination of figure 10.3 shows that the distribution divides at Flitwick into two regular parts, each with even but different distribution of points. Like all such statistics, S can oversimplify the situation and hide details which will appear from a more careful examination of the data.

10.7. Further points

Besides the problem of end points which become negligible when a large number of points is considered, there is the problem encountered in section 10.5 of whether measurements should be crow's flight or along the line. In many cases the latter is preferable, but the user will have to decide in each case which is more appropriate, and whether the extra work of measuring along a curved line is worthwhile.

The nearest neighbour technique will work equally well for points round a circle, when there is no need to worry about end points. The expected mean is $L/2n$. The result can then be found simply by dividing the sum of the nearest neighbour lengths by half the total length. For example a study of the twenty-one lifeboat stations around Ireland gives a nearest neighbour sum of 102 km (sea distances), and a total distance of 141 km. Thus

$$S = 1021 \div (1414 \div 2) = 1.44$$

This suggests some regularity of provision in spite of long stretches of the west coast without lifeboat stations.

Dacey, 1960, suggests an easier way of analysing randomness of linear distribution by examining the proportion of reflexive pairs of nearest neighbours. Unfortunately the method does not seem very successful with the small numbers of points likely in many geographical examples.

10.8. An alternative graphical approach

Figure 10.4 shows an alternative approach for the example of section 10.6. The idea develops out of the cumulative frequency curve used in statistics and geographers do not seem to have used this method, which is visually effective but has theoretical difficulties. The figure will explain how the situation can be illustrated by a step function. The points to be plotted are numbered evenly up the y-axis of the graph starting at zero and ending (since there are nineteen stations between London and Leicester) at 18. Along the x-axis the distances of these stations are plotted. The graph is then drawn in a series of steps. If the points were evenly distributed, then they would lie along a diagonal line from the origin to the top right-hand corner of the graph, and this line is drawn in for comparison purposes. This method assumes that the first and last points are members of the set and thus lie on the diagonal, unlike the method used previously in this chapter.

If we require a measure of the way in which the graph departs from the diagonal, we measure the maximum distances a and b of the step function above and below the diagonal. These can readily be read off the graph, or can be calculated exactly by working out the equation of the diagonal. In figure 10.4, since a is read off from the thirteenth station at $40\frac{1}{4}$ miles and the equation of the diagonal is

$$y = \frac{18}{99} x$$

(the gradient is $\frac{18}{99}$ and the line passes through the origin), we have

$$a = 13 - \frac{18}{99} \times 40\frac{1}{4} = 5.68$$

Similarly

$$b = 18 - 17 = 1$$

(These results may be read off rather less accurately from the graph.) The statistic is

$$V_n = \frac{a+b}{n} = \frac{5.68 + 1}{18} = 0.37$$

where n is the number of points, not counting the initial point. V_n varies from $1/n$ for a regular distribution to one for a clustered distribution, so it is unfortunately 'the other way round' to S. It is incorrect to compare values of V_n from cases with different values of n (Pearson, 1963), and this is a real drawback.

When the end points are not members of the set of points, the y-axis is numbered from $\frac{1}{2}$ to $n + \frac{1}{2}$, otherwise the procedure is similar. The value of V_n for a random distribution is not known, so that until this is found the method is unlikely to be of great value except for its clear visual representation of the situation. V_n can also be used for points distributed round a circle, the starting point may then be chosen quite arbitrarily.

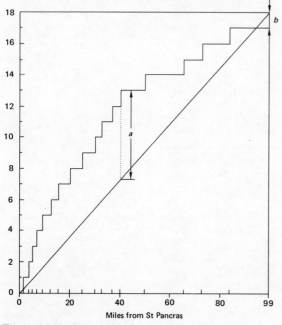

Figure 10.4. Step graph for stations from London St Pancras to Leicester.

Exercises

1. Use either of (or both) the above methods to examine any linear distribution of points, e.g.
   (a) Dates of accession of kings and queens of England from 1066.
   (b) Starting pages of each of the books of the New Testament.
   (c) Position of main roads or railways through gaps in an escarpment (e.g. the Chilterns).
   (d) Times of passage of heavy lorries outside a school.
   (e) Birth dates of children in a class at school.
   (f) Position of bridges across a river. (As rail and road bridges are often close, this can give a clustered distribution.)
   (g) Position of ferry ports along the east and south coasts of England (compare with the distribution along the continent).
   (h) The exit points for the first twenty exits on the M1 (England) and A1 (France) motorways. (Compare figure 24.1.)
   (i) The service stations along the M1-M6 (England).
2. Check the values for S given in section 10.4 for figure 10.1 (b) and (c).
3. Use a graphical method to calculate V_{18} for the first eighteen stations out of a major town on various rail routes. Compare with the result of section 10.8 for London–Leicester and with each other.
4. Check the result given in section 10.7 for the Irish Lifeboat stations. (See, for example, *Reader's Digest Complete Atlas of the British Isles*.)
5. Draw a circle of radius 10 km around any major inland road centre (e.g. Salisbury, Lincoln, Madrid, Milan, Winnipeg) and write down the bearings of the points at which major roads cross this circle. Analyse these bearings for regularity by finding S. (Compare also the ideas in chapter 7.)
6. Examine some main road in an urban area with which you are familiar and investigate the distribution of facilities along it (e.g. grocery or other shops, supermarkets, pillar boxes, churches).

Further reading

Dacey, 1960
Pearson, 1963 (difficult)
Pinder and Witherick, 1975
Selkirk, 1973–4
Smith, 1975, pp. 175–80

11 Points in areas

11.1. Introduction

The study of the distribution of points in an area is a logical extension of the work of the last chapter and is of interest to economists and biologists, for example, outside the field of geography. The technique, which is surprisingly recent, was first described in Clark and Evans, 1954. As in the linear case we develop a statistic, which, while it hides the finer details, at the same time highlights underlying patterns. Its success can only be judged by relating it to the real world, and if this does not happen, its use is not justified.

11.2. Use of nearest neighbour statistic in studying settlement patterns

The technique of nearest neighbour analysis depends on the fact that if points are uniformly distributed over an area, then the distances from each point to its neighbours are as large as possible, while if the points are clustered, then the nearest neighbours will tend to lie close together. The first step is to decide as precisely as possible the area and the points which are to be analysed. The area should have a minimum of about fifteen points, and up to thirty or forty can be fairly readily dealt with. The area should be defined independently of the points within it, and it should be possible to define further points outside the area in many cases. A useful ploy can be to use grid squares, whose area is easily calculated; if irregular areas are used it will save calculating them if they can be obtained from published statistics.

In order to illustrate the process involved, an area of south Devon has been chosen corresponding to the areas covered by the former Kingsbridge Rural District and the Kingsbridge and Salcombe Urban Districts. This fairly compact area is illustrated in figure 11.1.

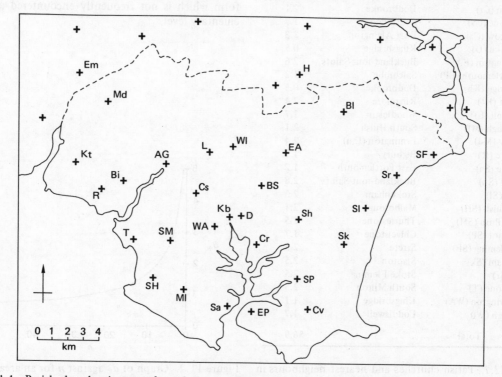

Figure 11.1. Parish churches in part of south Devon. (For abbreviations see table 11.1.)

Concepts

The points chosen are the centres of the civil parishes in the area. These are usually nucleated villages, and the church has been chosen as the most easily identifiable point to take in each parish. When parishes have no identifiable centre, and the church is isolated, then the church has been retained as the point for consistency. Kingsbridge formerly consisted of two parishes Kingsbridge and Dodbrooke, so both churches have been included. This choice has led to three areas of substantial population being neglected; the villages of Chillington, Hope and Bigbury-on-Sea, which have grown up away from parish churches.

It is helpful to begin with a tracing such as figure 11.1 marking boundaries and points, as well as any points close outside the boundary which might be nearest neighbours to those inside. The next step is to draw up the equivalent of table 11.1 (which also serves to identify the villages on the map in our case). From this we must calculate the average observed nearest neighbour distance, d_o, which for the twenty-eight

villages is $56.9 \div 28 = 2.03$ km. This has to be compared with the expected mean distance in the random case, d_e.

11.3. Calculation of nearest neighbour statistic, R

It can be shown that if p is the number of points per unit area, then

$$d_e = 1/2\sqrt{p}$$

To find p we calculate n/A, that is the number of points divided by the area. In the example above, $n = 28$ and $A = 296$ km^2, so that $p = 28/296 = 0.095$. This gives $d_e = 1/2\sqrt{0.095} = 1.62$. Finally we calculate the nearest neighbour statistic, R, using

$$R = d_o/d_e = 2.03/1.62 = 1.25$$

Alternatively, if Z is the sum of the nearest neighbour distances, in this case 56.9 km, we can put all these together to give

$$R = 2Z/\sqrt{(nA)}$$

but this formula, while quicker to use, is less informative.

It is an interesting mathematical exercise to plot the graph of $d_e = 1/2\sqrt{p}$ for a fixed area, say 100 km^2. This is done in figure 11.2 and the graph is of a simple form which is not frequently encountered at an elementary level.

Parish	Nearest neighbour	Distance (km)
Aveton Gifford (AG)	Churchstow	2.5
Bigbury (Bi)	Ringmore	1.7
Blackawton (Bl)	Halwell (H)	3.5
Buckland-tout-Saints (BS)	Dodbrooke	2.4
Charleton (Cr)	Dodbrooke	2.1
Chivelstone (Cv)	South Pool	1.7
Churchstow (Cs)	West Alvington	2.3
Dodbrooke (D)	Kingsbridge	0.5
East Allington (EA)	Buckland-tout-Saints	2.6
East Portlemouth (EP)	Salcombe	1.2
Kingsbridge (Kb)	Dodbrooke	0.5
Kingston (Kt)	Ringmore	2.4
Loddiswell (L)	Woodleigh	1.7
Malborough (Ml)	South Huish	2.1
Modbury (Md)	Ermington (Em)	2.4
Ringmore (R)	Bigbury	1.7
Salcombe (Sa)	East Portlemouth	1.2
Sherford (Sh)	Buckland-tout-Saints	2.8
Slapton (Sl)	Stokenham	2.5
South Huish (SH)	Malborough	2.1
South Milton (SM)	Thurlestone	2.5
South Pool (SP)	Chivelstone	1.7
Stoke Fleming (SF)	Strete	2.5
Stokenham (Sk)	Slapton	2.5
Strete (Sr)	Stoke Fleming	2.5
Thurlestone (T)	South Milton	2.5
West Alvington (WA)	Kingsbridge	1.1
Woodleigh (Wl)	Loddiswell	1.7
Total		56.9

Table 11.1. Parish churches and nearest neighbours in part of south Devon.

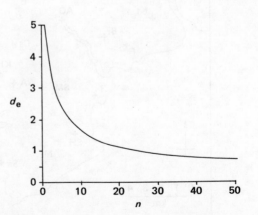

Figure 11.2. Graph of d_e against n for an area of 100 km^2.

11.4. Accuracy

(This section may be omitted if desired.)

Statistical calculations based on samples are always subject to random variations. It can be shown that a measure of this is the standard error, which for d_e is approximately

$$0.261\sqrt{A/n}$$

This means that we can be 95% sure that the true value of d_e is within

$$1.96 \times 0.261\sqrt{A/n}$$

of its calculated value. (This assumes that the sampling distribution of d_e is normal, which is only approximately true.) In the example of sections 11.2 and 11.3 we can be 95% sure that

$$d_e = 1.62 \pm 0.31$$

This means that d_e probably lies between 1.31 and 1.93, corresponding to values of R of 1.05 and 1.55. These are known as the 95% confidence limits for d_e and R respectively.

11.5. Interpretation

It can be shown that for a random distribution of points, the value of the nearest neighbour statistic R is one. We shall show in section 11.6 that complete regularity will give a value of R which is not 2, as in the linear case, but approximately 2.15 (compare section 10.3). Perfect clustering would make all the nearest neighbour distances zero and make R zero also. The value of R obtained in section 11.3 was 1.25, and this suggests some tendency towards regularity, a conclusion which is confirmed by the confidence limits found in section 11.4 since the value one does not lie between them. Values of R around 1.25 or a little higher are typical of villages in many areas of lowland Britain, suggesting economic forces were tending to keep villages from clustering in the middle ages.

11.6. Regular patterns

(This section may be omitted if desired.)

Figure 9.5 illustrates regular patterns of triangles, squares and hexagons in the plane. If we imagine points at the centres of these shapes, in each case of distance one unit from its nearest neighbour, then each point can be thought of as controlling its surrounding territory. For many reasons, points can most easily control circular areas around them. The triangular pattern is therefore a poor one, and while the square pattern

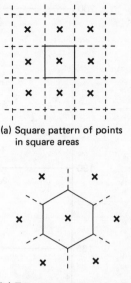

(a) Square pattern of points in square areas

(b) Triangular pattern of points in hexagonal areas

Figure 11.3. Two regular patterns in the plane.

in figure 11.3(a) is quite a good one, the hexagonal pattern of figure 11.3(b) is even better. Notice that for a pattern of hexagons, the centre points then form a pattern of triangles.

Since the calculations are easier with the square pattern, we shall begin by calaculating R for a regular square pattern of points one unit apart using the formulae from section 11.3. Clearly $d_o = 1$ since every point is one unit from its neighbours, and since there is one point per unit square, $p = 1$ also. Thus $d_e = 1/2\sqrt{p} = \frac{1}{2}$, giving $R = 2$, which is the same as the maximum value for the linear nearest neighbour statistic (section 10.3).

In figure 11.3(b), the calculation is a little harder. Once again $d_o = 1$, but we now need the area of the hexagon surrounding each point. It is a trigonometrical exercise to show that the area of a hexagon with diameter one unit is $\frac{1}{2}\sqrt{3} \approx 0.866$, so that the number of points per unit area is

$$p = 1 \div (\tfrac{1}{2}\sqrt{3}) = 2/\sqrt{3} \approx 1.155$$
$$\text{Hence } \quad d_e = 1/2\sqrt{p} = \sqrt{\sqrt{3}}/2\sqrt{2} \approx 0.465$$
$$\text{giving} \quad R = 2\sqrt{2}/\sqrt{\sqrt{3}} \approx 2.149$$

This is the maximum possible value of R. The unusual occurence of the square root of the square root, which may be written $\sqrt[4]{3}$, should be noted.

Concepts

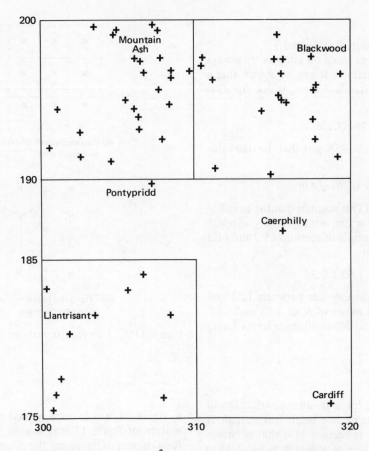

Figure 11.4. Patterns of stations in three 100 km² areas of south Wales, 1954 OS map.

11.7. Discussion example

Figure 11.4 shows the stations (closed and open) marked on parts of the 1954 edition of Ordnance Survey 1:63 360 map 154 (Cardiff). Three ten kilometre squares, as shown, were surveyed. Subsequent demolition of stations will lead to substantially different results from later maps. For those who use them, railways are in one sense point features since trains can only be boarded at stations. For the squares shown (which may be identified on the Ordnance Survey map from the grid numbers in the figure) we may calculate

Llantrisant square $n = 10$ $R = 1.23$
Mountain Ash square $n = 25$ $R = 0.93$
Blackwood square $n = 20$ $R = 0.80$

These suggest respectively regular, random and clustered distributions, although the figures do not differ sufficiently from one in the first and third cases to be as sure as one would like of this point.

However, these results agree with the historical and geographical reasons for the distributions. The first square covers a fertile and low-lying farming area where there are no major barriers to the construction of railways, and stations would be fairly regular, though tending to lie along lines constructed for other reasons. The Mountain Ash square is a coalfield area of deep valleys, where coalmines tend to be evenly scattered for access to the coal seams, but settlements and mines have to be located in the valleys. Thus there are two opposing forces. In the Blackwood square, the slightly easier topography allowed two railways to compete in each valley leading to a number of pair-clustered stations.

11.8. Randomness in geographical distributions

A variety of geographical patterns can be investigated by the methods of this chapter. Other examples are the distribution of confluences in a stream network

68

(compare chapter 30) and the distribution of farm-steads in rural areas leading to the definition of nucleated and scattered settlements.

It is worth emphasising that in these two chapters the idea of randomness is a mathematical rather than a geographical one. Just as there are reasons why a distribution should be clustered or regular, so there are non-random reasons for an apparently random distribution. No distribution is, in fact, ever truly random, there are always causal factors for points to be where they are found. A random value of S or R will usually indicate, therefore, that these factors are either conflicting or insufficiently clear-cut to produce extreme values.

Exercises

1. (Mathematical) Complete the proof in section 11.6 by showing that the area of the hexagon is $\frac{1}{2}\sqrt{3}$, and show that for a hexagonal pattern of points at the centres of triangles $R \approx 1.54$.

2. (Mathematical) Choose twenty random points in a square 1000 x 1000 units by using six random numbers to give the two coordinates for each point. Plot nearby points from selections of twenty similarly selected for the eight surrounding squares to allow for nearest neighbours over the boundary, and calculate R. (As a group exercise, the values of R obtained may be illustrated on a block diagram.)

3. Analyse the pattern of market towns in an area such as East Anglia, and try to account for any departures from the regular ideal pattern.

4. Analyse the pattern of towns over a given population (say 200 000 people) in three countries (e.g. UK, France and Italy) and compare them.

5. Analyse the distribution of facilities in an urban area (in the UK the Yellow Pages Telephone Directory is useful). Consider for example banks, post offices, secondary schools, branches of a building society, supermarkets. Try to account for the values of R obtained.

6. Compare values of R for village patterns in various areas, or for farmsteads, or for stream confluences, and try to account for any variations.

Further reading

Clark and Evans, 1954
Cole and King, 1968, pp. 176–217
Continuing Mathematics Project, 1977a
Daugherty, 1974, pp. 12–22
Davis, 1974, pp. 23–8, 32–6
Dawson, 1975
Dinkele, Cotterell and Thorn, 1976e, pp. 57–8
Fitzgerald, 1974, p. 33
Gibbs, 1961, pp. 451–9
Haggett, 1972, pp. 279–81
Hammond and McCullagh, 1974, pp. 32–43, 237–43
Holt and Marjoram, 1973, pp. 244–6
Ling, 1977, pp. 104–5
Lloyd and Dicken, 1977, pp. 86–9
Meyer and Huggett, 1979, pp. 30–3
Pinder and Witherick, 1972, 1973
Smith, 1975, pp. 180–94
Theakstone and Harrison, 1970, pp. 41–63
Tidswell, 1976, pp. 185–201
Wilson and Kirkby, 1975, pp. 266–70

12 Centres

12.1. Introduction

The most important point of a set of points along a line or in an area is often the central point. In this chapter we shall attempt to locate the centre of a given collection of points, while in the following chapter we shall locate the boundaries when given the centres. We have already used the idea of centre in sections 8.7 and 11.6, which is some indication of its importance; although in many applications the concept is not made explicit. As we shall see, a variety of centres can be developed depending on the particular situation, so that care needs to be taken to select the correct mathematical idea.

12.2. Continuous linear distributions

When Robert Stephenson built the London to Birmingham railway, he had to decide where to place his engineering works. The length of the line is 182 km, and if one supposes that a breakdown is equally likely to occur anywhere along the route, an obvious question is to find the most efficient point to locate the works. If these were placed at one end, the average distance travelled to the works would be $182 \div 2 = 91$ km. If the works were at the centre, then the average distance would only be $91 \div 2 = 45.5$ km, and this is in fact the best point from considerations of symmetry as well as by calculation.

In fact Stephenson placed the works at Wolverton, 84.5 km from London (see figure 12.1). The average distance to be travelled from the south by a breakdown was $\frac{1}{2} \times 84.5$ km and the chance of a breakdown occurring in this section was 84.5/182 since that is the proportionate length of line. Similarly the average distance from the north was $\frac{1}{2} \times 97.5$ km, and the chance was 97.5/182. Thus the average distance which a breakdown would have to travel was

$$(\tfrac{1}{2} \times 84.5 \times \frac{84.5}{182}) + (\tfrac{1}{2} \times 97.5 \times \frac{97.5}{182}) = 45.7 \,\text{km}$$

This is so little different from the optimum situation as not to matter, and Wolverton had the advantage of a nearby town (Stony Stratford). It is surprising that the large variation of 6.5 km from the optimal position has so little effect on the mathematical suitability of the point, but this means that there is scope for geographical detail to play an important part in the final choice.

12.3. An example with a branch

A similar problem faced Isambard Kingdom Brunel in building the Great Western Railway from London to Bristol via Bath, a distance of 190 km. In spite of suitable choices near the half-way point, the town of Swindon was chosen, 124 km from London. One reason for this was the heavier gradients between Swindon and Bath. However a very early branch was built from Swindon to Gloucester and Cheltenham, shown diagrammatically in figure 12.2.

The problem of determining the optimal site in this diagram is now much more complex, demanding the use of quadratic equations or the equivalent graphs. It is also likely to be far more heavily affected by the varying amounts of traffic along the different lines. Ignoring this latter point it is in fact possible to show that Swindon is the best position, but it is clear that our mathematical ability to handle more and more complex situations will rapidly get out of hand.

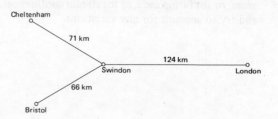

Figure 12.2. Diagram of early lines of the Great Western Railway.

Figure 12.1. Diagram of London and Birmingham Railway.

12.4. Discrete points on a line

Sometimes, instead of wishing to locate the centre of a continuous distribution of points along a line, it is necessary to locate the centre of a number of isolated points along the line. For example, suppose a chain of retail stores wishes to build a new distribution depot to serve five stores along the south coast of England. The towns in which the stores are situated together with the relevant road distances are shown in figure 12.3. Where would be the most advantageous point to locate the depot, assuming there is an available site? We shall ignore any effect caused by the supply of goods to the depot, considering only the distribution of goods from it.

One assumption we might make is that the best site is the one where the sum of the distances to all the stores is the least. A little trial and error should soon convince the reader that the best site is at the most central town, Worthing, since the total distance from all five stores is $27 + 16 + 0 + 8 + 18 = 69$ km. Any movement away from the central store will reduce distances to two stores on one side of Worthing, but increase distances to two stores on the other side of Worthing by an equal amount. In addition, there will be a journey to Worthing itself which was hitherto at the depot and this will increase the total distance. On this criterion, the best point of a linear set of points is the middle one; if there is an even number of points, anywhere at or between the two middle points will do.

Even if retail sales of the individual stores are taken into account, this method can be used. Suppose the trade of the stores is distributed in the ratio 2 parts to Bognor Regis, 1 part to Littlehampton, 5 parts to Worthing, 1 part to Shoreham and 11 parts to Brighton. This problem is now exactly the same as if there were $2 + 1 + 5 + 1 + 11 = 20$ equally sized stores. The procedure is known as *weighting* the points. The optimum position would be at or between the tenth and eleventh stores, that is at Brighton. This method is difficult to extend to non-linear sets of points. A partial mathematical solution is given in chapter 15, and a mechanical method of solution in section 15.5.

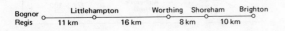

Figure 12.3. Five south coast towns in England with road distances (diagrammatic).

12.5. Discrete points on a line - alternative solution

Another type of centre can be found by a different method. Suppose that in figure 12.3 the depot is located x km east of Bognor Regis. The distances of the stores from this point are 0, 11, 27, 35 and 45 km respectively, so since there are five stores we solve

$$5x = 0 + 11 + 27 + 35 + 45 = 118$$
$$\Rightarrow \quad x = 23.6$$

Using this method the depot would be placed 23.6 km east of Bognor Regis or 3.4 km west of Worthing. Whatever starting point is used, the point determined by x remains the same provided that all westward distances are counted as negative.

Even if we wish to take the trading ratios in figure 12.4 into account the method still works, this time we will assume the depot is located y km to the east of Worthing:

$$(2 + 1 + 5 + 1 + 11)y = \{2 \times (-27)\} + \{1 \times (-16)\} + \{5 \times 0\} + \{1 \times 8\} + \{11 \times 18\}$$
$$\Rightarrow \quad 20y = -54 - 16 + 8 + 198$$
$$\Rightarrow \quad y = 6.8$$

This time the solution is a point 6.8 km east of Worthing or 33.8 km east of Bognor Regis.

Unfortunately it is difficult to justify this solution in preference to that of section 12.4. It minimises not the sum of the distances, but the sum of the squared distances to the stores, which tends to give additional emphasis to the most distant points from the centre. This method is, however, mathematically much more tractable, and can be extended to cover points in areas as we shall see in section 12.11. We shall return to some of the problems raised in the above sections in chapters 14 to 16.

12.6. Statistical averages

There are four common statistical measures of central tendency, each giving a different type of average. Readers should not need to have met these to read the following sections, but some knowledge of them will enhance understanding. We shall examine each of the four averages in turn and show how it can be adapted to solving the problem of finding the centre of an irregular area. In each case as an example we shall use England and Wales including Anglesey and the Isle of Wight, but excluding small islands further off-shore. To locate points we shall use the National Grid. This interesting problem has never been satisfactorily solved; although the village of Meriden in Warwickshire has often claimed to be the centre of England, the grounds for this are not clear. In other cases where the map has no grid, it will be possible to use degrees of latitude and longitude. Alternatively an arbitrary grid may be drawn on the map.

12.7. Mid-point of range

This is the simplest form of statistical average and is the number mid-way between the largest and smallest numbers of the set being examined. It is a rapid but very rough and ready form of average to calculate. With an area we can use both west–east and south–north measurements to find an appropriate centre. For England and Wales:

most westerly point	Land's End	135 km east of origin
most easterly point	Lowestoft	655 km east of origin
most southerly point	Lizard	012 km north of origin
most northerly point	Berwick-on-Tweed	658 km north of origin

This gives the coordinates of the centre as $(\frac{1}{2}[135+655], \frac{1}{2}[012+658]) = (395, 355)$. This is the point shown in figure 12.4 near the village of Hilderstone in Staffordshire, 5 km east of Stone.

Since none of the defining points is in Wales, it makes no difference whether we include that country or not. A similar point for the whole of Great Britain including inhabited off-shore islands lies, surprisingly, near the town of Hawick in Scotland.

As an example of how latitude and longitude may be used to determine this centre, consider Thailand, exluding off-shore islands. The resulting point is $\frac{1}{2}(97°23' + 105°37')$ E and $\frac{1}{2}(5°40' + 20°28')$ N. The centre is then 101°31' E, 13°4' N, a point about 125 km south-east of Bangkok, which is thus well-placed on this criterion. Readers should compare this process with that in section 8.8. Here, as there, a drawback is the arbitrary imposition of lines in fixed directions, a criticism which also applies to the method of section 12.8.

12.8. Mode

The mode is the member of a set which occurs most frequently. Any map can be considered as a sort of frequency graph in which the columns have a length equal to the length of territory covered by them. The longest length is then the modal distance in that direction. For England and Wales this 'longest vertical distance' is the line between Berwick-on-Tweed and St Aldhelm's Head in Dorset along grid-line 397 km east shown in figure 12.5. If we turn the map sideways and repeat the

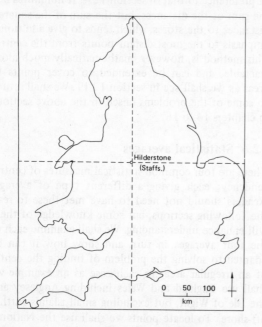

Figure 12.4. Lines along middle of west–east and south–north ranges of England and Wales crossing near Hilderstone, Staffordshire.

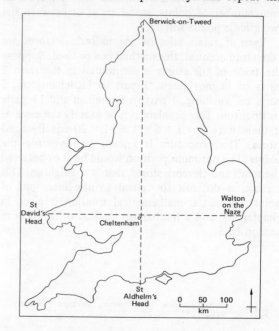

Figure 12.5. Locating the centre of England and Wales by using maximum south–north and west–east lines.

process, the line is a little more difficult to select because the cavity of Cardigan Bay is opposite the bulge of East Anglia, but the longest grid-line appears to be 224 km north, between St David's Head and Walton-on-the-Naze. These two lines locate a centre whose grid reference is 397224, which is 3 km north east of Cheltenham and well over 100 km south of the previous centre.

Thailand illustrates one practical difficulty of this process because the south–north line has a gap caused by the Gulf of Siam. If this gap is allowed for, the centre is about 190 km north-west of Bangkok. This type of centre probably has no practical use, but helps to illustrate the variety of methods which can be used in locating the centre of an area.

12.9. Median

If a set of numbers is arranged in numerical order, the median is the central one. For an area, a median line would separate it into two halves of equal areas. This line could be in any direction, but it would be logical to use west-east and south-north lines. Unfortunately these would be very difficult to determine practically.

12.10. Arithmetic mean

The arithmetic mean is often loosely called the average, although the three measures above are other examples of an average. The equivalent in an area is the *centre of mass* (or centre of gravity as it is popularly known) of a thin uniform sheet or lamina the shape of the area.

A reasonable approximation to this point can be made by cutting out a map of the required area drawn on thin card. This is no simple task if the area is an awkward one, and impossible when the area has more than one piece. A small knot can then be made in the middle of a piece of cotton and this is threaded using a needle through a corner of the card map. If the needle is left at one end of the cotton, the whole can be hung up by the other end until it comes to rest. The cotton line with the needle on the end should now pass through the centre of gravity, and this process is illustrated in figure 12.6. This can be repeated for several corners and three such lines are drawn in the figure. They should meet in a point, but the experimental error is just detectable in the figure.

The experiment demonstrates the uniqueness of the centre of mass; the points of suspension chosen do not affect the result. The point is often called the *centroid*, and its uniqueness makes it the best centre to use in many applications. For England and Wales it is situated about 8 km north-east of Birmingham

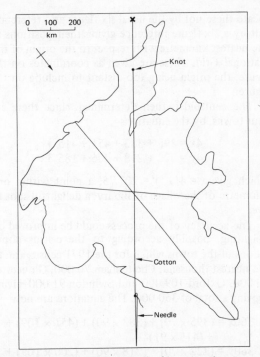

Figure 12.6. Practical method of locating the centroid of England and Wales. (Note that the three lines do not meet in a point, indicating experimental error.)

(pessimists might see some significance in the fact that it lies close to the motorway intersection popularly known as Spaghetti Junction). The centroid is difficult to determine exactly, but an approximate method of determining it will be given in section 12.12.

12.11. Centroid of points in an area

The method used to find the centroid of several points in an area is analogous to that used in section 12.5 for points along a line. Suppose, for example, that a travelling salesman has to visit Swindon, Oxford, Cheltenham and Gloucester (figure 12.7). We shall

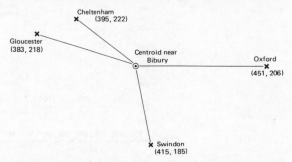

Figure 12.7. Centroid of four south Midlands towns.

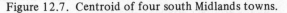

73

locate these not by the usual six-figure grid reference, but by a six-figure reference giving their positions to the nearest kilometre with respect to the origin of the National Grid. These are given as coordinates on the figure, the origin being too distant to include on the figure.

The centroid is then determined, since there are four towns, by the equations

$$4x = 395 + 383 + 451 + 415$$
$$4y = 222 + 218 + 206 + 185$$

which give $x = 411$, $y = 207.75$, a point within one kilometre of the village of Bibury, a delightful spot to live.

The accuracy of the process could be improved by weighting, possibly according to the census populations of the towns which for the 1971 census are, to the nearest thousand, Cheltenham 70 000, Gloucester 90 000, Oxford 109 000 and Swindon 91 000, giving a giving a total of 360 000. The equations are now

$$360x = (395 \times 70) + (383 \times 90) + (451 \times 109) +$$
$$+ (415 \times 91)$$
$$360y = (222 \times 70) + (218 \times 90) + (206 \times 109) +$$
$$+ (185 \times 91)$$

which give $x = 414.0$, $y = 206.8$. This is easily calculated with an electronic calculator, and it is easy to improve its accuracy by adding in further smaller towns in the area. Because the four towns are roughly

equal in population, the result is very close to that for the unweighted centroid.

12.12. Finding an approximate centroid for an area

An effective way of obtaining an approximate centroid for an area is to divide it into several smaller regions and guess the centre of each one. The areas of the regions are then used as weights in the calculation of the centroid as in section 12.11. If a grid is available it can be used; if not, it is probably easier to super-impose an arbitrary grid rather than try to use latitude and longitude. This is shown using the states of Australia as an example in figure 12.8. The data may be obtained from the first three columns of data in table 12.1. In spite of the arbitrary nature of the choice of centroids, the answer will be surprisingly accurate because the errors for each individual region will tend to cancel out, and will anyway be pro-portionately smaller in the context of the whole area than for each individual state. The calculation for the easting is

$$7715x = (805 \times 143) + (1358 \times 87) + \ldots + (2531 \times 36)$$

This gives $x = 090$ and similarly $y = 085$. The individual estimated centroids and the national centroid are shown on figure 12.8. The point is some 250 km south of Alice Springs.

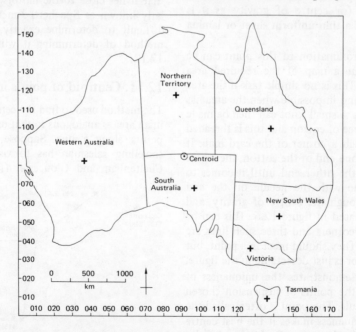

Figure 12.8. Finding the centroid of Australia (the state centroids marked have been obtained by guesswork). Note the arbitrary grid coordinates.

	Area centroids			Population centroids		
	Area (000 km²)	E	N	Popn. (000)	E	N
New South Wales and Canberra	805	143	053	4 748	151	048
Northern Territory	1 358	087	117	86	082	140
Queensland	1 739	138	100	1 823	154	086
South Australia	986	097	068	1 173	110	049
Tasmania	68	136	009	390	138	008
Victoria	228	127	036	3 496	131	031
Western Australia	2 531	036	082	1 027	024	054
Totals	7 715			12 743		

Table 12.1. Data for states of Australia showing areas and estimated centroids (columns 1–3) together with population and estimated population centroids (columns 4–6).

12.13. Estimation of population centre of an area

In many practical cases the effective centre of a country is asymmetrical because of uneven population distribution. Australia is a good example of this, the main centres of population being in the south-east. An attempt to estimate the population centre of Australia is given in figure 12.9, taken from data in the last three columns of table 12.1. The state population centres have been guessed, allowance being made for the high proportions of population in and around the major cities. The equations are analogous to that in section 12.12 using population instead of area. The equation for the easting is

$$12743x = (4748 \times 151) + (86 \times 82) + \ldots + (1027 \times 24)$$

The solutions are $x = 131$, $y = 049$. This is a point in the fork of the Murray and Darling Rivers in New South Wales. Although it is nearer to the area centroid than the actual capital, Canberra, the position of Canberra looks less surprising than when compared with the area centroid.

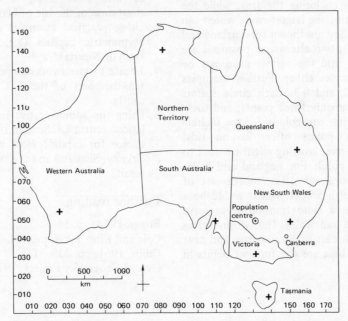

Figure 12.9. Finding the population centre of Australia (the state population centres marked have been obtained by guesswork).

Concepts

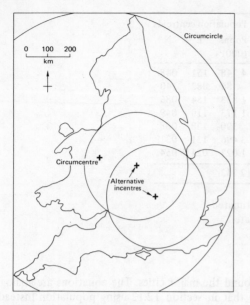

Figure 12.10. Circumcentre and alternative incentres for England and Wales.

12.14. Circumcentre and incentre

These centres have already been met in section 8.7 and in chapter 9, but it is convenient to remind the reader of them here. The *circumcentre* is the centre of the smallest circle enclosing the area, while the *incentre* is the centre of the largest circle which can be drawn within it. They are shown for England and Wales in figure 12.10; two alternative positions are given for the latter, and the former need not be unique in other examples either. Further examples appear in figures 9.2 and 9.3. Each circle suffers from being defined by only three points, and these are often difficult to fix, particularly for the incircle since the important points often lie on tidal estuaries. The lowest river crossing might be used to determine the exact point. For England and Wales the circumcentre lies about 10 km north-east of Welshpool on the Welsh border, which would be a good point to locate a radio transmitter to serve the whole of England and Wales. The two incentres lie about 16 km north-east of Birmingham and near Buckingham Town. These are the furthest points in England from the sea.

Exercises

1. Suggest organisations which would most effectively be placed at the various centres considered above. Assuming that all points of the coastline are equally vulnerable, how, in theory, would an effective centre for a coastguard service be located?
2. Consider the vector **d** joining the circumcentre to the capital city for several countries and in each case examine the hypotheses:
   (a) the direction of **d** tends to coincide with the direction of a country's population centre from its circumcentre (e.g. Australia).
   (b) the direction of **d** tends to coincide with the direction of a country's main links with the outside world (e.g. Eire).
   (c) the direction of **d** tends to indicate the area of a country which was first settled (e.g. USA, ignoring Alaska and Hawaii).
3. Locate the various centres of Brazil and see how they compare with the positions of Rio de Janeiro and Brasilia.
4. Locate the area centroid and population centroid of Wales using the method of sections 12.12 and 12.13. Which of the following towns would you favour for the site of a new capital: Brecon, Llandrindod Wells or Aberystwyth?
5. Locate the population centre for the UK using regions, not counties. How does a suggested site for a new capital between York and Harrogate fit in with your ideas, or would the alternative suggestion of the Isle of Man be better?
6. Using practical examples discuss the dangers of asymmetric capitals (e.g. Pakistan with Bangla Desh or Nigeria).
7. Locate by guesswork the population centres of the ten members of the EEC, and find the overall centre.
8. Using the administrative regions locate the population centre of Scotland. Is Edinburgh a good choice for capital? How would the omission of Orkney, Shetland and the Western Isles affect your result?

Further reading

Briggs, 1974, pp. 56-8
Cole and King, 1968, pp. 491-7
Gibbs, 1961, pp. 235-51
Oxford Geography Project, 1975, pp. 91-3, 126

13 Boundaries

13.1. Introduction

Boundaries have been important throughout history, both on the local and national scale. Ceremonies of 'beating the bounds' survive from mediaeval times (e.g. at Hawick, Scotland) on the local level; while many boundaries are in dispute (e.g. Israel, Kashmir). The early development of geometry in Egypt is said to have received impetus by the need to re-determine boundaries from a few landmarks after the annual Nile floods. Boundaries are the complementary concept to centres, and we shall deal with them explicitly here as a fitting introduction to the following two chapters.

We can begin with fixed boundaries and choose centres as was done in the last chapter, or we can begin with centres and choose boundaries. The results are not the same. Western Europe may readily be broken into six major regions, roughly Scandinavia, West Germany, France, Italy, Iberia and the British Isles. If we start with these units and fix centres, a centre for the British Isles would not be in London (see chapter 12). If on the other hand, we were to fix six major cities as in section 13.4 and figure 13.4 by choosing the largest one in each region and then decide the boundaries, London would be given the British Isles and only very minor parts of the continent. The approach must depend on the circumstances; in many cases the two ideas interlock. Capital cities are, however, more permanent than national boundaries.

13.2. The boundary on the map

On the national scale, boundaries may be determined by defensive needs, ethnic considerations or geographical features. They may also be geometrically determined as in the examples given in section 4.2. Often they appear almost accidental as in the case of Switzerland.

On the local scale boundaries have received far less attention, but are often remarkably persistent – property boundaries in York, for example, still follow lines laid down in Viking times. Figure 13.1 shows the boundaries of two parishes taken from the 1:50'000

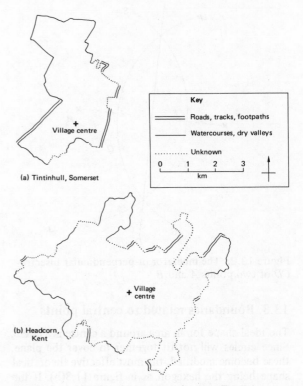

Key

═══	Roads, tracks, footpaths
────	Watercourses, dry valleys
·········	Unknown

0   1   2   3
km

(a) Tintinhull, Somerset

(b) Headcorn, Kent

Figure 13.1. Types of boundary for two English parishes.

map of Great Britain (first edition, they do not appear on the second edition). The boundaries follow either natural or man-made features or are independent of both these. Analysis shows that Tintinhull has 56% of the boundary following natural features and 24% man-made features, while for Headcorn the proportions are 30% and 17%. While examination of larger scale maps would determine more of the unknown sections (for example where they follow field boundaries), these proportions are sufficiently different to suggest that some external factor has a bearing on choice of boundary. It is possible that the Headcorn area was more heavily settled when the boundaries were drawn. The boundaries would then follow the land ownership boundaries in more cultivated areas. It is worth noting that watercourse boundaries may have their lengths inflated by river meanders.

An exercise such as this may be carried out for parishes in several areas and the results contrasted. National and regional boundaries can be analysed in the same way; for example state boundaries in the U.S.A. may be almost completely classified as rivers and geometrical lines, with a few mountain divides.

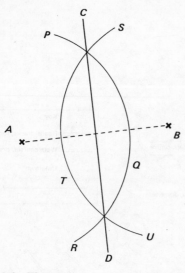

Figure 13.2. The mediator or perpendicular bisector *CD* of two points *A* and *B*.

13.3. Boundaries related to central points

The ideal shape for an area around a centre is a circle. Since circles will not fit together to cover the plane, these become modified, the most effective theoretical shape being the hexagon as in figure 11.3(b). If the centres are not regularly distributed, however, where should the boundary lie? If the control exerted by competing centres is equal, it seems reasonable for each point to associate with its nearest centre and for boundaries to lie midway between two neighbouring centres. In figure 13.2, the geometric construction is given which enables us to divide the plane between two neighbouring points *A* and *B*. Draw two equal arcs *PQR* and *STU* with centres *A* and *B* respectively so that the arcs meet in two points. Draw the straight line *CD* through these two meeting points, then every point on *CD* is equidistant from both *A* and *B*, and *CD* forms an obvious 'boundary' between *A* and *B*. Mathematicians traditionally call *CD* the *perpendicular bisector* of *A* and *B*, but we shall use the more succinct modern title of *mediator*. The mediator is also the mirror line which will reflect *A* into *B* and vice versa and is commonly met in most elementary geometry courses.

In figure 13.3, there are three points *A*, *B* and *C* between which three mediator lines can be drawn, one for each pair. It is not difficult to see that all three must meet in a single point equidistant from *A*, *B* and *C*. (This point is the circumcentre of triangle *ABC*, see sections 8.7 and 12.14.) The boundaries between the three points are now the thicker portions of the mediators in the figure.

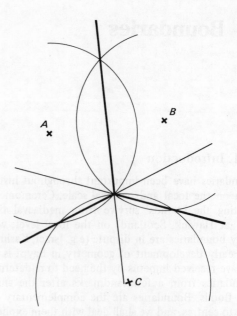

Figure 13.3. The mediators of three points meet in a point. (The thicker portions of the mediator give the boundaries between the three points.)

13.4. Mediators – a geographical example

Figure 13.4 shows how mediator lines may be drawn on the map. The largest cities in each of the six major regions of Western Europe have been chosen as centres, and the mediator lines have been drawn on the map, omitting the construction lines (Stockholm is slightly larger than Copenhagen). It is very noticeable how closely the theoretical regions correspond with actual boundaries; the smaller nations act as buffers, and major mountain and water barriers also modify the geometrical lines. Readers might care to examine the effect of replacing the Rhine–Ruhr conurbation with the prewar German capital of Berlin.

Figure 13.5 gives a similar example with the re-organised counties of England. Care must be taken in drawing such a map especially where four mediator lines come close together. The theoretical inconsistencies can be highlighted by shading the incorrectly allocated portions of land, assuming each point should be allocated to its nearest centre. Anomalies may be due to geographical barriers (south-west France in figure 13.4, parts of north Derbyshire in figure 13.5), historical reasons (note the position of Chester in Cheshire in figure 13.5), political considerations (the French border on the Rhine) or ethnic considerations (southern Austria).

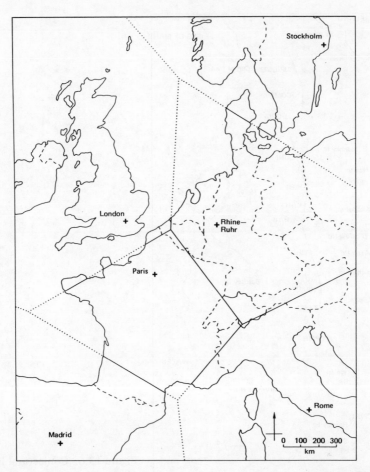

Figure 13.4. Mediator lines for six major Western European cities (compare national boundaries).

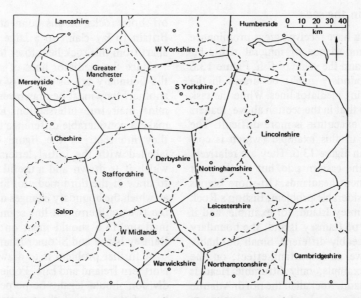

Figure 13.5. Mediator lines between county towns of new English counties (county towns shown as circles).

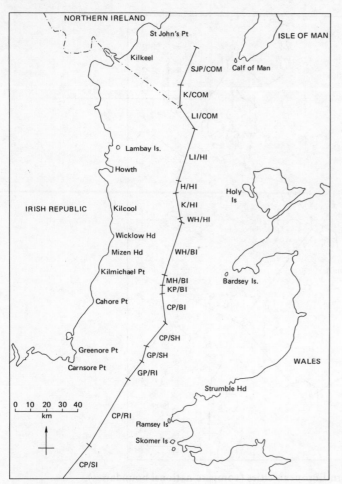

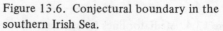

Figure 13.6. Conjectural boundary in the southern Irish Sea.

13.5. Boundaries in the sea

Boundaries in the sea have received great prominence recently with the importance of mineral rights beneath the ocean bed and the value of fish. Figure 13.6 illustrates how a boundary might be drawn in the southern Irish Sea using mediator lines. While the task is similar in nature to that in the section above, readers are warned that the execution is more difficult. The various points used in this example (which is conjectural) are shown in figure 13.6. They are relatively easy to identify on the eastern side, but on the west there are few prominent headlands. Off-shore islands also constitute a considerable problem; Bishop's Rock is some 5 km off Ramsey Island, for example, and if it were used instead of Ramsey Island, the boundary given would be noticeably different. Small but habitable islands also have an important effect; on the eastern shore, for example, only Strumble Head is actually on the mainland. Rockall in the north Atlantic Ocean is a prominent example of the importance of

off-shore rocks in this connection; it enables Great Britain to lay claim to a large tract of ocean which apart from this rock lies closer to Eire.

Since the mediator lines of successive segments of the boundary are usually very nearly parallel to one another, they must be drawn very accurately to determine their true intersection. Even small errors will make a considerable difference to the points at which they intersect. In the figure each line segment is labelled with the initial letters of the points from which it is drawn and a useful check on accuracy is to draw in the third mediator line through each point at which the boundary changes direction. For example the two southernmost line segments on the boundary in figure 13.6 should meet on the mediator line of Ramsey Island and Skomer Island.

A further problem is to draw the division between Northern Ireland and Eire. Poole, 1976, states that the division should legally be perpendicular to the trend line of the coast at the border. The difficulty is to agree on a trend line. In our figure we have avoided this problem by using the dividing line between the nearest land points. Poole's article has an interesting discussion of the division line between England and Scotland in the North Sea.

An attempt to construct a map such as that in figure 13.6 illustrates vividly the problem of defining sea-bed boundaries, even in theory. In practice, of course, it is even harder to pinpoint somewhere which is covered in water anyway. Mediator lines in the context of this section are often (incorrectly from a mathematical point of view) referred to as *median lines*. We have however avoided using this term, which has a different specific mathematical meaning.

13.6. Mediator lines in local geometry

In section 3.6 the idea of measuring distances only along transport routes was suggested, and in sections 3.7 to 3.9 we gave geometrical and practical examples (see figure 3.15 for another example of a mediator line). Figure 13.7 shows a local geometry for the road system of the village of Keyworth, Nottinghamshire. Various facilities are shown on the map such as letter boxes and public houses. The pecked lines indicate the mediators between the six letter boxes, the distances being calculated by measurement along the roads (the inclusion of public footpaths would alter the geometry considerably). Each of the six areas therefore shows that part of the village nearest to each of the six letter boxes. Around each letter box could be drawn isograms or lines of equal distance,

rather as is done for the town of Lientz in figure 3.9.

Similar studies can be done for other facilities. Bus routes would give differently shaped areas because they are linear rather than point features. A local study of this nature can reveal much about the social cohesion of a neighbourhood. The lay-out of estates can have a considerable effect upon the local geometry, and linear barriers such as railways, rivers or even long parallel streets with no cross connections can make a large difference to neighbourhood boundaries which is not at first apparent. Some facilities have a greater impact on social contacts than others. School catchment areas often define contacts between young mothers with primary school children, but in an age of car ownership public houses are less local centres than they used to be.

Exercises

1. Complete figure 13.5 for other parts of England, or repeat the exercise for another country. Discuss any discrepancies between theory and reality.
2. Try constructing sea boundaries for the Baltic or part of the Mediterranean. Note the importance of islands.
3. Construct sea boundaries on a map of the north Atlantic Ocean. Examine the varying effects of assuming Rockall belongs to the UK, Eire and Denmark, and of ignoring it.
4. Analyse the proportions of various types of boundaries for the states of the USA, and plot a scatter-graph of the proportion of geometrical boundary against the date of incorporation of the state into the Union.
5. Analyse the proportions of some parish boundaries over a small region as outlined in section 13.2. Compare and contrast your results with another region. Ascertain the areas (e.g. from census tables) and calculate the circularity ratio C_2 for each parish (see section 9.4).
6. Analyse the areas served by the other facilities given in figure 13.7, or carry out a similar survey for some area known to you.

Further reading

Abler, Adams and Gould, 1972, pp. 476-8
Briggs, 1974, pp. 56-7
Cole and King, 1968, pp. 569-71, 613-26
Gibbs, 1961, pp. 263-85
Haggett, 1972, pp. 365-91
Haggett and Chorley, 1969, pp. 47-50, 226-57
Meyer and Huggett, 1979, pp. 80-93
Prescott, 1965

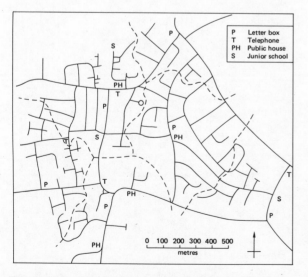

Figure 13.7. Local (non-Euclidean) geometry showing mediator lines dividing six letter boxes in a village (Keyworth, Notts, England).

PART 2
MODELS

Histories make men wise; poets, witty; the mathematics subtile; ...

Francis Bacon, *Essay, 50. Of Studies*

If you once cross the county boundary, you cannot come back.

Beatrix Potter, *The Tale of Pigling Bland*

14 The area around a point

14.1. Concepts and models

There is not a clear boundary between part 1 and part 2 of this book; the division rather consists of a change in emphasis. The reader will have noticed that most chapter titles have consisted of mathematical ideas, not geographical ones, but we have frequently used geographical examples to illustrate these ideas; for instance, when we discussed how to find the area of irregular shapes in chapter 3, we used geographical illustrations of the process. In later chapters we have tended more and more to take these geographical illustrations back into geography and to try to interpret them in the light of reality. This is the essence of a mathematical model. It is a simplified mathematical description of a real situation which can be manipulated mathematically before being used to throw light on the real world.

The word *model* is a valuable one because it implies incompleteness. A small child can use a block of wood as a model of a car, while an older child may use something very much more elaborate. Both models are, however, imperfect, and there are many advantages in using simpler models, at any rate to begin with. One characteristic of model builders is that they are never satisfied with the accuracy which they have attained. Just as there is a constant search for a closer approximation to reality in building a model car, so the mathematical model builder constantly seeks to improve the accuracy of his model, returning again and again to the real world to test his ideas and predictions against reality. In this book the models we shall use will essentially be very simple ones, and usually the problem of improving them will involve us in mathematics which is too complicated. From time to time however we shall be able to enlarge upon an idea which is a first approximation, and in this chapter we can see how von Thünen's basic model can be improved by considering various additional features.

There is one way in which a mathematical model differs from a child's model. A child builds a model chiefly for his own enjoyment, although as adults we might find other reasons for encouraging him to spend his time in this way, such as development of manual dexterity or improvement of his ability to conceptu-

alise. In mathematical model building we deliberately attempt to obtain a deeper understanding of what goes on in the real world. The differences between the model and reality are as important as the similarities, and we can often learn more from them. The ultimate test of a mathematical model is its ability to predict a situation, as we might use the gravity model of chapter 16 to predict where new motorways are needed most.

14.2. Von Thünen's model

J.H. von Thünen, writing in 1826, studied the economics of producing a farm crop which was to be sold at a city. For simplicity he chose an isolated city and the rural area immediately surrounding it. Since a particular crop theoretically costs all farmers the same price to produce, and all farmers will receive the same amount for it in the city, the only important variable which will make the crop worth producing will be the distance which the farmer needs to take his crop to market; that is his transport costs. The further the farm is from the city, the more transport will cost him, and the lower his profit margin will be. Eventually, at some stage the farmer will not be able to sell the crop at a profit at all. The margin of profit determines what the farmer can afford to pay for his land (not what he actually pays) and is known as his *locational rent* or *economic rent*. The relationship between this and the distance from the market is illustrated in figure 14.1, which makes the reasonable assumption (certainly likely to be valid in 1826 before the railway era, except possibly for canals) that transport costs are proportional to distance.

Von Thünen realised that the gradient of the graph in figure 14.1 depends upon the crop; some crops are more expensive to transport than others, partly because

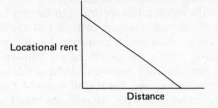

Figure 14.1. Relation between locational rent and distance.

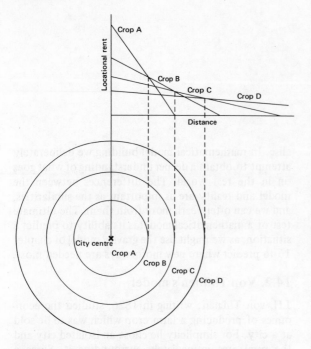

Figure 14.2. Von Thünen's model of agricultural location around a city (see text for explanation).

of bulk and partly because of perishability. If there are four different crops produced for sale in the city, then the four different graphs may be combined to produce the graph shown in the upper part of figure 14.2. The uppermost line in each section of the composite graph gives the crop which can be most economically grown at that distance from the city. The lower half of the figure shows the effect on the crop utilisation of the area around the city, producing a series of concentric rings.

The actual crops grown will vary with time and depend on climate, demand and history. In Europe and North America they might correspond to market gardening, dairying, cereal growing and meat production respectively, although this pattern was upset by the coming of the railways. In any case there would be many local variations depending on local problems such as suitability of land, and of course the rings would overlap considerably at the edges.

While the model is less applicable to farming today because of lowered transport costs, it still applies to other ways in which land is used around a city, and in particular it models the growth of the built-up area through time, basically because underlying this model of city growth is a graph like that of figure 14.1 which connects travel cost with distance. As travel costs have become less compared with incomes, the slope of the graph has become more nearly horizontal en-

abling land further out from the city to be developed. Thus cities have tended to grow outwards in rings as in figure 14.2. A more detailed economic approach to this model is given in Abler, Adams and Gould, 1972, pp. 346–61.

14.3. Barriers to circular growth

The circular rings of figure 14.2 reflect the symmetrical nature of unrestricted growth around a point source. Until some asymmetry is introduced, no other pattern is possible. By a consideration of various types of barrier the applicability of the model is increased. In the simplest case a barrier might be the coast, which would reduce the shape of the theoretical city to a major segment of a circle, that is rather more than a semi-circle. Examples are Kingston-upon-Hull and Chicago.

More interesting is a barrier such as a river which can be crossed only by a single bridge. The effect of this is shown in figure 14.3. All distances to the right of the barrier from the city centre A have to be measured via the bridge B rather than directly. Many towns exhibit this type of growth; sometimes the barrier is so strong that the portion of the town across the river is separately administered as at Newcastle-upon-Tyne and Gateshead which are separate metropolitan boroughs. Traffic congestion often increases the effect of the barrier. Other examples are St Louis in the USA, Ottawa in Canada, and Sydney in Australia.

Other barriers can be simulated in similar ways. Many small English towns have had their growth stunted by the presence of important estates where building was not permitted, for example Woodstock in Oxfordshire and Stamford in Lincolnshire are obvious examples. If the town is larger compared with the barrier, then the town will spill round it, but

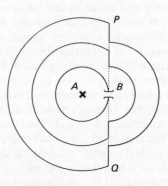

Figure 14.3. Effects of a linear barrier PQ such as a river with a bridge B on zones around a city centre A.

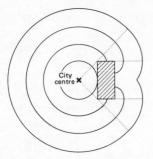

Figure 14.4. Effect of a partial barrier upon development of a city.

growth will be restricted beyond the barrier. This is illustrated in figure 14.4. The Bois de Boulogne in Paris and Sutton Park in Birmingham are examples of this.

14.4. Aids to growth outside the circle

Von Thünen's model thus demonstrates a feature of models, that they can often be applied to different situations. In this way a model developed to explain agricultural practices applies to a different situation to that envisaged by its author. Positive departures from the circular growth model also occur and are usually due to a reduction in transport cost or time by a new or improved facility. Even in a mediaeval city, the major routeways provided incentives to development. Thus a city with six major routes leading from it would tend to develop in the shape of a six-pointed star as in figure 14.5. This tendency is visible in many towns, for example Perth in Scotland; though it is sometimes obscured by the presence of modern estates in between the major routes. Its worst exemplification was in the between-the-wars ribbon development around many cities, which was the result of a sudden drop in road transport costs combined with a lack of planning controls. Road improvements along major routes tend to magnify this effect, but 'green-belt' policies have reduced it in many major cities.

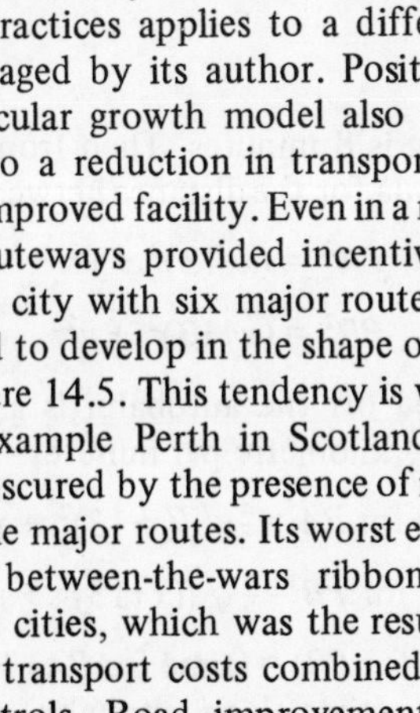

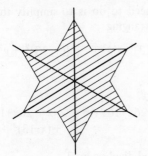

Figure 14.5. Star development of a city along easy traffic routes.

Sometimes such expansion is particularly noticeable in one direction, as in the industrial expansion of Manchester after the construction of the Manchester Ship Canal, producing the shape of figure 14.6. If access to the new facility is intermittent this becomes modified to the shape of figure 14.7, typical of development outside a large metropolis on a suburban railway route such as the line from London to Aylesbury. Near the metropolis successive developments coalesce, further away they remain independent. Urban motorways may produce similar effects if there are no planning controls.

14.5. Effects of an improved transport link on time of travel

In many cases the effects of improved travel facilities can easily be quantified, and lines of equal time saving may be constructed. These curves are not circles but *hyperbolae*. Figure 14.8 shows the effect of a section of new autobahn built from Kassel in West Germany to near Fritzlar, about 25 km to the south east. Applying the circular model to Kassel and assuming average travel speeds of 45 km.p.h. using crow's flight rather than road distances, a set of concentric circles may be drawn around Kassel whose radii are multiples of 6 km distance or 8 minutes time.

The autobahn route itself is about 26 km long from the centre of Kassel, and a convenient time to take for this distance is 16 minutes, which fortunately is a multiple of eight. We now draw a second set of circles with the same radii starting at the end of the autobahn. These indicate times of 8, 16, 24, 32, ... minutes

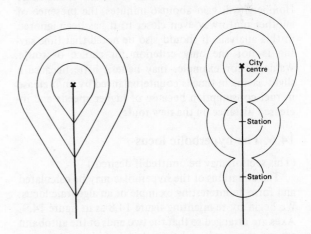

Figure 14.6. *left* Effect of a transport corridor on the growth of a city.

Figure 14.7. *right* Effect of an intermittent corridor such as a railway on the growth of a city.

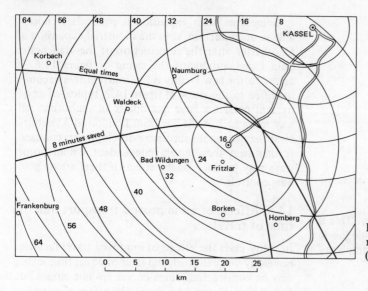

Figure 14.8. Time saving on a new autobahn near Kassel (West Germany) (units in minutes).

from the autobahn exit, or 24, 32, 40, 48, ... minutes from Kassel. Finally we can draw a line through the points of equal travel time for the two routes, and another one through the points for which 8 minutes is saved.

The map now shows that the time saving to Frankenburg is over 8 minutes, to Waldeck it is about 4 minutes, and Korbach will not benefit at all. While Homberg will gain about 6 minutes, the presence of another motorway even closer to it has been ignored in this analysis. It should also be noted that time saving is not the only criterion for choice of route. Waldeck, for example, may benefit little because a slight saving in time is counterbalanced by an increase in fuel consumption because of higher speeds and increased distance on the new route.

14.6. The hyperbolic locus

(This section may be omitted if desired.)

The equations of the hyperbolae may be calculated and form an interesting example of an algebraic locus. We begin by re-orienting figure 14.8 as in figure 14.9. Axes are arranged so that the two ends of the autobahn are on the x-axis and the origin is mid-way between them. Since the autobahn distance is 26 km, we shall make Kassel the point B $(-13, 0)$ and the Fritzlar exit the point A $(13, 0)$ (assuming the autobahn to be a straight line). Consider now a point $P(x, y)$ for which

the time saving is 8 minutes. Then from section 3.2, using the formula for the distance between two points,

$$PA^2 = (x-13)^2 + y^2$$
$$PB^2 = (x+13)^2 + y^2$$

Since the speed off the autobahn is assumed to be 45 km.p.h., or $\frac{3}{4}$ kilometre per minute,

$$\text{time for } PA = \tfrac{4}{3}\sqrt{\{(x-13)^2 + y^2\}}$$
$$\text{time for } PB = \tfrac{4}{3}\sqrt{\{(x+13)^2 + y^2\}}$$

But   (time for PB) = (time for PA) +
                (time along autobahn) + (time saved)

$$\Rightarrow \tfrac{4}{3}\sqrt{\{(x+13)^2 + y^2\}} = \tfrac{4}{3}\sqrt{\{(x-13)^2 + y^2\}} + 16 + 8$$

All we now need to do is to simplify this awkward equation. Rearranging

$$\sqrt{\{(x+13)^2 + y^2\}} - \sqrt{\{(x-13)^2 + y^2\}} = 18$$

Squaring

$$(x+13)^2 + y^2$$
$$-2\sqrt{\{x^2+26x+169+y^2\}}\,\sqrt{\{x^2-26x+169+y^2\}}$$
$$+ (x-13)^2 + y^2 = 324$$

Rearranging and dividing by 2

$$x^2 + y^2 + 169 - 162 = \sqrt{\{(x^2+y^2+169)^2 - (26x)^2\}}$$

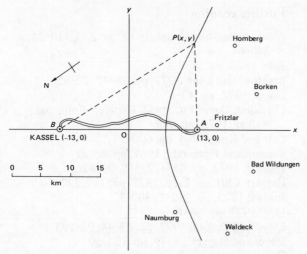

Figure 14.9. Figure 14.8 re-oriented to fit a suitable coordinate system.

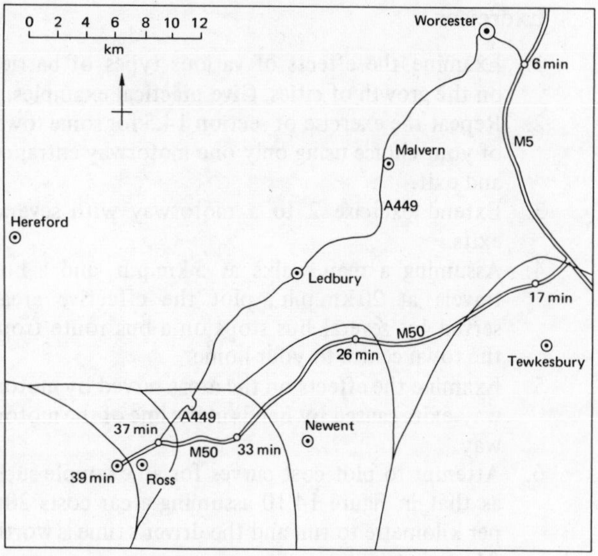

Figure 14.10. Best exits from M50 for traffic travelling from Worcester.

Squaring
$$(x^2+y^2)^2 + 14(x^2+y^2) + 49 =$$
$$(x^2+y^2)^2 + 338(x^2+y^2) + 169^2 - 676x^2$$

This now simplifies to

$$352x^2 - 324y^2 = 28\,512$$

This is usually written

$$\frac{x^2}{81} - \frac{y^2}{88} = 1$$

This is the equation of a hyperbola which is well known in algebraic geometry. In the general case, if the distance AB is $2a$ and

$$c = \frac{\text{(time along autobahn)} + \text{(time saved)}}{\text{speed off the autobahn}}$$

then the equation is

$$\frac{x^2}{\frac{1}{4}c^2} - \frac{y^2}{\frac{1}{4}(4a^2-c^2)} = 1$$

14.7. The effect of multiple exits

In section 14.5 it was assumed that the autobahn has no exits *en route*. In fact, most motorways have intermediate exits and these will affect the fastest route. The method of section 14.5 can be used to determine the best exits to use for traffic travelling from any given point. Figure 14.10 shows the favoured exits for traffic travelling from the city of Worcester along the motorway M50, and illustrates the complicated nature of the resulting areas. Times assumed from Worcester to the various exits are shown, and speeds of 50 km per hour for cross-country driving are assumed. In the diagram there are parts of ten different hyperbolae shown, and this ignores the influence of exits further south along the M5. The exercise is carried out by the method of figure 14.8, although in this case six sets of concentric circles have been omitted. Particularly noticeable is the effect of the orientation of the M50 to one side of Worcester, which means the first two exits produce little saving in time.

Models

Exercises

1. Examine the effects of various types of barrier on the growth of cities. Give practical examples.
2. Repeat the exercise of section 14.5 for some town of your choice using only one motorway entrance and exit.
3. Extend exercise 2 to a motorway with several exits.
4. Assuming a man walks at 5 km.p.h. and a bus travels at 20 km.p.h., plot the effective areas served by several bus stops on a bus route from the town centre to your home.
5. Examine the effects on the areas served by motorway exits caused by bends in the line of the motorway.
6. Attempt to plot cost curves for an example such as that in figure 14.10 assuming a car costs 20p per kilometre to run and the driver's time is worth £4 per hour.
7. (Mathematical) Where do the other branches of the hyperbolae in figure 14.8 lie, and what do they mean?

Further reading

Abler, Adams and Gould, 1972, pp. 230, 319-23, 340-64
Bale, 1976, pp. 54-9
Bradford and Kent, 1977, pp. 28-41, 70-85
Briggs, 1972, pp. 43-8
Chapallaz, Davis, Fitzgerald, Grenyer, Rolfe and Walker, 1970, pp. 2-5
Cole and King, 1968, pp. 600-5
Everson and Fitzgerald, 1969, pp. 26-32
Haggett, 1972, pp. 255-72, 389-90, 426
Haggett, Cliff and Frey, 1977, pp. 199-230
Jordan, 1973, pp. 232-7, 300-3
Ling, 1977, pp. 86-8
Lloyd and Dicken, 1977, pp. 33-44, 95-102
Meyer and Huggett, 1979, pp. 124-50
Oxford Geography Project, 1974b, pp. 31-3, 77-8
Oxford Geography Project, 1975, pp. 50-1, 140-6
Tidswell, 1976, pp. 70-98, 230-55

15 Competing points

15.1. Introduction

In this chapter we shall consider situations involving more than one centre, since few locational problems depend on one point alone. This takes us a step nearer to reality, improving the model discussed in chapter 14. The model used in this chapter was first developed by Alfred Weber in discussing the location of industries in 1909, but his work was not translated into English until 1929. In setting up an industry in an optimal situation, construction and labour costs, transport costs for raw materials and finished product and government grants will all have to be taken into account. While a complete solution is possible, it will demand much data gathering (see for example Abler, Adams and Gould, 1972, pp. 546-9), and we shall be content with simpler examples here.

15.2. The two-centre case

The simplest case possible concerns two centres of equal importance. For a manufacturer this might represent a situation where the transport costs per unit distance of raw material and finished product are equal. Suppose, for example, the source of raw materials is a point A with coordinates $(a, 0)$ and the market is a point B with coordinates $(-a, 0)$. The total transport costs will be proportional to $PA + PB$,

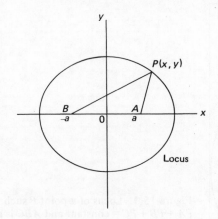

Figure 15.1. Elliptical locus $PA + PB$ = constant.

where P is the position of the factory. For any given factory site we can write

$$PA + PB = c$$

and the manufacturer will endeavour to reduce c to a minimum, which will occur when P lies on the direct line between A and B. However this ideal case might not be attainable in practice, perhaps due to a lack of factory sites, and the manufacturer might well have to accept a value of c larger than the minimum possible.

This equation is remarkably similar to that discussed in section 14.6 which is $PB - PA$ = constant, and the mathematical analysis is almost identical, although the resulting curve looks quite different. The locus is illustrated in figure 15.1, and the curve is known as an *ellipse*. Its equation is

$$\frac{x^2}{\frac{1}{4}c^2} + \frac{y^2}{\frac{1}{4}(c^2 - 4a^2)} = 1$$

where $2a$ is the distance between the centres, and c is the distance $PA + PB$. It is familiar to astronomers as the path of a planet moving round the sun, which must be either at A or at B. For the manufacturer it means that having decided on the maximum permissible transport cost, he can locate the factory anywhere within the ellipse.

15.3. The asymmetric two-centre case

Figure 15.2 illustrates the slightly more complicated situation where the transport costs for raw materials from A are double those of the finished product to B. The method of construction is that of figure 14.8, but in this case the formula is $2PA + PB$ = constant. Circles are drawn at radii 1, 2, 3, 4, . . . units about A and at radii 2, 4, 6, 8, . . . units about B. Thus successive circles represent lines of equal transport costs from their centres. The curves giving three different values of c are plotted, the outermost curve, for example, passes through the intersections of the third circle from A and the second from B, and also the second circle from A and the third circle from B.

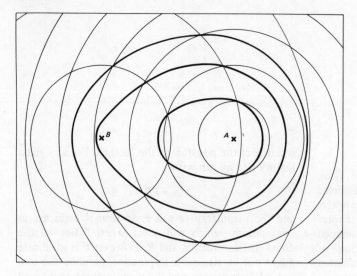

Figure 15.2. The asymmetric two-centre case $2PA + PB$ = constant. Three separate values of the constant are shown.

Readers wishing to repeat this process are advised to draw more circles than are shown in the figure. The resulting curves of constant cost are called *isodapanes*. In this case they are not ellipses, although their shape is similar.

15.4. The three-centre case

This is still more complicated, and the simplest case is illustrated in figure 15.3 where transport costs per unit distance are all assumed to be equal and the three points lie in an equilateral triangle. The reader can verify that the two curves in the figure are the loci (paths) of points P and Q such that $PA + PB + PC = 6.5$ and $QA + QB + QC = 8$, the centres being $3\frac{1}{2}$ units from each other and the circles drawn at one unit intervals. These are surprisingly difficult to plot, suggesting that in still more difficult situations a better approach would be to calculate total costs from several points at suitable selected sites rather than attempt a general solution. We shall return to a similar problem from a rather different angle in section 17.5.

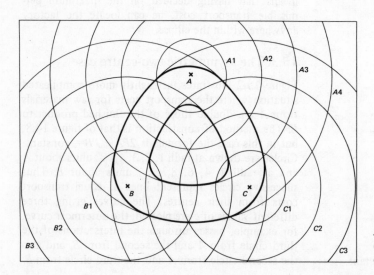

Figure 15.3. Locus of a point P such that $PA + PB + PC$ = constant and ABC is an equilateral triangle. Two different values of the constant are shown.

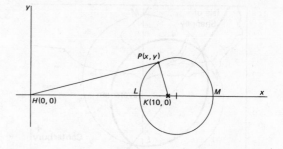

Figure 15.5. The locus $PH = 4PK$ showing the inverse linear law and the neutral points L and M.

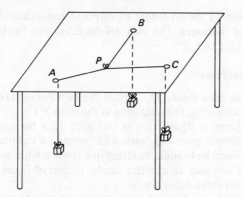

Figure 15.4. Determining optimal location by using a mechanical analogue.

15.5. A mechanical solution to the location of the optimal point

A simple mechanical solution to the difficulty above exists. The three points are located on a table top through which holes are drilled at the appropriate places. Three strings are tied together and one dropped through each hole as in figure 15.4. Equal weights are fastened to the free ends of each string. If the table and holes are reasonably friction-free and the string is light and flexible, the knot P will assume to optimum location required. This is because the system takes up the position of least potential energy, so that the weights are in the lowest possible positions, and the amount of string above the table is as small as possible. Different weights can be used, thus giving different 'pulls' towards each of the three holes, and extra holes and strings can easily be added. Thus the model can be made quite complicated, and one national British food retailer is reputed to have used it to help to fix the location of a distribution depot.

Since tables are expensive, the whole table top can be turned on its side and the weights hung over pulleys. This variation is known as a Varignon frame.

15.6. Boundaries in the weighted case

Mediator lines were used to define boundaries in sections 13.3 to 13.5. Other criteria can, however, be used to draw boundaries; for example transport costs per unit distance from two different sources might differ because only one is served by railway, and the mediator will then no longer be the break-even line. A more homely example is the shopping expedition where goods may be available more cheaply by travelling further to a larger town with more competition, especially for larger occasional purchases.

Suppose for example a person has the choice of shopping in two towns H and K, 10 km apart with populations 40 000 and 10 000 respectively. The towns may be given coordinates $(0, 0)$ and $(10, 0)$ as in figure 15.5. We shall suppose that the likelihood of a person living at $P(x, y)$ shopping in a given town is proportional to its population and inversely proportional to its distance. In this case, the break-even line is

$$\frac{40\ 000}{PH} = \frac{10\ 000}{PK}$$

$$\Rightarrow\ PH^2 = (4PK)^2$$

Using the formula for distance from section 3.2,

$$x^2 + y^2 = 16\{(10 - x)^2 + y^2\}$$
$$\Rightarrow\ 15x^2 + 15y^2 - 320x + 1600 = 0$$

This is in fact a circle with centre $(10\frac{2}{3}, 0)$ and radius $2\frac{2}{3}$, which surrounds K. Within the circle, K is the preferred shopping centre, while outside it, H is chosen. This surprising result is familiar to many suburban shop owners; shoppers once embarked on a journey often prefer to go all the way to the town centre.

The locus here is known as Apollonius' circle (see, for example, Durell, 1939, p.477, exercise 18). It may be plotted by finding the points L and M on HK for which $HL = 4LK$ and $HM = 4KM$. The line LM is then the diameter of the circle. In a more general case if H is p times more attractive than K (the populations need not be used) the positions of L and M are found by $HL = pLK$, $HM = pMK$.

Models

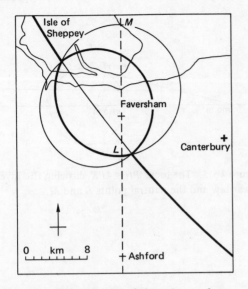

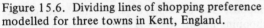

Figure 15.6. Dividing lines of shopping preference modelled for three towns in Kent, England.

15.7. A practical example

A practical example will illustrate the above idea, and we shall continue to use the populations of the towns as a measure of their 'attractiveness'. We shall attempt to determine the zones of influence of three towns in Kent, Ashford (population 36 000), Canterbury (33 000) and Faversham (14 000). Ashford (A) and Faversham (F) may be separated by finding the points L and M on figure 15.6 for which $AL:LF = 36:14$ and $AM:FM = 36:14$. (These two points are known as *break points* or *neutral points*.) A circle (the larger complete circle in figure 15.6) is drawn on diameter LM. A similar circle divides Faversham and Canterbury. The circle dividing Ashford and Canterbury has a very large radius since those towns have nearly equal populations, and only an arc may be drawn on the figure. It may be approximated by a straight line.

The figure may be interpreted by a Venn diagram as in sections 1.3 and 1.4, each of the zones into which the map is divided indicating a different order of influence for the three towns. The thickened portions of the dividing arcs split the area into the three first preferences. The figure shows only three towns; it must be remembered that there are others nearby (Dover, the Medway towns) which will influence the complete picture still further. The map will, however, be accurate in the centre. It should also be noted that a portion of the Isle of Sheppey will not, in fact, fall under the influence of Faversham because of the lack of a bridge which means that crow's flight

distances are no longer an effective approximation to road distances. The idea will be developed further in section 16.6.

Exercises

1. Redraw figure 15.2 giving the two towns (a) equal weighting, (b) weighting in the ratio 3:1.
2. Draw a figure similar to figure 15.3 for another simple case, e.g. with ABC forming a right-angled isosceles triangle, or giving one town double weight.
3. Carry out an exercise similar to that of figure 15.6 for three other towns.
4. Compare figure 15.6 or your solution to exercise 3 above with the mediator line solution of figure 13.5. If you have local knowledge of the area, which do you think constitutes the better model?

Further reading

Abler, Adams and Gould, 1972, pp. 328–39
Bale, 1976, pp. 82–8
Bradford and Kent, 1977, pp. 42–7
Briggs, 1974, pp. 28–33
Chapallaz et al., 1970, pp. 23–30
Everson and Fitzgerald, 1969, pp. 95–100
Haggett, 1972, pp. 193–8
Lloyd and Dicken, 1977, pp. 81–6, 120–39
Smith, 1975, pp. 295–303
Tidswell, 1976, pp. 141–55
Wilson, 1973a, pp. 9–21

16 Interaction between points

16.1. Introduction

This chapter forms the climax of a group of four chapters whose theme is the action of points at a distance. We have considered cases where the actions may be considered as additive (section 15.2) or subtractive (section 14.5), and we have determined boundaries drawn by considering lines where the action of two points is equal (chapter 13 and section 15.6). In this chapter we shall extend the latter idea to develop a more general model which can also be used to model problems about the amount of traffic between points. This is generally known as the gravity model.

16.2. The gravity model

The gravity model is called by this name because it was first used effectively by Sir Isaac Newton late in the seventeenth century in describing his theory of universal gravitation. This postulated that the force between two point masses is proportional to the masses and inversely proportional to the square of the distance between them. That is, if the masses are m_1 and m_2, and they are a distance d apart, then they mutually attract each other with a force proportional to $m_1 m_2 / d^2$. This quantity must be multiplied by a constant to obtain the force itself in the appropriate units. The theory explains the real world remarkably well – it is an excellent model. Only in certain very extreme cases does it become inaccurate, and there it has been superseded by Einstein's theory of relativity, of which it is a simplification. The gravity model, often called the inverse square law because of the d^2 underneath the fraction bar, has later found important applications in two other areas where the action of a point at a distance is important, namely in electrostatics and in magnetism.

It is not surprising, therefore, that geographers, casting around for a model to explain the action of a 'point' town at a distance, should hope that the gravity model would be of value to them. There is, however, one important difference between the examples suggested above, and the geographical example of towns acting as attractors, and this has

usually been ignored. It is that in the gravitational, electrical and magnetic situations, the attraction acts in three-dimensional space, while in the geographical situation it acts in only two dimensions. In the former, the point mass can be imagined surrounded by a series of spherical shells, each being the set of points for which the attactive force has a certain value. The sphere of radius r has surface area $4\pi r^2$, and it is this r^2 term which has sometimes been held to account for the squared term in the inverse square law. If this is the case, in the geographical example, the spherical shell must be replaced by a circular ring whose circumference is of length $2\pi r$. Thus one might expect that the geographical equivalent of the inverse square law would be an inverse linear law.

It should be emphasised that this is speculation. Geographical data are not, in any case, susceptible to interpretations as precise as those in physical phenomena. We may choose whichever law we please to model the situation, but only by testing the model as a predictor against a real situation can we see whether it is realistic or not. We shall return to this point later in the chapter.

In the meantime, we can introduce the idea of a generalised inverse power law which leads to a gravity model where the distance component is d^n, giving the expression $m_1 m_2 / d^n$. The number n need not be a whole number, though we would expect it to be positive for otherwise the action of the point would become more powerful with distance. In this book we shall confine ourselves to the values $n = 1$ and $n = 2$ for simplicity. The first case has already been met in sections 15.6 and 15.7, and we now turn to a similar example with $n = 2$.

16.3. Circles of equal attraction

In several examples in the last two chapters we have drawn circles around points, and von Thünen's model points out that these are circles joining points of equal attractiveness (equipotentials, as the physicist would call them). We have used these to develop different loci, and also to show in section 15.6 that the points at which the attraction to two towns is equal lie on a circle around the smaller town provided that the law of attraction is the inverse linear law $h/PH = k/PK$ as in figure 15.5. If we alter this to an inverse square law $h/PH^2 = k/PK^2$, then we can adjust the equation by taking square roots to $\sqrt{h}/PH = \sqrt{k}/PK$. This is equivalent to replacing the populations (or whatever other quantities are used) by their square roots. Thus the dividing curves are still circles, but the ratio of the populations is replaced by its square root. Similarly for an inverse cube law, the ratio would be replaced by its cube root. While the locus of points of equal attraction may be found from this, it is probably easier to proceed as in section 16.5.

16.4. The neutral or break points

As an example, figure 16.1 repeats figure 15.5 which was discussed in section 15.6, but using the inverse square law. The circle is proportionately larger, and its diameter may now be found by determining L and M so that $HL = \sqrt{4LK}$ and $HM = \sqrt{4KM}$, the ratio of the town's populations being 4:1. These points have coordinates $(6\frac{2}{3}, 0)$ and $(20, 0)$ respectively, and are the neutral or break points for this model. Once again we have the 'hole' effect; for people to the right of M in the figure, the town at H constitutes a more powerful attraction than that at K, even though they must pass through K to reach H. The hole is now comparatively larger than in the inverse linear case.

16.5. Reilly's law of retail gravitation

We shall obtain the general formula for the distance HL in figure 16.1 since some geography texts give an unnecessarily complicated version of the proof. If the populations of towns at H and K are h and k, then

$$h/HL^2 = k/LK^2$$

as in section 16.3 above. By writing $LK = a - HL$ where a is the distance between H and K, and taking square roots,

$$\sqrt{h}/HL = \sqrt{k}/(a - HL)$$
$$\Rightarrow a\sqrt{h} - HL\sqrt{h} = HL\sqrt{k}$$
$$\Rightarrow \qquad HL = \frac{a}{1 + \sqrt{(k/h)}}$$

In this form, the inverse square law is known as *Reilly's law of retail gravitation*. It may be checked with reference to figure 16.1 by inserting the populations $h = 40\,000$, $k = 10\,000$, and the distance $a = 10$ km, which give $HL = 6\frac{2}{3}$ km. To find M, the negative sign must be taken with one of the square roots, which leads to the replacement of the plus sign by a minus sign in the denominator of the formula.

16.6. Practical example, first method

One practical approach to Reilly's law is by an extension of the circle drawing method used in section 15.7 and figure 15.6, but with the inverse square law. As an example we take the four major regional centres in Ghana, which (with populations) are Accra (738 000), Kumasi (345 000), Sekondi–Takoradi (161 000) and Tamale (49 000). These are shown in figure 16.2 and the problem is to determine the six circles which separate the areas of influence for each pair of towns. For example Accra and Kumasi are 197 km apart. The distances of the neutral points from Accra are therefore

$$\frac{197}{1 + \sqrt{(345/738)}} = 120 \text{ km}$$

and

$$\frac{197}{1 - \sqrt{(345/738)}} = 620 \text{ km}$$

These are easily calculated by using an electronic calculator with a square root facility. A circle is now easily drawn on these two points as diameter; its centre is $\frac{1}{2}(120 + 620) = 370$ km from Accra on the extended line from Accra to Kumasi, and its radius is 250 km. The centre is marked with a cross on the Ghanaian border north-west of Kumasi on the map.

It the same way we can draw five more circles, although in fact the one between Tamale and Sekondi–Takoradi turns out to be redundant. An interesting geometrical property of the six centres is

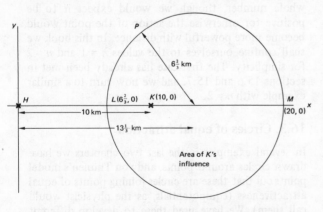

Figure 16.1. The locus $PH = \sqrt{4PK}$ (see for comparison figure 15.5) illustrating the inverse square law and the neutral points L and M.

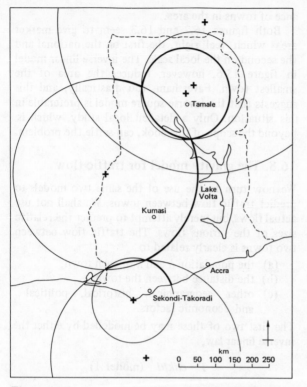

	Population (1971)	Attraction	$d^2 = P/A$	d (km)
Lincoln	74 000	200	370	19
		100	740	27
		50	1480	38
Grimsby	96 000	200	480	22
		100	960	31
		50	1920	44
Scunthorpe	71 000	200	355	19
		100	710	27
		50	1420	38
Boston	26 000	200	130	11
		100	260	16
		50	520	23
Grantham	28 000	200	140	12
		100	280	17
		50	560	24
Newark (Notts)	25 000	200	125	11
		100	250	16
		50	500	22

Table 16.1. Calculation of radii of circles of attraction around six towns in the Lincolnshire area of England.

Figure 16.2. Theoretical market divisions for six pairs of the four major towns of Ghana based on the inverse square law. First preference areas are divided by thicker lines.

that they lie on four straight lines, three on each of the lines. This forms a useful check upon their accuracy. The reader may care to verify this on the figure.

We have still to finish the problem by deciding which town predominates in each of the areas formed by the circles, and it can be helpful to note that, because of the collinearity property of the centres, where two circles intersect, so will a third (mathematicians may recognise systems of coaxal circles). The first preference towns for each area may now be sorted out and are distinguished on the map by thicker arcs. The result is a very effective division of the country apart from the areas north and east of Tamale which theoretically belong to Accra. In some areas, however, Lake Volta forms a barrier to travel which has not been taken into account.

16.7. Practical example, second method

When the circles used in plotting the areas in figure 16.2 become very large, they are difficult to draw. This happens when the populations of the towns

involved are nearly equal. We illustrate a method which overcomes this difficulty by considering the theoretical market areas of six towns in Lincolnshire. This method works well for evenly spaced towns of approximately equal populations, and with similar market functions. In this case we restrict the towns chosen to those with a population of over 20 000.

If a town has population P, then we can define its attraction A at a distance d by $A = P/d^2$. This may be rearranged as $d = \sqrt{(P/A)}$. We can then choose three values of A (or more if we require great accuracy) which give suitable values of d. In figure 16.3, for example, we want the smallest value of d to be about 10 km, and the largest about 40 km. By choosing values of A equal to 50 and 200, we can achieve this as shown in table 16.1, and a convenient intermediate value of A is 100. (The choice of values for A may require some trial and error before the final decision is made.) Table 16.1 can then be worked out, an electronic calculator with a square root facility being useful. For each town we take the three chosen values of the attraction (A) and divide into the population (P) to give d^2, and the square root of this, d gives the radius of circle corresponding to this attraction.

We can then turn to the map, figure 16.3, and around each town draw three circles. On the figure they are shown in different styles, double for $A = 200$, single for $A = 100$ and pecked for $A = 50$. We can then draw in the arcs of the other circles (shown in thicker lines) which are the circles of equal attraction between adjacent towns. As can be seen in the diagram, these have a large radius; that between Lincoln and Scunthorpe cannot be distinguished from a straight line. In a few cases the exact position of these circular arcs may not be very clear. It is then always possible to draw circles for additional values of A.

There are no 'holes' as in figure 16.2 because the towns are nearly equal in size. The addition of much larger towns outside the area such as Hull and Doncaster might alter this. Some small towns are marked on the map and it is interesting to note that many of these lie very close to the divisions between the larger towns. Brigg and Louth are the least well situated of these, perhaps due to the modern development of Scunthorpe and Grimsby upsetting the bal-

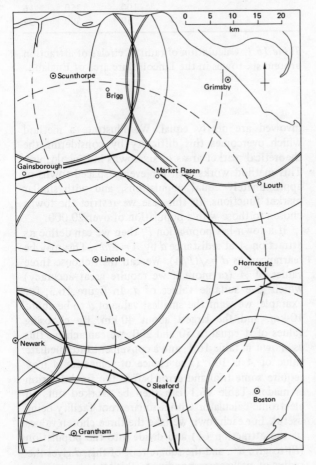

Figure 16.3. Circles of attraction and theoretical market areas based on inverse square law in part of Lincolnshire, England. See text for explanation.

ance of towns in the area.

Both figures 16.2 and 16.3 seem to give market areas which 'feel' right, the first on the national and the second on the local scale. The inverse linear model in figure 15.6, however, reduces the area of the smallest town, Faversham, too drastically, and this suggests that the inverse square model is preferable in this situation. Only a detailed local study, which is beyond the scope of this book, can settle the problem.

16.8. The gravity model for traffic flow

We now turn to the use of the same two models to predict traffic flow between towns. We shall not use actual flows, but merely attempt to predict the relative sizes of the various flows. The traffic flow between two towns is clearly related to

(a) the population h and k of each town,
(b) the distance between the towns,
(c) other geographical, historical, political and economic factors.

The first two of these may be modelled by either the inverse linear law,

$$T = chk/d \quad \text{(model } A\text{)}$$

or by the inverse square law,

$$T' = c'hk/d^2 \quad \text{(model } B\text{)}$$

In each case T and T' are the expected traffic flows and c and c' are some constants which we can ignore since in each model we shall only be interested in comparisons of the sizes of flows. Other models can also be used, for as pointed out in section 16.2, d may have any power greater than zero.

The multiplication of the populations of the towns sometimes causes difficulty. However if, for example, we double the size of one town only, there are twice as many contacts with the other town and twice as many reasons for making the journey between the towns. If we now double the size of the other town as well, that will again produce twice as many journeys, quadrupling the original traffic flow. Thus the two doublings have produced a four-fold increase in traffic, and multiplication of populations satisfies this situation rather than addition.

16.9. Example

As a simple example we return to the towns of Ghana used in section 16.6 and illustrated in figure 16.2. The distances between the towns are given in table 16.2 (we use crow's flight distances for simplicity). We shall also need the populations given in section 16.6.

For each pair of towns we now work out the product of the populations and divide it by d for model A or d^2 for model B. For example for Accra and Kumasi,

$$T = \frac{c \times 738\,000 \times 345\,000}{197}$$

and

$$T' = \frac{c' \times 738\,000 \times 345\,000}{197^2}$$

$$\Rightarrow T = 1\,292\,000\,000\,c$$

and

$$T' = 6\,560\,000\,c'$$

	Accra	Kumasi	S–T	Tamale
Accra		197	175	432
Kumasi	197		200	312
Sekondi–Takoradi	195	200		510
Tamale	432	312	510	

Table 16.2. Crow's flight distances between four Ghanaian towns (km).

	Accra	Kumasi	S–T	Tamale
Accra		1292	679	84
Kumasi	1292		278	54
Sekondi–Takoradi	679	278		15
Tamale	84	54	15	

Table 16.3. Relative traffic flows for Ghanaian towns (multiply by 1 000 000 c for figures given by formula), model A.

The complete figures for model A are given in table 16.3; those for model B are left as an exercise for the reader. We must be careful to compare figures only within each model, the figures are not comparable across the two models because we have no way of calculating the constants c and c'.

The figures in the two tables might be used for planning purposes, though if this were the case, we should want to refine the model considerably. We might, for instance, wish to estimate the relative importance of various through routes. Since Kumasi lies close to the direct route between Sekondi-Takoradi and Tamale, it has been assumed that traffic between these towns will pass through Kumasi and the resulting flows have simply been added together. The results for the two models are shown in figures 16.4 and 16.5 respectively. Notice that model A emphasises the population more, and that the order of importance of the two routes into Tamale is

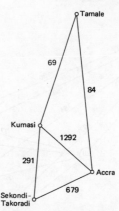

Figure 16.4. Theoretical relative traffic flows for Ghana, model A (inverse linear). (Not directly comparable with figure 16.5.)

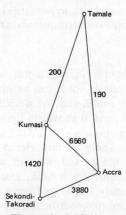

Figure 16.5. Theoretical relative traffic flows for Ghana, model B (inverse square). (Not directly comparable with figure 16.4.)

different for the two models. Since the distances between the three southern towns are almost equal, there is little difference between the relative predictions of the two models for the corresponding routes.

16.10. A more complicated example

The second example will be initially regarded as theoretical. The government of a developing country decides to build a system of all weather roads to link its six major towns, A, B, C, D, E and F. Since money is limited, they wish to know in which order to build the roads in order to obtain the greatest economic benefit as quickly as possible. The consultants decide to begin by building a mathematical model of the traffic flow, and accordingly obtain as initial data the populations of the six towns in thousands, and the distances between them in kilometres. These are shown in figure 16.6 in diagrammatic form. Clearly

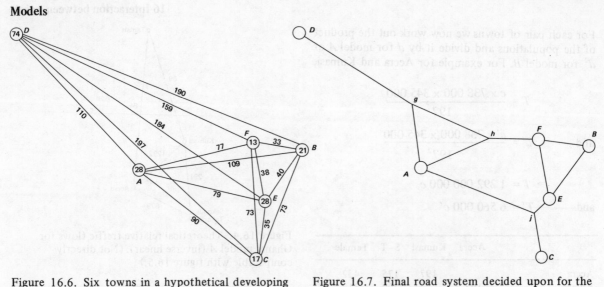

Figure 16.6. Six towns in a hypothetical developing country showing populations (thousands) and distances (kilometres).

Figure 16.7. Final road system decided upon for the six towns of figure 16.6.

all the possible routes in the figure will not be necessary because certain roads can be made to serve for more than one route, and the simplified system eventually decided upon is shown in figure 16.7. For convenience the junctions which are not at towns are labelled g, h and j. There are now eleven sections of road to be constructed, and we can assume, for example, that if section Dg is built, existing poorer quality roads will carry traffic on from g. We need to determine the order of construction of the eleven road sections, which will be in the theoretical order of traffic volumes for a first approximation. (In the next chapter we shall examine the optimum place of

	A	B	C	D	E	F
A		49	59	171	126	61
B	49		67	43	368	251
C	59	67		32	389	41
D	171	43	32		61	38
E	126	368	389	61		252
F	61	251	41	38	252	

Table 16.4 Relative traffic flows for six hypothetical towns of figure 16.7 using model B (inverse square). Multiply by 1000 c' to obtain figures given by the formula.

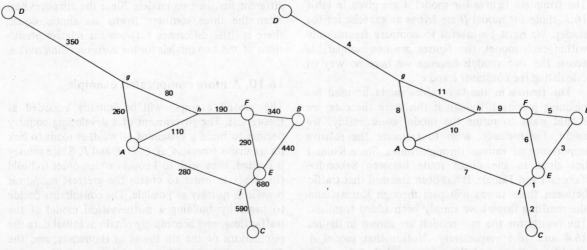

Figure 16.8. Comparative traffic volumes on road system of figure 16.7 model B (inverse square).

Figure 16.9. Order of establishment of links in figure 16.7, model B (inverse square).

Order of construction	1	2	3	4	5	6	7	8	9	10	11
Inverse linear, model *A*	Dg	jE	gA	jC	Aj	hF	FB	EB	gh	FE	Ah
Inverse square, model *B*	jE	jC	EB	Dg	FB	FE	Aj	gA	hF	Ah	gh

Table 16.5. Relative order of construction for the road links of figure 16.7 under the two models.

junctions such as that at *j*; we could of course combine *g* and *h* to build one road into *A* from the north.)

The traffic flows are worked out as in section 16.9, those for the inverse square law are given in table 16.4, the inverse linear model being left as an exercise for the reader. Figure 16.8 shows the total traffic flow for the inverse square model on each section of road. All traffic between the six towns is assumed to take the shortest possible route, so that, for instance the traffic flow between *B* and *F* includes traffic from *B* to *A* and *D*. From figure 16.8, the proposed order of construction is calculated in figure 16.9. This data is repeated together with the equivalent data for the inverse linear model in table 16.5. While there are general similarities in the two orders, the inverse square model tends to emphasise the shorter links in the system more.

16.11. Agreement of models with the historical situation

The remaining sections of this chapter should not be read before a detailed study of section 16.10. There are few figures in order to avoid the visual clues which they inevitably give. The reader may therefore find sketch diagrams a helpful aid. There are three ways in which the model of section 16.10 may be tested, and these will be examined in turn in sections 16.11 to 16.13. There are, of course, many factors which the models do not allow for; terrain, capital cities, ports, pre-established road systems, smaller towns and established patterns of trade and industrial links.

We begin by comparing our models with a system which had already been developed. Rotate figure 16.9 so that *D* is at the south or bottom of the map, and then reflect it about a vertical axis (this idea will be considered further in chapter 24). The six towns can then be interpreted as the six major conurbations of England, excluding Tyne and Wear. *D* is Greater London, *A* is West Midlands, *F* is South Yorkshire, *B* is West Yorkshire, *E* is Greater Manchester and *C* is Merseyside. The populations in figure 16.6 are then in hundreds of thousands and the distances in miles rather than kilometres, but these changes of scale will

not affect the relative order of the predictions. The various roads can then be interpreted as the basic motorway system of part of Britain. In figure 16.7, *DghFB* is the M1, *gAj* is part of the M6, and *BejC* is the M62. *Ah* is the proposed M42, while *FE* is the now abandoned Manchester–Sheffield motorway through the Peak District National Park. The order of construction of the nine links built is difficult to give because of piecemeal construction, but is roughly that given down the left-hand scale of figure 16.10. This is compared with the actual order of construction for model *B* by joining corresponding points across the diagram.

The number of crossings of lines in this figure gives an indication of the success of the model, the fewer the better. (Kendall's rank correlation coefficient τ may be derived from this figure by calculating $1 -$ (no. of crossings)/(half maximum number of crossings). See, for example, Hammond and McCullagh, 1974, pp. 201–6.) Both models are bad on this criterion, and model *B* is even worse than model *A*.

Why is the model so poor at predicting reality? There are a number of reasons. Three of the links *Ej*, *jC* and *gA* were preceded by other improved roads (the East Lancashire Road and the M45/A45 improvements). Another difficulty is the low priority the model gives to *gh*, which is nevertheless an essential link; its omission would be a great disadvantage. Finally figure 16.10 does not include two links which

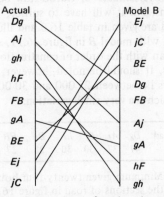

Figure 16.10. Comparison of rank order of construction, actual and model *B*.

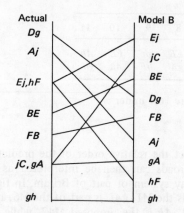

Figure 16.11. Comparison of rank order of traffic density, actual and model B.

come bottom of the list in reality and in the model. All these suggest that model A has some validity in the British context. Model B should not be dismissed too readily since in an underdeveloped country the 'friction' of distance is much more powerful and provides justification for preferring a model which gives increased emphasis to shorter links.

16.12. Agreement of models with statistical observations

Another way of testing the models is to count the actual traffic using the motorways and compare the predictions with it. This can be done by making use of published statistics (Department of Transport, 1978). The figures available are twenty-four hour traffic counts of different sections of motorway taken in 1976. To eliminate the effects of local traffic as much as possible, the census point with the lowest volume of traffic given for each of the nine sections of motorway has been used. This gives a very crude overestimate of traffic flow between the conurbations, but it will have to suffice. The actual figures used are given in table 16.6 and illustrated in comparison with model B in figure 16.11. Agreement is better than with the order of construction, but still rather poor. It should be noted, however, that most of the flows lie between 25 000 and 30 000 vehicles per day, which is a very small variation.

16.13. Internal consistency of models

Models can also be tested by examining their internal consistency, that is by seeing how they change with alterations to the data. The models were tested by adding the next two conurbations for size in England, ignoring the rather remote north-east. The conurbations added were Avon county and the Derby-Nottingham area with populations estimated at 910 000 and 750 000 respectively. Of these, the latter had more effect on the system because of its central position, but the rank orders in both models were never altered by more than one position except that the section of the M1 north of Derby-Nottingham went up three rank places in model B. This suggests a fair degree of consistency about the rank orders. A surprising feature was the low traffic flows predicted for the two motorways to the Avon (Bristol) area, far below any other predicted flows. This emphasises that the model does not allow for the additional traffic flows created by ports and exceptional flows created by holiday traffic which are important on these routes.

On the showing above the gravity model of traffic flow comes out rather poorly, the inverse linear model generally being slightly better than the inverse square model. The models do, however, provide a basis for more complicated models and lead us to ask relevant and important questions. In fact the models are not sophisticated enough to cope with the complex problems of traffic flow in such a complicated area as Britain.

Section of road	Dg	Aj	Ej	hF	BE	FB	jC	gA	gh
Traffic flow	47	37	30	30	28	27	26	26	25

Table 16.6. Minimum given twenty-four hour traffic flows for nine of the sections of road in figure 16.7, in thousands of vehicles per day (Department of Transport, 1978).

Exercises

1. Repeat exercise 3 of chapter 15 using the inverse square rather than the inverse linear law.
2. Redraw figure 16.2 or figure 16.3 using mediator boundaries and compare the results with the original figure.
3. Redraw figure 16.2 or figure 16.3 using the inverse linear law and compare the results with the original figure.
4. Discuss the factors which will tend to invalidate results such as those of figures 16.2 and 16.3.
5. Complete the analysis of section 16.9 for the inverse square law.
6. Complete the analysis of sections 16.10 to 16.12 for the inverse linear law.
7. Repeat the analysis of section 16.10 for some other country, e.g. Scotland, France, Italy or Spain.
8. Repeat the analysis of sections 16.10 and 16.11 for some other mode of transport, e.g. turnpike roads, canals or railways. This will require some historical research.
9. Use one of the models to plan the number of airline flights between five major cities, e.g. London, Paris, Rome, Brussels and Madrid. If possible compare with reality and comment on differences.
10. Repeat question 9 for train services, e.g. for Dublin, Galway, Limerick, Cork and Waterford.
11. Discuss whether the gravity model should use crow's flight or actual route distances. Is there an appreciable difference?

Further reading

Abler, Adams and Gould, 1972, pp. 216–25, 502–6
Bradford and Kent, 1977, pp. 114–27
Briggs, 1974, pp. 59–64
Cole and King, 1968, pp. 502–7
Continuing Mathematics Project, 1977d
Daugherty, 1974, pp. 10–12
Dinkele, Cotterell and Thorn, 1976d, pp. 45–51
Everson and Fitzgerald, 1969, pp. 95–100
Graves and Talbot White, 1974, pp. 190–209
Haggett, 1972, pp. 329–32
Haggett, Cliff and Frey, 1977 pp. 30–40
Hammond and McCullagh, 1974, pp. 75–85, 201–6
Hay, 1973, pp. 126–32
Ling, 1977, pp. 97–8
Lloyd and Dicken, 1977, pp. 56–8, 106–9
Meyer and Huggett, 1979, pp. 94–109
Oxford Geography Project, 1974b, pp. 114–5
Oxford Geography Project, 1975, pp. 122–3
Smith, 1975, pp. 286–95
Tidswell, 1976, pp. 215–29, 291–7

17 Finding the best route

17.1. Introduction

A frequent mathematical concern is that of finding an optimal solution to a problem. For example in chapter 9 it was assumed that the optimal shape for an area is a circle. By optimal in that case was meant the shape with the smallest perimeter which would enclose a given area. Another example was hinted at in section 16.10 when the network of figure 16.7 was derived from figure 16.6. This was done in an arbitrary way, but the general solution to the best set of routes linking a number of towns depends on what we are trying to achieve. This chapter examines some geometrical ideas which can be used in the solution of such problems in geography (and some also in physics). Because the proofs are mathematically interesting and not too difficult, we shall in some cases outline them, especially where they are not well known. Non-mathematical readers can, of course, omit them. In this chapter we shall concern ourselves with setting up a network in order to optimise some aspect of it. We will return to the problem of finding optimal routes through established networks in chapter 29.

Bunge, 1962, quoted in Haggett, Cliff and Frey, 1977, suggests five ways of optimising the routes between a set of towns. These are illustrated in figure 17.1:

(a) the 'Paul Revere' net which starts at one town and connects it by the shortest possible route to all the other towns without returning to the starting point. This will be dealt with in chapter 29.

(b) the travelling salesman net which is similar to (a) but returns to the starting point. This also will be dealt with in chapter 29.

(c) the complete network of direct links for one town.

(d) the complete network of direct links for all towns. Figure 16.6 has another example of this.

(e) the minimum length of links to connect all towns, which will be discussed in this chapter.

(f) a compromise solution such as is usually found in practice.

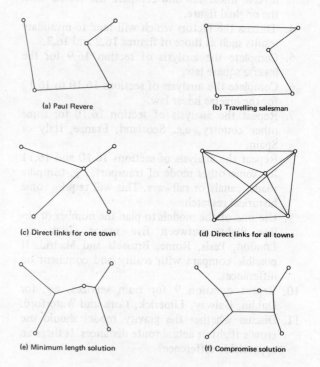

(a) Paul Revere (b) Travelling salesman

(c) Direct links for one town (d) Direct links for all towns

(e) Minimum length solution (f) Compromise solution

Figure 17.1. Various solutions to the problem of optimising the routes connecting five towns. (See text for interpretation.)

It is the tendency for compromise solutions to occur which often makes it difficult to pick out geographical examples of these solutions. For example it is difficult to find examples of figure 17.1(c) in practice, but a tendency towards it is apparent in the rail networks of many countries, for example the situation of Dublin in Ireland and Paris in France.

17.2. The reflection model

We begin with two models which are borrowed from the theory of light in physics, although their wider applicability is sometimes not realised. Suppose, for example, a jetty is to be erected on a straight stretch of coast to serve two off-shore oil-rigs. In figure 17.2(a), AB is the coastline, P and Q are the oil-rigs and J is the jetty. If the oil-rigs generate equal amounts of

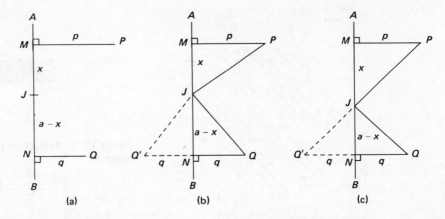

Figure 17.2. Stages in the location of the optimal position of J using the reflection model.

(a)   (b)   (c)

traffic, where should the jetty be placed to ensure that the distances to be travelled by ships are as small as possible?

Suppose that PM, QN are the perpendiculars from P, Q to the coastline and that $PM = p$, $QN = q$, $MN = a$ and $MJ = x$. Pythagoras' theorem (section 3.2) gives

$$PJ = \sqrt{[p^2 + x^2]}, \quad QJ = \sqrt{[q^2 + (a-x)^2]}$$

The problem is to minimise $PJ + QJ$ by a suitable choice of x. This looks like a problem in differential calculus, which is outside the scope of this book. Fortunately, a much simpler solution can be found by an ingenious trick which is illustrated in figure 17.2(b) and (c).

Produce QN to Q' so that $QN = NQ' = q$ as in figure 17.2(b). Then $PJ + JQ = PJ + JQ'$ by symmetry about line AB, and the problem is now equivalent to selecting J so that PJQ' is a minimum. The shortest distance between P and Q' is the straight line PQ', and so we choose J at the intersection of PQ' and AB as shown in figure 17.2(c).

The value of x may be found by scale drawing, or by using the fact that triangles JMP and JNQ' are similar in shape giving

$$x/p = (a-x)/q$$
$$\Rightarrow \quad x = ap/(p+q)$$

A further property of the figure is that $P\hat{J}M = Q'\hat{J}N = Q\hat{J}N$, which means that the coastline may be regarded as a mirror, so that looking from P in the direction of the reflection of Q, the line of sight passes through J.

The property is of value in several simple locational problems where we wish to find a point on a line to service two points away from the line on the same side of it. An example is the location of an electricity substation on a power line to provide power supplies for two villages on the same side of it. (If the villages lie on opposite sides the optimal solution lies on the line joining the two villages.)

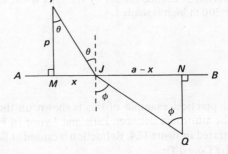

Figure 17.3. Route between P and Q using the refraction model.

17.3. The refraction model.

Since the reflection property of light provides a useful model, it is natural to investigate whether the refraction model is also of value. It turns out that this is the case. Suppose a road or railway has to be constructed between two points P and Q as shown in figure 17.3. The line AB divides two types of country, the cost of construction on the P side of the line being greater than that on the Q side. Suppose that these costs are £h and £k per kilometre respectively, where h is greater than k. Then the total cost of construction is

$$C = hPJ + kJQ$$
$$= h\sqrt{[p^2 + x^2]} + k\sqrt{[q^2 + (a-x)^2]}$$

By use of calculus it may be shown that the minimum cost solution to the location of the point J in figure 17.3 is given by $h \sin \theta = k \sin \phi$, θ and ϕ being the angles marked in the figure. This result is known in physics as Snell's law, and is used to find a value of x which produces the minimum cost of production. A

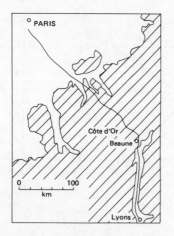

Figure 17.4. Autoroute from Paris to Lyons showing refraction at Beaune caused by the Côte d'Or. Land over 200 m high is shaded.

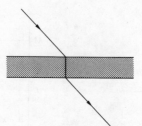

Figure 17.5. Refraction through a layer of denser material.

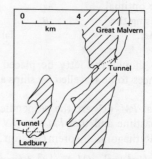

Figure 17.6. Railway from Malvern to Ledbury showing refraction at tunnel mouths. Land over 150 m high is shaded.

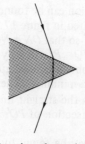

Figure 17.7. Refraction through a wedge of denser material.

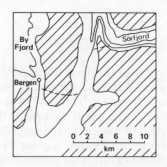

Figure 17.8. Tunnelling through spurs to improve a route. The new railway out of Bergen is shown pecked. Land over 200 m high is shaded. (The railway began life as a local line to Voss and is now a main line to Oslo.)

good practical example of this is shown on the map of the autoroute between Paris and Lyons in France illustrated in figure 17.4. Refraction is caused at Beaune by the Côte d'Or.

17.4. More complicated refraction models

Two common uses of refraction in physics both have interesting geographical analogues. Figure 17.5 shows the path of a ray of light passing through a layer of denser medium, for example a sheet of glass. This illustrates the most economical way of crossing a river or tunnelling through a mountain ridge. The reader should have no difficulty finding examples; figure 17.6 shows the path of the railway line between Malvern and Ledbury in England where it tunnels through two ridges of very hard rock, and countless bridges display the same principle.

Figure 17.7 shows the path of a light ray through a prism and again geographical analogues are easy to find; they are frequent in the construction of railways in river valleys where meanders cause problems. Solutions vary so much that it is sometimes possible to infer how easily finance was obtainable. The railway from York to Scarborough had its winding route through the Derwent Valley altered precisely because of the shortage of finance. Sometimes increased traffic has led to subsequent shortening of the route as on the northern end of the Oxford Canal in the English Midlands, and the railway out of Bergen in Norway (see figure 17.8).

17.5. Shortest set of links joining three towns

A rather different optimisation problem is that of finding the shortest set of links joining three towns. This is the problem first hinted at in figure 16.7, and a more general case has been illustrated in figure 17.1(e). This problem involves finding a point somewhere in the triangle formed by the three towns so that the sum of the distances to the three towns is a minimum. This point or 'centre' is different to the centres used in chapter 12, although there is a relationship to the centroid of the three points, which will be explained later.

Suppose the three towns, labelled A, B and C in figure 17.9, are to be connected at P by three roads so that $AP + BP + CP$ is a minimum. The problem of locating P is known as Fermat's problem or Steiner's problem and has a simple but little-known proof which is worth repeating in full.

First assume A, B and C are not too nearly in a straight line (we shall make this restriction clearer later). In figure 17.9, construct an equilateral triangle BCC' on the outside of BC so that $BC = BC' = CC'$. For some point P inside the triangle ABC, construct another equilateral triangle BPP' so that P' lies on the opposite side of BP to A. If triangle BPC is rotated clockwise about B through an angle of $60°$, it will map onto triangle $BP'C'$ since $BP = BP'$ and $BC = BC'$. Hence triangles BPC and $BP'C'$ are equal in size and shape, that is congruent. Thus $CP = C'P'$ so that

$$AP + BP + CP = AP + PP' + P'C'$$

Now C', by definition, is a fixed point, and $AP + PP' + P'C'$ will be a minimum length when its line segments lie along the straight line AC'. Thus the

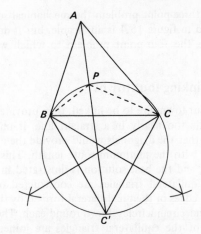

Figure 17.10. Construction for the solution of Fermat's problem.

optimal position of P is on AC' and we have a method of constructing P which is given in figure 17.10. First draw an equilateral triangle on the outside of BC and join its third point to A. The point P may then be determined as in the figure by drawing the circumcircle of the equilateral triangle, or by constructing a second equilateral triangle on another side of triangle ABC.

It is now easy to show that $B\hat{P}C = C\hat{P}A = A\hat{P}B = 120°$ for the best position of P. The proof breaks down, however, if any angle of triangle ABC exceeds $120°$. In that case the best solution is obtained by using the two shorter sides of triangle ABC.

It is quite difficult to find good examples of this minimum property, partly because it is comparatively rare for transport links to be designed to connect three towns simultaneously and partly because the solution, while economic to build is not particularly economic to operate and therefore only occurs when initial finance is limited. A British example is illustrated in figure 17.11 and a French example is the autoroutes radiating from Orange. In many examples it is difficult to be certain how much of the effect is due to the physical geography of the area and how much is an attempt to produce a minimum distance solution.

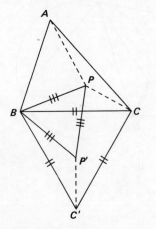

Figure 17.9. Figure for the proof of Fermat's (Steiner's) problem.

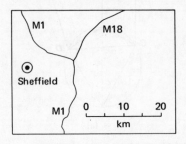

Figure 17.11. Junction of M1 and M18 near Sheffield.

Models

For the three-point problem the mechanical solution suggested in figure 15.4 is applicable, but it does not apply to the four-point problem to which we now turn.

17.6. Linking four towns

When four towns are to be linked, then provided they do not lie too nearly in a straight line, it might be thought that the diagonals would provide the optimal solution with the minimum route length. This is not the case, and the best solution is illustrated in figure 17.12. Equilateral triangles are constructed on two opposite edges of the quadrilateral formed by the four points and circumcircles drawn round each. The third vertices of the equilateral triangles are joined by a straight line, and this line cuts the circumcircles again at the two required junctions. There are two alternative solutions depending on which pairs of opposite sides of the quadrilateral one starts with, and only one alternative gives the optimum solution (unless they are equal). In figure 17.12, the reader should have no difficulty in verifying that (a) gives a better solution than (b) by measurement. Notice the stretch of route between the two junctions which will normally be the busiest link in the network. This means that the capacity of the network is lower than in the system consisting solely of two diagonals.

In the case of a square the two solutions are equally good. This situation can be observed practically at the kitchen sink. The blades of an electric mixer

often consist of four wires symmetrically disposed, so that in cross-section they form the corners of a square. If a blade is immersed in a soap solution so that soap films join all four blades, then the cross-section of the films takes up one of the positions shown in figure 17.13. By shaking gently, one can sometimes flip the film of soap from one solution to the other. If the film to one wire of the blade is pricked, the three-point solution for a right-angled triangle shown in figure 17.14 is obtained.

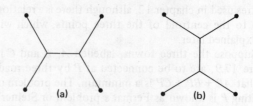

(a)   (b)

Figure 17.13. Alternative solutions to the four-point problem when the points form a square.

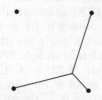

Figure 17.14. Solution of Fermat's problem for a right-angled isosceles triangle.

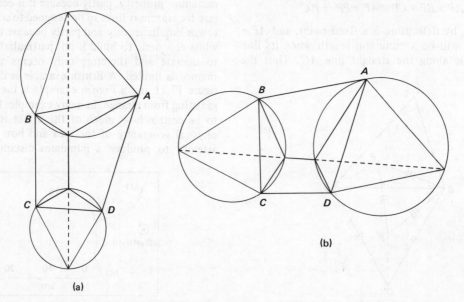

(a)

(b)

Figure 17.12. Alternative possibilities for the four-point version of Fermat's problem ((a) is the optimal solution).

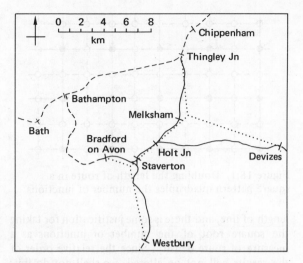

Figure 17.15. Example of real (solid) and theoretical (dotted) solution of Fermat's problem for railways connecting four points in north Wiltshire. (Other railways shown pecked.)

Practical examples of the four-point solution are even harder to obtain than the three-point case, and it is sometimes clear that apparent examples are accidental. A good example is the railway system of north Wiltshire, England, shown in figure 17.15, which was built as two lines connecting Devizes with Bath, and Chippenham with Westbury. Pre-existing routes and the deep valley between Bath and Bradford-upon-Avon effectively meant that the routes had to connect Bradford-upon-Avon, Devizes, Thingley Junction and Westbury. For these four towns the adopted solution is quite close to the theoretical one. Staverton with a triangular junction is very well placed, but Holt Junction would have been better placed at the small town of Melksham.

17.7. Relation of the least-distance point with the centroid

The centroid (sections 12.10 to 12.13) is not the same point as the one P used above. In fact for the centroid G, $AG^2 + BG^2 + CG^2$ is a minimum. It is more important in practice, and, surprisingly, easier to calculate. The relationship between these two points is somewhat similar to that between median and arithmetic mean in statistics, where the median is the point about which the sum of the absolute deviations is least, while for the arithmetic mean the sum of the squared deviations is least. The minimum distance problem can be extended to more points, but becomes less useful with increasing complication.

Exercises

1. Construct other examples of the reflection model with different configurations of points.
2. (Mathematical) Complete the proof of the minimum value property of C in section 17.3.
3. Find practical examples of the refraction model. How would you walk diagonally up a steep hillside of varying slope?
4. Find practical examples to illustrate the optimal solutions for the three- and possibly the four-point problems. Measure the angles involved and try to account for departures from the best value of 120°.
5. (Mathematical) Find the minimum lengths of road needed to connect (a) three points 10 km apart in an equilateral triangle, and (b) four points 10 km apart in a square.
6. Construct solutions to Fermat's problem for rectangles of various shapes: parallelogram, rhombus and isosceles trapezium. Treat separately the cases where obtuse angles are under and over 120°, and where there are two constructible solutions find the better one.
7. (Mathematical) What happens in the solution to Fermat's problem for four points when the constructed circles intersect?
8. Examine the routes of oil and gas pipelines in the North Sea or elsewhere in relation to Fermat's problem and the reflection model.

Further reading

Abler, Adams and Gould, 1972, pp. 272–88, 455–90
Bale, 1976, pp. 82–4
Bradford and Kent, 1977, pp. 45–6, 88–93
Chorley and Haggett, 1967, pp. 768–71
Courant and Robbins, 1941, pp. 329–61
Coxeter, 1961, pp. 21–3
Haggett, 1972, pp. 339–45
Haggett and Chorley, 1969, pp. 114–16, 193–226
Haggett, Cliff and Frey, 1977, pp. 64–76
Hay, 1973, pp. 65–70
Lloyd and Dicken, 1977, pp. 158–66
Oxford Geography Project, 1974b, pp. 114–16
Tidswell, 1976, pp. 280–4

18 Density of networks

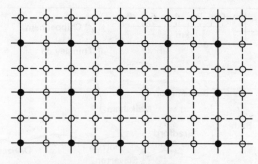

Figure 18.1. Doubling the length of route in a square pattern quadruples the number of junctions.

18.1. Introduction

The rather awkward problem of measuring the density of a set of lines in an area may be solved by using a somewhat unexpected model. If we wish to measure the density of the road system in an area, then we face two apparent difficulties. One is the problem of measuring the lengths of many segments of road, and the other is that of deciding in what area we should measure them. The second problem has already been met briefly in section 8.4 and in this chapter we shall develop the idea more fully. The method used in this chapter is suggested in Briggs, 1972, but the details here are rather different to those given by him.

18.2. Points for lines

The difficulty of measuring lengths of roads leads to two simplifications. For a major survey we may restrict ourselves to main roads only, thus avoiding a common difficulty in towns of knowing at what point to stop counting. Secondly, instead of measuring lengths, it is much quicker to count intersections, a simplification which has been shown to give very effective results (see Haggett and Chorley, 1969, p. 83). Counting junctions is not the same thing as measuring lengths; for example a series of parallel roads with few cross connections will have relatively few intersections for a considerable length of road. Usually, however, road systems are not planned in such an orderly fashion. In any case, the purpose of the exercise is really to measure the accessibility of the area, and it can be argued that the junctions are a better measure of this, especially on motorways with limited access.

Another effect of counting junctions is illustrated in figure 18.1, in that case for a square pattern. The original pattern is shown with solid lines for roads and solid dots for junctions. If the density of lines is doubled by inserting the pecked lines, then the number of junctions is quadrupled, the new ones being indicated by small circles. The same effect occurs with other patterns, and the reader may check this, for example with triangular line systems. Thus the number of junctions increases as the square of the

length of line, and there is some justification for taking the square root of the number of junctions as a measure of route density. Since the relative order of the results will not be altered, we shall not do this; counting junctions rather than their square roots will tend to emphasise the high points on the resulting map.

18.3. Relative importance of junctions

The number of routes meeting at a junction is a measure of its relative importance. Figure 18.2 illustrates two contrasting junctions. The first shows six roads meeting at one junction (the road lay-out has lately been altered at this junction) while the second shows four roads which, because of routes cutting off the corners, meet in eight junctions. It seems incorrect to count these as one junction and eight junctions respectively. The problem may be partially overcome by arbitrarily giving each junction a value of two less than the number of routes leading from it as in table 18.1. When the number of possible traffic routes through the junction is worked out, it can be seen that this is quite well related to the arbitrary value, especially if some allowance is made for the lower likelihood of very acute turns at junctions with five or more routes.

No. of routes leading from junction	Arbitrary value of junction	No. of possible traffic routes through junction
3	1	3 x 2 = 6
4	2	4 x 3 = 12
5	3	5 x 4 = 20
6	4	6 x 5 = 30
7	5	7 x 6 = 42

Table 18.1. Arbitrary method of counting value of route junctions.

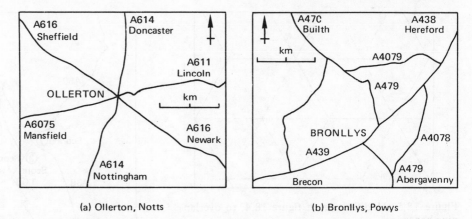

Figure 18.2 Two
contrasting types
of road junction

(a) Ollerton, Notts

(b) Bronllys, Powys

This convention also avoids the problem of whether a slightly staggered crossroads should count as one or two junctions. Complicated junctions such as occur in towns are often produced by one-way street systems. An arbitrary ring can be drawn round the complicated area and the value of the junctions taken to be two less than the number of routes leading out of it. It is difficult to generalise about how large the ring should be, but it is best to keep it quite small. This system can also be developed to deal with motorway junctions with incomplete access.

18.4. Choosing areas in which to count junctions

Briggs, 1972, suggests that this should be done by taking a set of points on the map in a square lattice of unit side 12.6 km. Around each of these points a circle is drawn of radius 12.6, so that its area is $\pi \times 12.6^2 \approx 500 \text{ km}^2$. This produces the pattern of circles in figure 18.3. The junctions are then counted within each circle. This means that some junctions fall within two circles while others fall in three or four circles, thus having considerably more effect on the count of junctions around each lattice point.

This can be partially remedied as in figure 18.4 by using a triangular system of points, which means that every part of the pattern is now covered by three or four circles. If the cireles are modified to hexagons as in figure 18.5, then each junction appears in exactly three hexagons.

The last suggestion is theoretically the soundest, but all the suggestions suffer from the need to draw a complicated grid on the map. Thus it is suggested that a much easier solution is to use the grid lines which already appear on many maps. The saving of

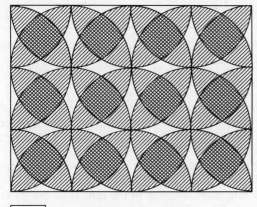

Areas covered by two circles
Areas covered by three circles
Areas covered by four circles

Figure 18.3. Overlapping circles in a square pattern.

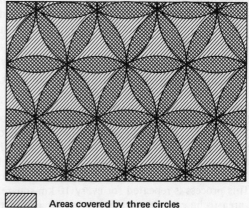

Areas covered by three circles
Areas covered by four circles

Figure 18.4. Overlapping circles in a triangular pattern.

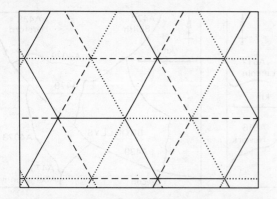

Figure 18.5. Modification of figure 18.4. to overlapping hexagons.

time and the ease with which this can be put into effect encourages the use of the technique. We could simply count the number of junctions in each grid square, but the overlapping technique smooths the results considerably and makes them much easier to interpret. It also emphasises that accessibility is something which affects the whole area around a given junction; unless there is overlapping of squares, a junction near the edge of a square will only affect the accessibility count on one side of it.

Thus we shall count the junctions in 20 km grid squares, overlapping by 10 km so that each junction falls within four squares. The central points of the 20 km squares will thus lie at the intersections of the 10 km grid lines, and each square will cover 400 km^2 rather than the 500 km^2 of Briggs' circles. There is a problem caused at coastlines and similar boundaries which we shall deal with in a practical example in section 18.7. The process of overlapping squares outlined above is known as calculating the *areal running mean* and is similar to that used in computer aided weather forecasting. (See, for example, Lighthill, 1978, pp. 13–69.)

18.5. Calculating the junction densities. Example

Figure 18.6 shows an example of the 'A' class road system in one 10 km grid square around Burton-on-Trent, England. The arbitrary values for each junction are given in table 18.2 and may be checked by the reference numbers to the map. The total score is 7. This process is repeated for every 10 km square in the area to be covered, including a border around the edge to allow for the overlaps. A finished map is displayed in figure 18.8, and the stages in producing a portion of this are given in figure 18.7. The scores for

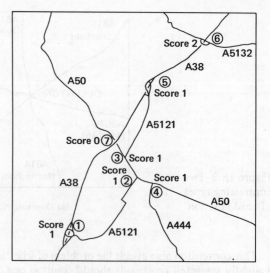

Figure 18.6. Main roads in the 10 km grid square around Burton-on-Trent showing arbitrary junction scores. Circled numbers refer to table 18.2.

Junction	No. of routes	Score
1. A38/A5121 (flyover)	3	1
2. A5121/A50	3	1
3. A5121/A50 (again)	3	1
4. A444/A50	3	1
5. A38/A5121 (again, flyover)	3	1
6. A38/A5132 (flyover)	4	2
7. A38/A50 (bridge only)	–	0
Total		7

Table 18.2. Scores for various road junctions shown in figure 18.6.

each 10 km grid square are first entered up as in (a), the score of 7 for the Burton area is shown ringed, and the count can be made very rapidly with a little practice.

Next the totals for the four squares surrounding each internal grid point of (a) are entered in (b), the grid references referring to the centres of the 20 km squares. Since Burton-on-Trent lies on the edge of the area, its score of 7 only affects two 20 km squares; these are ringed in figure 18.7(b). The ringed value 33, for example, is 2 + 23 + 7 + 1.

18.6. Drawing the contour map. Example

Figure 18.7(b) is now used to prepare an isogram or contour map by interpolation as in section 8.4. The range of values for the whole area is from 2 to 60, so contour lines are drawn for values of 10, 20, 30, 40 and 50. Initial attempts to draw these contours are best made on a copy of figure 18.7(b) as illustrated in (c), remembering that the numbers refer to the centres of the squares. Interpolation between adjacent numbers can be diagonally as well as horizontally and vertically. When a rough idea of the contours has been obtained, the final map can be prepared, plotting one contour at a time, interpolating between each pair of points and drawing a smooth curve to connect up the interpolated points. It is wise to use a pencil and have an eraser handy, but the exercise is an excellent one in curve sketching.

Some difficulties occur. The first is in deciding the exact shape of the contours near the boundary because interpolation is not possible there, and a second is when figures such as the 20 at grid reference 450360 give saddle points in the system. This can be overcome by plotting contours 9.5, 19.5, .., which is inconvenient, or more easily by including the point within a narrow saddle of contours.

Geographers will wish to spend some time interpreting figure 18.8. The M1 motorway lies from south to north along a ridge of high density. The overlapping places high spots between pairs of large towns (Sheffield–Rotherham and Nottingham–Derby) and emphasises the locational attractiveness of such points. The low position of Mansfield and Chesterfield is surprising, but emphasised by major conurbations to south and north. The low accessibility of the hills on the west is also emphasised.

Figure 18.7. Stages in the production of figure 18.8.

	400	410	420	430	440	450	460
380							
370	6	0	2	5	7	6	
360	0	2	3	1	3	8	
350	0	0	1	2	6	3	
340	3	6	0	4	11	21	
330	3	3	2	23	5	23	
320	1	0	⑦	1	9	5	

(a) Entering total values for each 10 km grid square

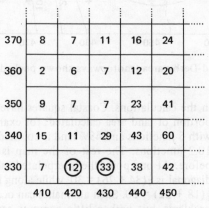

(b) Calculating total values for overlapping 20 km grid squares

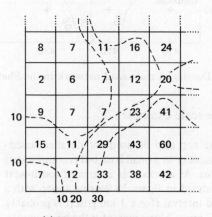

(c) Making a rough sketch of density contours

113

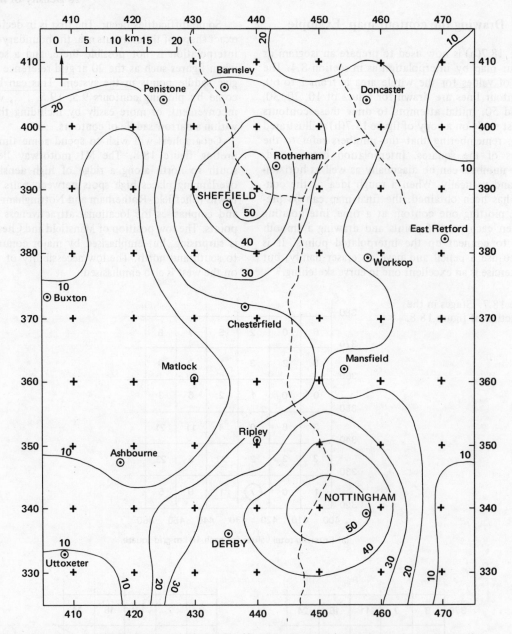

Figure 18.8. Density of main road network in the Sheffield-Derby area (motorways shown pecked).

18.7. A large-scale example

The technique can also be used for detailed assessment of accessibility in a small area, but is complicated to use in towns. As an example an area of south-west Jamaica is analysed in figure 18.9 using a map with a 10 000 ft grid interval (for a 1 km grid it is probably better to use 2 km x 2 km squares for the basic count). All road and track junctions of any sort are included in the calculations. Coastal squares have had the proportion of land area calculated; for example a square with 5 junctions and 49% land is counted as $5 \div 0.49 = 10.2$ junctions. The rest of the map is produced as before. At one point the interpolated value along one diagonal is $\frac{1}{2}(34 + 26) = 30$, while along the other it is $\frac{1}{2}(18 + 22) = 20$. Such anomalies can occur and cause problems, but with a little common sense an acceptable answer can usually be achieved.

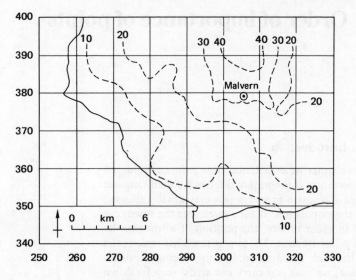

Figure 18.9. Local accessibility map for part of south-west Jamaica (isogram values are arbitrary).

18.8. General points

The production of contour or isogram maps is best adapted to continuous variables over the map; it is for example difficult to illustrate an overhanging cliff. While meteorological variables suit this method well, others are less suitable, especially when as in this chapter or in population density maps it is really isolated points which are being illustrated. In such cases, enlarging the map does not help; it becomes impossible to use. On the other hand, the visual impact of the contour map is considerable, and this is the chief purpose of a map, so that it is worth putting up with some disadvantages to obtain this end, as in sections 25.1 to 25.4.

Exercises

1. Use figure 18.7(a) to attempt to draw contours directly, and compare your results with the south-west corner of figure 18.8. Use contour values 5, 10, 15 and 20.
2. Reproduce a map similar to figures 18.8 and 18.9 for an area of interest to you.
3. Adapt the methods of this chapter to deal with railway lines. Here junctions are much more specific and 1:50 000 maps will show the number of possible traffic routes through each junction. Bridges should be ignored. Would it be better simply to count stations?
4. Use the methods of this chapter to plot the density of other point features on the map, e.g. churches, bridges, stream confluences and stations. When would it be more suitable to ignore the overlapping technique?

Further reading

Abler, Adams and Gould, 1972, pp. 502–6
Briggs, 1972, pp. 27–9
Haggett and Chorley, 1969, pp. 82–7
Haggett, Cliff and Frey, 1977, pp. 87–92, 293–301

19 Order of importance of points

19.1. Introduction

In this chapter we shall discuss how points are ordered in importance; in geographical terms we shall examine the size of towns in an area, a property usually assessed from the population. If for a given area the towns are listed in order of size, the position of a town in the list is called its *rank*. The largest town has rank 1, the next has rank 2 and so on. Because of considerations of space, we shall not carry our study very far down the scale. A more extended example is given in Everson and Fitzgerald, 1969. In some statistical books rankings are made from the smallest to the largest which has advantages, but in geographical examples the smallest is often difficult to define and we must start with the largest and work downwards.

19.2. The rank ordering graph

When the towns in an area are ranked in size, they usually display some pattern of population. Some of this is a natural result of the ranking procedure, but the patterns show more regularity than is justified by chance alone. Table 19.1 shows the populations of the twenty largest towns in Italy, and then every fifth town to the fiftieth ranked. These can be found in official figures, but sometimes tourist guides such

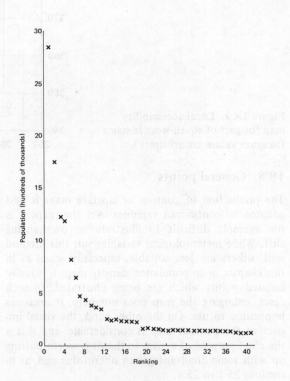

Figure 19.1. Population and rank for forty largest Italian towns.

Town	Population (thousands)	log.	Rank	Town	Population (thousands)	log	Rank
Rome (Roma)	2833	6.45	1	Messina	256	5.41	14
Milan (Milano)	1743	6.24	2	Padua (Padova)	237	5.38	15
Naples (Napoli)	1222	6.09	3	Taranto	235	5.37	16
Turin (Torino)	1199	6.08	4	Cagliari	233	5.37	17
Genoa (Genova)	813	5.91	5	Brescia	214	5.33	18
Palermo	658	5.82	6	Leghorn (Livorno)	177	5.25	19
Bologna	494	5.69	7	Parma	176	5.24	20
Florence (Firenze)	461	5.66	8	Foggia	149	5.17	25
Catania	397	5.60	9	Pescara	129	5.11	30
Bari	367	5.57	10	Monza	117	5.07	35
Venice (Venezia)	366	5.56	11	Forli	108	5.03	40
Trieste	272	5.44	12	Udine	103	5.01	45
Verona	270	5.43	13	Torre del Greco	95	4.98	50

Table 19.1. Population (in thousands), logarithms of population and ranking of towns in Italy (first twenty and then every fith rank to fiftieth).

116

as the Michelin guides are more easily obtained. The logarithms of populations will be required later in the chapter and are also included. Figure 19.1 shows a graph of the populations and ranks of the first forty towns; this is a characteristic shape not dissimilar to many river profiles (see chapter 5). It is difficult to interpret because so many points fall close to the x-axis.

19.3. Using logarithms of population

This difficulty of interpretation may be overcome by adopting the method of section 5.10 and figure 5.7 and plotting the logarithms of the population against the rank as in figure 19.2. The terms in that figure seem to fall into three groups with ranks 1–11, 12–18, and 19–40 and these are emphasised by the lines drawn in that figure. Each of these lines separately suggests a relationship connecting the logarithm of the population ($\log p$) and the rank of the town (r) of the form

$$\log p = -mr + \log k$$

where m and k are convenient constants, the m having a negative sign before it to emphasise that the line is sloping downwards. Some readers may know that this can also be written

$$p = k\,10^{-mr}$$

where the 10 is raised to a negative power. (We assume the logarithms are to base 10.) This type of equation is a very common mathematical model known as the exponential model.

In this model the jumps between the lines might be said to signal changes in the functions of the cities. Figure 19.3 shows the members of the first two groups on the map of Italy, and the groups might be identified as regional and area centres respectively. The identification of the first group is reasonably convincing in terms of Italian geography, but the second group is oddly scattered and the model is not very convincing in this example.

19.4. Using logarithms of both population and rank

Instead of the semi-logarithmic model above we can also take logarithms of the ranks. Geographers do not always seem to be quite clear that in this case we have a completely different model. The logarithmic model is most easily performed using special logarithmic graph paper as in Continuing Mathematics Project,

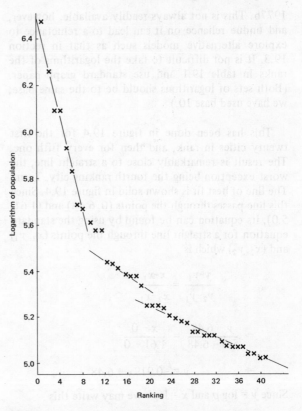

Figure 19.2. Rank and logarithm of population for forty largest Italian towns.

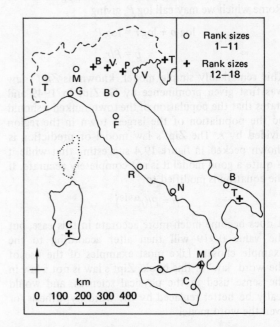

Figure 19.3. The eighteen largest cities of Italy.

1977b. This is not always readily available, however, and undue reliance on it can lead to a reluctance to explore alternative models such as that in section 19.3. It is not difficult to take the logarithms of the ranks in table 19.1 and use standard graph paper. (Both sets of logarithms should be to the same base; we have used base 10.)

This has been done in figure 19.4 for the first twenty cities in rank, and then for every fifth one. The result is remarkably close to a straight line, the worst exception being the fourth ranking city, Turin. The line of best fit is shown solid in figure 19.4. Since this line passes through the points (0, 6.48) and (1.61, 5.0), its equation can be found by using the standard equation for a straight line through the points (x_1, y_1) and (x_2, y_2) which is

$$\frac{y-y_1}{y_2-y_1} = \frac{x-x_1}{x_2-x_1}$$

$$\Rightarrow \frac{y - 6.48}{5.0 - 6.48} = \frac{x - 0}{1.61 - 0}$$

$$\Rightarrow \qquad y = -0.919x + 6.48$$

Since $y = \log p$ and $x = \log r$ we may write this

$$\log p + 0.919 \log r = 6.48$$

Now 0.919 is quite close to unity, and 6.48 is approximately the logarithm of the population of Rome which we may call $\log P$, giving

$$\log p + \log r = \log P$$

$$\Rightarrow \qquad p = P/r.$$

This remarkably simple model, known as *Zipf's law* was first given prominence by G. Zipf in 1949 and states that the population of the town ranked r should be the population of the largest town in the region divided by r. The Zipf's law model or prediction is shown pecked in figure 19.4 suggesting that while it is quite a good model it is not completely accurate. If the equation is modified to

$$p = P/(r^{0.919})$$

it does become much more accurate in this case, but the value 0.919 will then alter according to the example chosen. Like most examples of the use of the word 'law' in this book, Zipf's law is not a law in the sense used in the physical sciences, and would really be better replaced by the word hypothesis, or even the word model.

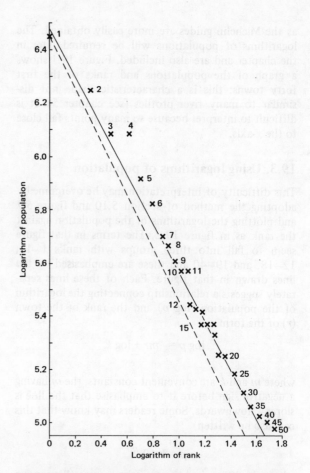

Figure 19.4. Logarithm of population and logarithm of rank for the fifty largest Italian towns (line of Zipf's law shown pecked).

19.5. Discussion of Zipf's law

The choice between the semi-logarithmic model of section 19.3 and the logarithmic one of section 19.4 is a personal one; both are attempts to discern patterns in natural phenomena. The choice will, of course, be made on the basis of many more examples than the one given here. Geographers have preferred the second model because it seems to fit a wider variety of situations, and because of its greater simplicity.

As always with mathematical models, the differences between the model and the reality are as important and as interesting as the similarities. As far as the Italian situation is concerned, Zipf's law suggests that the population of Rome is a little too small, while the towns ranking 2 to 6 are too large. This suggests that Italy has overemphasised the development of the regions at the expense of the central function. This is historically true, and Rome has been the capital of all Italy only since the last century. Both the United Kingdom and France display the reverse tendency, London and Paris appearing too large, which suggests over-centralisation. The size of the largest city is crucial in verifying the model since it occurs in the statement of the law. Both London and Paris also have wider rôles than within their own countries which survive from their days as capitals of empires.

So far little has been said about regions and how they are selected. The natural areas to test for Zipf's law are national territories. There is some evidence that Zipf's law does not work well with very large territories such as the USA and the USSR, but that in these cases it works well for regions. Clearly it cannot work for both because if the largest town is the 'right' size for the nation; it will be too large according to Zipf's law for its own region. For many smaller nations the law works well, and it also seems well suited to explaining clear geographical regions not too close to the capital such as East Anglia in Great Britain.

Figure 19.5 illustrates this property for the south of Italy including Sicily, roughly corresponding to the old Kingdom of Naples. This produces a good fit, since Naples seems to be about the right size. A similar exercise for the Po Valley and adjacent lowlands in the north, however, suggests that Milan and Turin are too large, although the other towns fit in well.

Rank order laws do not apply to city size alone but to other phenomena such as the sizes of commercial companies, populations of nations, personal incomes and number of species in biological genera, as is pointed out in Bradford and Kent, 1977.

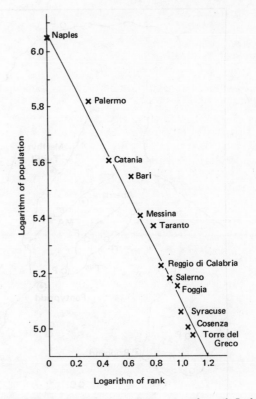

Figure 19.5. Zipf's law for the towns of south Italy and Sicily.

19.6. Ranking by services

Towns may also be ranked by studying the commercial services they provide such as banking, utilities and chain stores. About twenty of these need to be identified from the commercial telephone directory or a similar guide, and the towns are then ranked for number of services. Very often a step such as those in figure 19.2 becomes apparent and can be used to separate major and minor towns. Figure 19.6 illustrates this for the south-east Wales telephone area, a region where Zipf's law does not work well. The major centres are named, and minor centres are identified by their initial letters. The map shows an interesting example of a 'take-over', the new town of Cwmbran taking over the functions of Pontypool which has a restricted site with poor local communications. It is also interesting to note that Abergavenny, situated in a rural area, is a much more important centre than many larger towns in the industrial area.

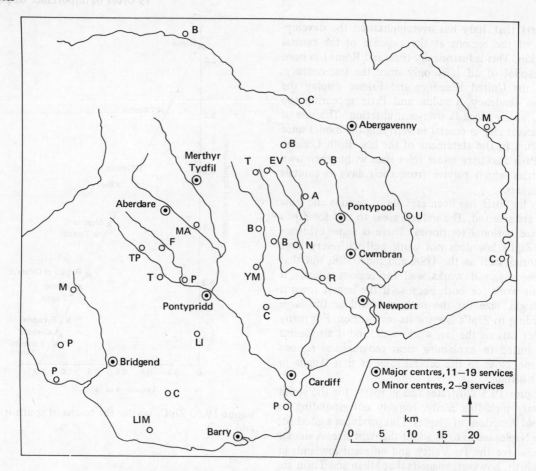

Figure 19.6. Towns of south-east Wales showing those providing major and minor services.

Exercises

1. Repeat the work on rank ordering by population size for other countries or regions, e.g. France, Ireland, Spain, USA, southern France, south-west England or north-east USA.

2. Repeat figure 19.5 for the towns in the Po Valley – northern lowlands area. These are ranks 2, 4, 7, 11, 13, 15, 18, 20 in table 19.1.

3. (Mathematical) Verify that the equation of the line in figure 19.5 is approximately $y + 0.95x = 6.05$. Draw a similar line for the result of question 2, and show that if no attempt is made to draw it through Milan and Turin, its equation is approximately $y + 0.99x = 6.15$.

4. Repeat the analysis of section 19.6 for another area. (See also Briggs, 1974.)

Further reading

Bradford and Kent, 1977, pp. 58-69
Briggs, 1974, pp. 23-7, 33-4, 52-5
Cole and King, 1968, pp. 481-3
Continuing Mathematics Project, 1977b
Dinkele, Cotterell and Thorn, 1976e, p. 57
Everson and Fitzgerald, 1969, pp. 45-73
Gibbs, 1961, pp. 436-51
Graves and Talbot White, 1974, pp. 291-8
Haggett, 1972, pp. 281-5
Haggett, Cliff and Frey, 1977, pp. 110-21
Lloyd and Dicken, 1977, pp. 68-81
Meyer and Huggett, 1979, pp. 22-9, 34-44
Tidswell, 1976, pp. 182-3, 201-6
Wilson, 1973b, pp. 60-5

20 Clustering into regions

20.1. Introduction

In this chapter we shall investigate the technique known as cluster analysis which has been widely used in the social sciences. However, we shall avoid using a computer or even statistical techniques by making a number of simplifications in the procedure. Cluster analysis groups together objects for which we have several statistical measurements by combining those which are mathematically closest together. A particularly geographical aspect of this is the idea of the region, although the clustering method does not always produce regions which are cohesive on the map. Mathematically there are at least two interesting ideas: one is that of 'trees' which will be met again in chapter 30, and another that of generalised distance. This latter idea covers not only the idea of distance between two points on a graph (where units need not be those of length), but also the idea of 'distance' in three and more dimensions. In this chapter we shall, however, remain in two-dimensional space. Because of this restriction and the necessity of keeping the data simple, the clusterings in this chapter will be rather crude. Only one criterion for clustering will be used (the hierarchic one), but others will be found in more advanced treatments. The ideas will be developed by a series of examples, each adding a little to an understanding of what the process is trying to achieve. While this makes for a lengthy explanation, it illustrates the formulation of a complicated mathematical model by a sequence of small steps.

20.2. Assembling a construction kit

The assembly of a plastic construction kit gives an example of the idea of clustering. Figure 20.1 shows a clustering diagram based on the instructions for assembling part of Lesney Toys $\frac{1}{32}$nd scale model of a Jaguar SS/100 car (kit number PK-304). Down the left-hand side of the diagram are the part numbers, and the network gives the order in which this must be put together to assemble the kit. (The numbers in brackets indicate the numbers of identical parts.)

One problem in drawing up such a figure is to

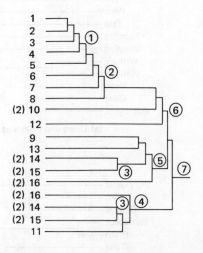

Figure 20.1. Cluster diagram for the building of part of a plastic toy car (Lesney Toys kit number PK-304).

determine the order in which the part numbers should be written down so that the lines in the diagram avoid crossings which cause confusion. Usually an initial rough drawing must be made first. If necessary it can be rearranged by working from right to left. The figure illustrates another convention which will be used in this chapter, that of associating the distance of the vertical lines from the left-hand edge of the figure with the order of construction, in effect giving an approximate time scale. In the case of the model kit, this order is not unique. There is also a primitive idea of distance in the chart since parts which are to be glued together will appear in general close together in the chart. However, the reverse may not necessarily be the case.

The numbers encircled in the figure give the main stages of construction as indicated in the kit, and thus show the major clusters in the course of construction. Networks which have no closed circuits like the ones in this chapter are known as *trees*. It has already been pointed out in section 1.7 that elements in a cluster diagram may be identified by a binary coding by starting from the right and coding 0 for a left turn and 1 for a right turn. Thus part number 13 in the figure may be coded 10110. The number of digits will vary with the number of choices to be made, so it may be helpful to fill up additional spaces with zeros on the right of the code.

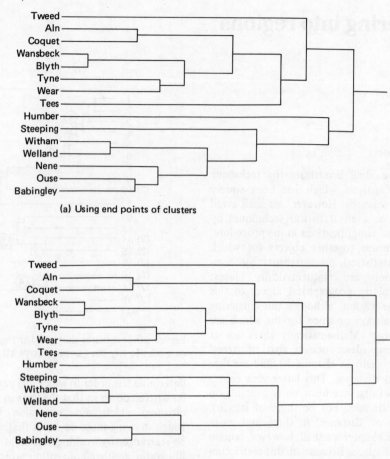

(a) Using end points of clusters

(b) Using centres of mass of clusters

Figure 20.2. Alternative groupings of the river mouths of figure 10.2 into clusters using two different criteria.

20.3. Clustering of points on a line. First method

We shall now develop the example encountered in section 10.5 to show the idea of clustering in a geographical context; the data are given in table 10.2 and illustrated in figure 10.2. The clustering is shown in figure 20.2(a) and begins by grouping together the two closest river mouths, namely the Wansbeck and the Blyth, only 7 km apart. Next are the Welland and Witham, and the joining of these is indicated by drawing the vertical line in the figure further to the right than in the first case. For the third cluster Aln and Coquet and also Ouse and Babingley are equal. Next comes the Tyne and Wear, 17 km apart, and at the same distance the Nene joins the Ouse–Babingley cluster. In this way the process can be continued until a single cluster is produced. The process is more helpful if stopped before this stage, producing a small

number of clusters. A natural clustering might be in four groups: (a) Tweed, (b) Aln–Tees, (c) Humber, (d) Steeping–Babingley. This could be reduced to three by joining the first two groups. We now have an objective criterion for forming clusters, perhaps with the practical need to set up such authorities as drainage boards.

The number of clusters chosen depends on the requirements of the situation, but can be helped by analysis of the arithmetic. The distance between river mouths can be written down in order of size with their successive differences underneath thus:

7 8 9 9 17 17 20 25 33 39 53 78 82 235
 1 1 0 8 0 3 5 8 6 14 25 4 153

The differences help to highlight sudden jumps in size which often occur in such sequences. There is a sudden jump of 8 quite early in the process, but this is too soon for effective clustering. The jumps of 14

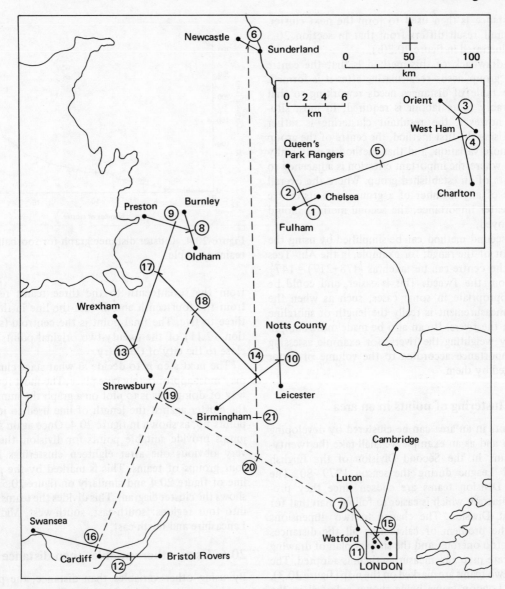

Figure 20.3. Clustering for football teams in the Second Division of the English Football League, season 1979–80 (London area inset).

and 25 are also larger, and suggest forming five or four clusters, although the final jump is exceptionally large and might also give an appropriate solution of only two clusters.

20.4. Clustering of points on a line. Second method

The clustering above has the disadvantage that it only takes account of the end point in each group. For

example, when the Tweed is added to the Aln–Tees group, the distance taken is that from the River Aln rather than from the centre of the group. This can be avoided by calculating the average river mouth distance of the group from the Tweed to find a 'centre' for the group. The calculation for the seven rivers in the group is

$$(78+87+120+127+147+164+217) \div 7$$
$$= 940 \div 7 = 134 \text{ km}$$

123

Models

This distance is then used to form the next cluster. The overall result differs from that in section 20.3 and is illustrated in figure 20.2(b).

The drawback of this method is that the centre of each group needs recalculating after it is formed, and the table of distances needs reworking so that considerably more labour is required. In most situations, however, the resultant clustering is rather better. Using the first method, the centre of the group shows more variation, and that method is only really suitable where the important criterion is adjacency to the limits of an established group. Where the overall distance of any member of a group from its centre is of greater importance, the second method should be employed.

The second method can be simplified by using the mid-point of the range; for example, in the Aln–Tees group, the centre can be taken as $\frac{1}{2}(78+217) = 147\frac{1}{2}$ units from the Tweed. This is easier, and could be more appropriate in some cases, such as when the crucial measurement is really the length of shoreline between the rivers. It can also be made more complicated by weighting the rivers, for example assessing their importance according to the volume of water discharged by them.

20.5. Clustering of points in an area

The points in an area can be clustered by developing this idea and as an example we shall take the twenty-two teams in the Second Division of the English Football League during the season 1979–80. The Second Division teams are chosen since they produce a diagram which is easier to follow than that for the First Division. The change to two dimensions makes the problem of calculating all the distances involved too onerous, and the simpler plan of drawing an accurate map and measuring them is adopted. The twenty-two teams are marked on the map (figure 20.3), the six London teams being shown enlarged in the inset. It happens that the two closest teams are Fulham and Chelsea in the inset, and these are joined and the mid-point of this line marked 1 replaces them. This reduces the twenty-two points to twenty-one, and of these the replacement point is closest to Queen's Park Rangers, and is joined to them. In this case one of the points represents two teams, and thus is twice as powerful. To compensate for this the line is divided in the ratio 2 : 1 taking the point of division marked 2 closer to the double point replacing Fulham and Chelsea. This procedure is repeated until after twenty-one junctions a single point is obtained. For example, the eighteenth junction joins the five teams resulting

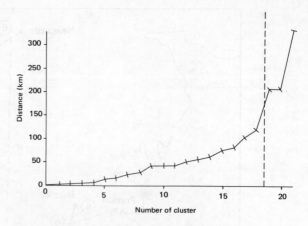

Figure 20.4. Cluster distance graph for football teams example.

from the seventeenth to the three teams resulting from the fourteenth and divides the line in the ratio three to five. The final point is the centroid (see section 12.11) of the twenty-two original points and is close to the city of Coventry.

The next step is to decide at what stage clustering may most appropriately take place. The most revealing way of doing this is to plot on a graph the number of the cluster against the length of line used to join the points up, as shown in figure 20.4. Once again sudden jumps provide suitable points for division, there is a very obvious one after eighteen clusterings leaving four groups of teams. This is marked by the pecked line of figure 20.4 and similarly on figure 20.5 which shows the cluster diagram. This divides the teams neatly into four regions: south-east, south-west, Midlands–Lancashire and north-east.

20.6. Using other variables than distance

By using other variables than distance, the process can be put to work in a variety of situations. Figure 20.6 shows the mean annual rainfall plotted against the mean annual sunshine for twenty-six seaside towns in England and Wales (Figure 20.7 shows the towns on the map). The clustering in figure 20.6 is carried out exactly as for that of figure 20.3. There is however a hidden trap in the process. This is that the spread of points in the graph must be the same along both axes, otherwise greater prominence is given to the variable which is more spread out. Roughly this can be achieved by ensuring that the scales on the graphs allow the ranges of both variables to cover about the same lengths. In fact, the ranges along the two axes are 1729 – 1339 = 462 hours for sunshine and 1100 – 530 = 570 mm for

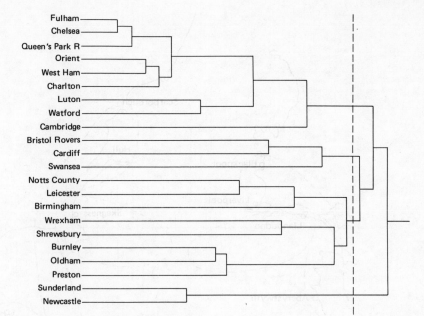

Figure 20.5. Cluster diagram for football teams example.

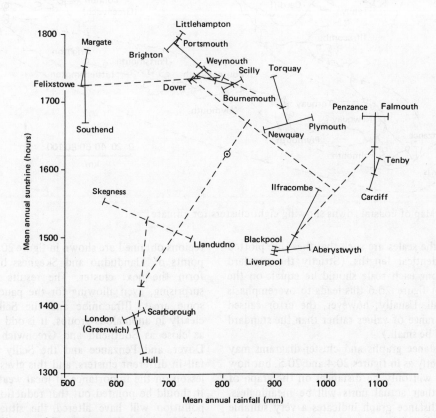

Figure 20.6. Climate of English and Welsh coastal towns.

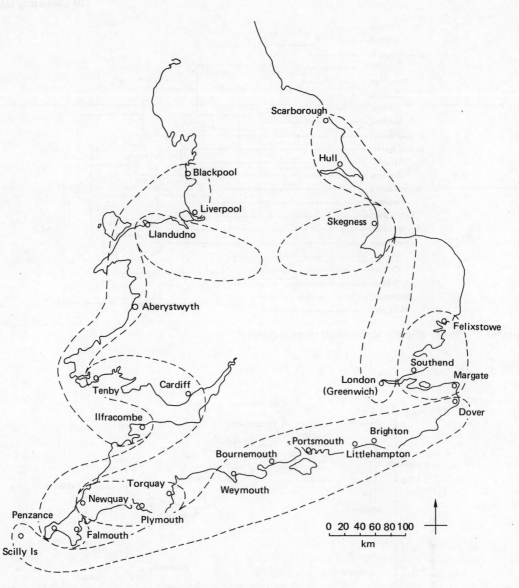

Figure 20.7. Map of coastal towns showing eight clusters for climate.

rainfall, and the scales are such that these are plotted on almost identical lengths. (Strictly the standard deviations along each scale should be equal; on the scales used in figure 20.6 this leads to overemphasis of the rainfall. Usually, however, the error caused by using the range of values rather than the standard deviation will be small.)

Cluster distance graphs and cluster diagrams may be drawn exactly as in figures 20.4 and 20.5, but now the distances will only be distances on the graph of figure 20.6, their actual units will be meaningless. The cluster distance graph indicates a very suitable break after the eighteenth cluster and the eight

regions obtained are shown in figure 20.7, the isolated points of Llandudno and Skegness being about to form the next cluster. The results are somewhat surprising, even allowing for the paucity of data in some areas. Ilfracombe and the Scilly Islands are clearly in anomalous groups. It is odd too that places as close as Southend and Greenwich, Margate and Dover, and Penzance and the Scilly Islands should fall in different clusters, and this gives an interesting lesson on the importance of local weather variations. It should be pointed out that reduction of industrial pollution will have altered the situation in figure 20.7 in recent years.

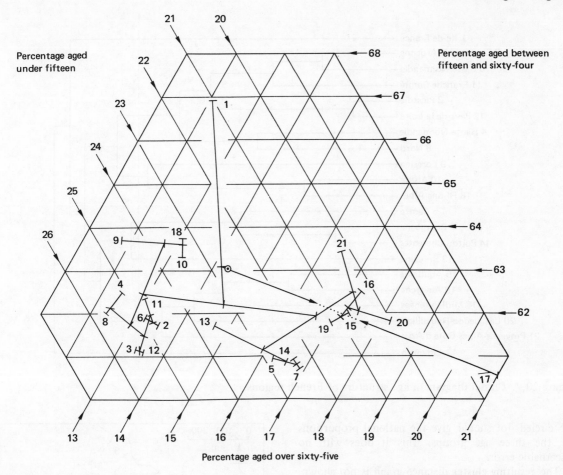

Figure 20.8. Clustering of age structure of French regions (see figure 20.9 for key).

It is tempting to use a process such as this to group areas into regions. The anomalies in figure 20.7 show how carefully this must be done if sensible results are to be obtained. A particular problem arises if it is desired that all parts of a region should be contiguous and it is quite easy to obtain regions whose shapes look like the worst excesses of gerrymandering.

20.7. Clustering into regions

As a final example of how an effective and meaningful result can be obtained without computer aid, the idea of the triangular graph used in section 2.11 will be used in producing regions. Figure 20.8 illustrates the proportion of the population aged under fifteen, aged fifteen to sixty-five and aged over sixty-five on a triangular graph. Since the percentages in the three groups add up to one hundred it is possible to illustrate this on such a graph. Only a small portion

of the whole triangle is shown in order to obtain clarity of detail since all the points fall quite close to one another. The regions chosen are the twenty-one French mainland economic planning regions and the data are from Institut National de la Statistique et des Etudes Economiques, 1977. The positions of the regions are numbered on the clustering and a key is provided to the regions in figure 20.9, which also gives the cluster diagram.

Once the points have been plotted, the clustering proceeds on figure 20.8 by measurement as before, but with one subtle sophistication. Each of the points is given a weighting according to the population it represents and the lines are divided in this ratio, the points of division being nearer the end of the line representing the greater population. This makes sure each region is represented fairly in relation to its population, and has the additional advantage that the final point of the clustering shown in figure 20.8 by

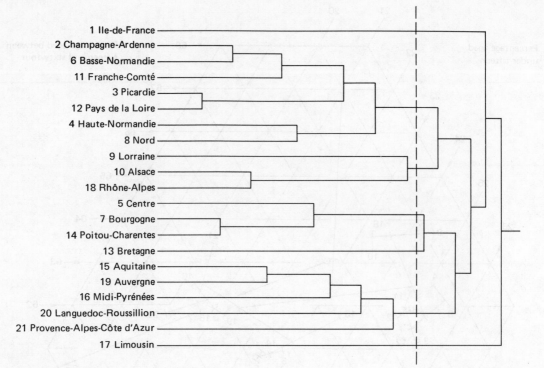

Figure 20.9. Cluster diagram of age structure of French regions.

the circled dot should give the national proportions for the three age groups. This it does with no discernable error.

The resulting cluster distance graph is not shown, but one jump on it suggests seven regions indicated by the pecked line on figure 20.9 and illustrated in figure 20.10. As it happens only one cluster does not consist of contiguous areas. Briefly the northern arc has a high under fifteen population and a low over sixty-five population. The southern region has a high population over sixty-five, while there is an intermediate region between these. The eastern region (in two portions on the map) is similar to the northern, but with a rather higher proportion of population between fifteen and sixty-four. The remaining three clusters are all isolated regions. Bretagne (region 13) falls between the central and northern regions. Limousin (region 17) has an extremely high proportion aged over sixty-five and the Ile-de-France around Paris (region 1) has an extremely high proportion aged between fifteen and sixty-four. The clustering emphasises the differing social problems faced by these exceptional areas. Readers might like to compare the treatment of this problem here with a related but more complex treatment in Cole and King, 1968, pp. 263–86.

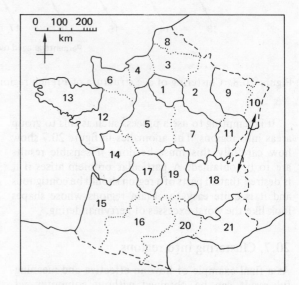

Figure 20.10. French regions, clustered by age structure of population.

128

20.8. Conclusion

The whole idea of clustering has considerable scope for development once the computer has removed the difficulties of computation. The example of section 20.6 could obviously be made three-dimensional by including a variable such as mean annual temperature; but mathematically there is no limit to the possible number of dimensions, and as many as fifty meteorological variables might be included in a cluster analysis. Similarly the age structure analysis in section 20.7 could be enlarged by dividing the age groups further and by using the figures for the ninety or so French departments rather than the twenty-one planning regions. The idea of cluster analysis is an example of multivariate analysis, a group of statistical techniques which require computer aid and which have become popular in recent years, not only in geography, but in psychology and other social sciences.

Exercises

1. Draw up a cluster diagram for a plastic model construction kit.
2. Draw the cluster distance graph and the cluster diagram for figure 20.6.
3. Draw the cluster distance graph for figure 20.8.
4. Work out a linear clustering for (say) food shops distributed along a suburban shopping street.
5. Using local telephone dialling codes work out clusters one digit at a time to determine the routing of calls to the various exchanges. Illustrate with a map.
6. Work out a clustering for a national or local league in some sport. Where is the centroid?
7. Work out a clustering of English universities and find the centroid. Try other alternatives such as regional centres. (Do not attempt more than twenty-five to thirty points.)
8. Work out a clustering for the main towns of some country using a road distance table and adapting the criterion for clustering used in figure 20.2(a) so that the problem of finding centroids is avoided. (The *Reader's Digest Complete Atlas of the British Isles* has a suitable one for twenty-three Irish towns).
9. Work out further clusterings for data which have two variables such as those of figure 20.6.
10. Repeat the clustering of section 20.7 for another nation.

Further reading

Abler, Adams and Gould, 1972, pp. 158-89
Cole and King, 1968, pp. 263-86, 583-7
Haggett and Chorley, 1969, pp. 239-57
Smith, 1975, pp. 328-39

21 Patterns of points

21.1. Hexagonal territories in a triangular settlement pattern

After examining the ordering and the clustering of points we shall now turn from a practical to a theoretical approach and examine how settlement patterns might develop on theoretical grounds. While this might appear of less geographical use, it provides an interesting mathematical study and raises some geographical points. Geographers who find it hard reading can easily omit the chapter if they wish.

The packing of regularly shaped areas in space has already been illustrated in figure 9.5. We can imagine the first settlers setting up farming communities in a new land. At first the villages will be independent of one another and there will be little opportunity or need for trade. Villagers will control an area around them of such a size that it is economic to walk, do a day's work and return to the village anywhere within the area, and this will tend to ensure an even pattern of villages. Circles will not fit together and so the shapes around villages will tend to be modified to the nearest shape which will fit into a pattern – the hexagon. Figure 13.5 (using mediator lines between county towns) shows a distorted view of this situation, albeit on a larger scale, while figure 21.1(a) shows the ideal of a triangular pattern of villages, each controlling a hexagonal area around it.

As population rises, specialisation develops and the need to trade brings the development of towns, or using the accepted jargon in this context, higher order *central places* develop. The spacing of these central places is determined by the distance it is economic to travel for the services they provide. The most obvious way this can happen is illustrated in Figure 21.1(b), where each town is surrounded by six villages. Since each of these villages is, however, equidistant from three different towns, all competing for custom, in theory the trade of the village will be equally shared among the three towns. Thus each town will serve one third of each of six villages, and of course its own area:

$$(\tfrac{1}{3} \times 6) + 1 = 3$$

We call this quantity, which is the effective number of settlements served by each central place, the K value of the central place.

If we enlarge the hexagons slightly and turn them through 30°, we have the pattern of figure 21.1(c), where the villages are at the mid-points of the sides of the hexagon, and each village has a choice between only two nearest towns. In this case

$$K = (\tfrac{1}{2} \times 6) + 1 = 4$$

Further enlargement of the hexagons and an oblique inclination to the basic pattern of villages will produce figure 21.1(d) where each central place controls six surrounding villages. Here

$$K = (1 \times 6) + 1 = 7$$

21.2. Possible values of K. Oblique coordinates

All values of K do not occur in regular hexagonal patterns, and in investigating which values can occur, a little-used geometrical device known as oblique coordinates is helpful. In figure 21.2, the axes Ox and Oy are not at right angles, and in our use we shall place them at an angle of 60°. The point P is then given coordinates (p, q) as illustrated so that P is at the opposite vertex of a parallelogram to O. We shall only need to consider points for which p and q are positive, and need not trouble about negative values.

The distance OP will be required, and may be calculated by the cosine formula which gives $OP^2 = p^2 + q^2 - 2pq \cos 120°$. Since the cosine of 120° is $-\tfrac{1}{2}$, we have

$$OP^2 = p^2 + pq + q^2$$

This should be compared with Pythagoras' theorem which uses $OP^2 = p^2 + q^2$ for rectangular coordinates.

We can now calculate OP^2 for various values of p and q, and some of the smaller values are given in table 21.1. It is not difficult to show that $K = OP^2$, since the number of settlements controlled by a central place must be proportional to the area it controls,

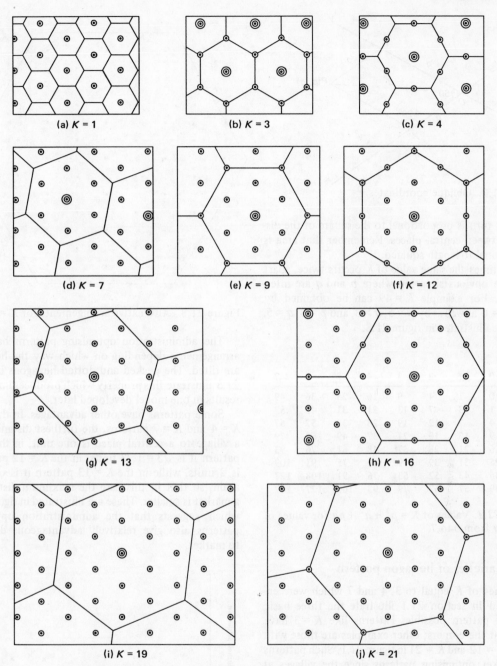

Figure 21.1. First ten hexagonal patterns on a triangular lattice.

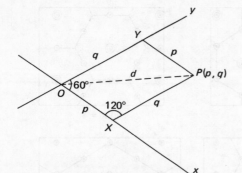

Figure 21.2. Oblique coordinates.

which in turn is proportional to the square of the distance between central places. Remember that area is proportional to length squared.

Sometimes the same value of K occurs twice, apart from the obvious situation where p and q are interchanged. For example $K = 49$ can be obtained by $p = 7$, $q = 0$ as well as by $p = 5$, $q = 3$, and $p = 3$, $q = 5$. These are illustrated in figure 21.3.

$q \backslash p$	0	1	2	3	4	5	6	7
0	0	1	4	9	16	25	36	49
1	1	3	7	13	21	31	43	57
2	4	7	12	19	28	39	52	67
3	9	13	19	27	37	49	63	79
4	16	21	28	37	48	61	76	93
5	25	31	39	49	61	75	91	109
6	36	43	52	63	76	91	108	127
7	49	57	67	79	93	109	127	147

Table 21.1. Values of $K = p^2 + q^2 + pq$ for values of p and q from 0 to 7.

21.3. Varieties of hexagon pattern

The values of K equal to 3, 4 and 7 which were encountered in section 21.1 illustrate the three basic types of pattern possible. Patterns like $K = 3$ have villages at the corners; other examples are those with $K = 9$, $K = 12$ and $K = 21$ in figure 21.1. Such patterns are market optimising patterns since the villages at the vertices have a choice of three central places in which to market their goods. Patterns such as $K = 4$, $K = 12$ and $K = 16$ have villages on the edges of the hexagons and are traffic optimising patterns since direct routes between adjacent central places pass through the greatest number of villages. Patterns like $K = 7$, $K = 13$ and $K = 19$ are administrative optimising patterns in which no village has divided loyalties. The $K = 12$ pattern is both market and traffic optimising.

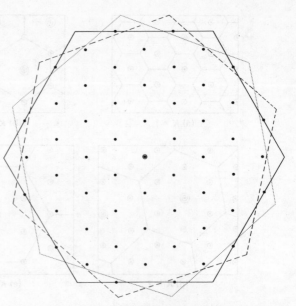

Figure 21.3. Alternative arrangements for $K = 49$.

The administration optimising patterns have two arrangements depending on which way the hexagons are tilted. The pecked and dotted hexagons in figure 21.3 illustrate this property which produces important results in one model developed later.

Some patterns have other advantages. In the $K = 3$, $K = 4$ and $K = 7$ patterns, the furthest distance from a village to a central place is one unit, in the $K = 9$ pattern it is $\sqrt{3} = 1.73$ units, in the $K = 12$ pattern it is 2 units, while in the $K = 13$ pattern it is $\sqrt{3}$ units again, so that in this case the maximum distance to a market is smaller. These are illustrated in figure 21.4, which suggests that the administration optimising patterns also give relatively advantageous distances to market.

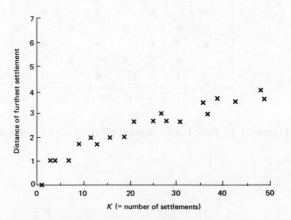

Figure 21.4. Distance of furthest settlement in hexagon from the centre plotted against K.

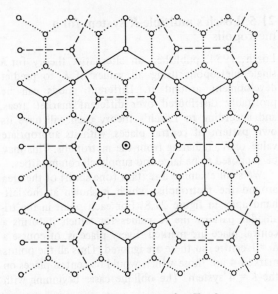

Figure 21.5. Christaller's system for $K = 3$.

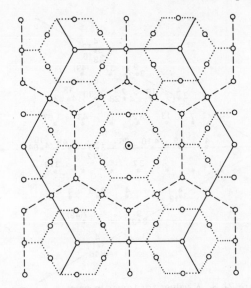

Figure 21.7. Christaller's system for mixed K
($K = 4$, $K = 3$, $K = 3$).

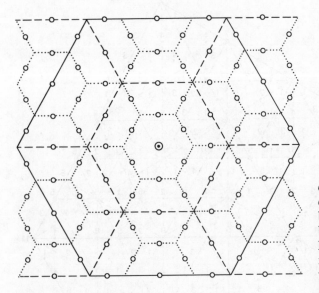

Figure 21.6. Christaller's system for $K = 4$.

21.4. Christaller's fixed-K theory

So far our model only allows for two levels of settlement. Christaller postulated a hierarchy of central places, each superimposed in tiers on the next one (see Christaller, 1966) as in figures 21.5 and 21.6. The first shows four orders of central places, each with $K = 3$ for the order below it, while the second has four orders each with $K = 4$. In the latter case all the hexagons are oriented in the same direction.

These patterns illustrate an inherent conflict in central places of different orders. Small hexagons cannot be fitted together to form larger ones, and so boundary conflict at different levels arises. The numbers of settlements in the two figures at different levels is 1, 3, 9, 27, ... in the first and 1, 4, 16, 64, ... in the second. There is no need to assume the same value of K at each stage, and figure 21.7 shows the situation with $K = 4$ in the first stage and $K = 3$ at each of the next two stages. The numbers of settlements controlled are respectively 1, 4, 12 and 36.

Christaller used southern Germany to illustrate his theory and found that while most places work on $K = 3$, there were many exceptions. Mining and border towns particularly betray exceptional characteristics. In some areas it is possible to identify Christaller's principles at work, but the distortions caused by varying physical factors make simple illustrations hard to find, so that most authors repeat Christaller's work, for example Bradford and Kent, 1977, pp. 6-27. An interesting attempt at a real application by Skinner is quoted in Haggett, Cliff and Frey, 1977, pp. 154-7.

133

Models

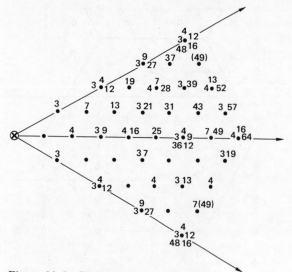

Figure 21.8. *K*-values for towns in part of one sextant of the Löschian landscape.

21.5. Lösch's multiple-*K* system for a metropolis

Lösch, 1954, published an alternative theory for a single metropolis using all values of *K* to predict development around it. Different goods can be profitably distributed over different market areas, and according to Lösch's theory each will have its own pattern of central places, with its appropriate value of *K*, radiating from the metropolis. This may be supposed to be large and supply all commodities.

We shall examine a sextant (one-sixth) of the area around the metropolis, which is shown at the left-hand apex in figure 21.8. For each point in the triangular pattern the *K* values for which it forms a central place are marked. Every place is, of course a *K* = 1 centre, so these are ignored. Thus all the points marked 4 are those which would be central places on the *K* = 4 system. The oblique cases beginning with

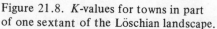

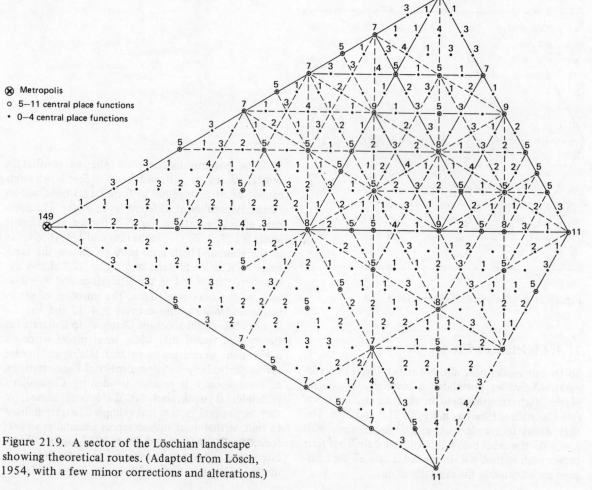

Figure 21.9. A sector of the Löschian landscape showing theoretical routes. (Adapted from Lösch, 1954, with a few minor corrections and alterations.)

$K = 7$ give two choices according to the direction of inclination. We shall choose to place the first $K = 7$ point in the upper half of the sextant, and shall do the same with all the oblique cases, thus fixing the rest of these patterns. Thus the next oblique case, $K = 13$, will have its first point placed as close as possible to the first $K = 7$ point. In other cases of choice, for example, the $K = 49$ case illustrated in figure 21.3, we shall place the pattern so that central places cluster as much as possible. The alternative $K = 49$ choices are shown in brackets in figure 21.8 for reference only.

If the process is continued, and the number of central place functions is written beside each point instead of the K values, then figure 21.9 is obtained. For example, the point six units east of the metropolis has five central place functions corresponding to values of K of 3, 4, 9, 12 and 36 in figure 21.8. In figure 21.9 the metropolis has no less than 149 central place functions, and the next highest number is 11. By the arrangement of the oblique cases the upper half of the sextant is much richer in central place functions, apart from the boundary lines there are eighteen places with five or more functions in the top half but only twelve in the bottom half. The same is true of each of the six sextants. Thus around the metropolis there are twelve sectors which are alternately rich and poor in central place functions.

The construction of figure 21.9 is complicated. It is helpful to begin by constructing an enlargement of table 21.1 giving values of K up to 600. The patterns in that table can be checked by examining the patterns of successive differences between entries. Where numbers occur more than once in the table, a decision has to be made over the placing of the appropriate pattern, and where possible this is done by reinforcing existing central places. In a few cases an arbitrary de-cision has to be made, and there Lösch's choice has been followed. The decision to stop when the metropolis has 149 central places is arbitrary, but gives a convenient eastern boundary.

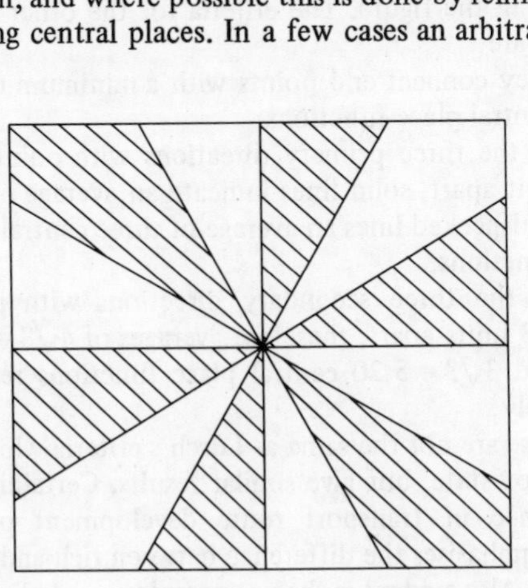

21.6. City-rich and city-poor sectors

There is no doubt that neither Lösch's nor Christaller's system is particularly convincing to the layman. It is not easy to find realistic examples which are both simple and yet work out in practice. The models, therefore, are somewhat unsuccessful in so far as theory and reality are not easily linked. Geographers have, however, persisted in trying to use them to explain the patterns which they observe, and it may be that further developments will enable them to be put to more practical use. Mathematicians can only be grateful for theories with such rich numerical and spatial patterns which are interesting in their own right.

Lösch's theory has been used to practical effect in the prediction of city-rich and city-poor sectors around a metropolis. Examples may be found in the literature, though it is not easy to be sure how much one is manipulating the data to fit preconceived theories. Figure 21.11 shows how Lösch's theory which is illustrated in figure 21.10 may perhaps be fitted into an area of about 200 km radius around Berlin, though the angles of the sectors need to be modified. Christaller's theory has also found some use in providing a focus for regional planning, and the effect of the theories upon planned landscapes may be more far reaching than in the interpretation of ones which arise naturally.

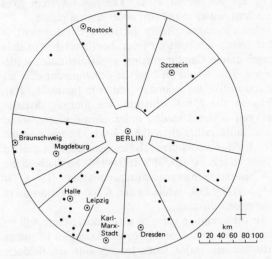

Figure 21.11. Conjectural city-rich and city-poor sectors around Berlin. Large towns are named, and smaller ones are indicated by dots.

Figure 21.10. Arrangement of city-rich and city-poor sectors around a metropolis under Lösch's theory.

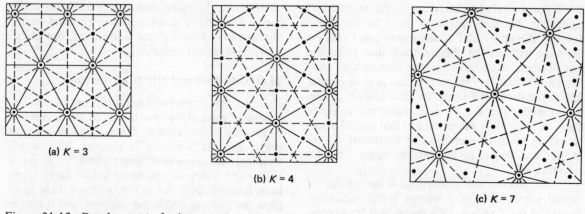

(a) *K* = 3

(b) *K* = 4

(c) *K* = 7

Figure 21.12. Development of primary and secondary routes on Christaller's *K* = 3, *K* = 4 and *K* = 7 systems.

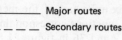

——————— Major routes
– – – – – – – Secondary routes

21.7. Routes on Christaller's and Lösch's landscapes

Both theories in this chapter can be developed to predict likely effects on transport routes. Figure 21.12 shows how these might develop under the *K* = 3, *K* = 4 and *K* = 7 systems. The routes between adjacent second order central places are shown solid, while those serving the next nearest set of second order central places are shown pecked. In the *K* = 3 system the first order central places are only served by those secondary routes, while in the *K* = 7 system they are not served at all. The *K* = 4 system gives excellent routes to the first order central places.

An alternative theory of route development is that routes are built up from short stretches of unit length connecting the original undifferentiated settlements. This would lead to the development of a set of routes like the secondary routes in figure 21.12(a). Thus in the *K* = 3 situation, the journey distance between adjacent second order central places would be 2 units rather than the $\sqrt{3} = 1.732$ units which direct roads would give. The excess distance travelled would be $[(2 - \sqrt{3})/\sqrt{3}] \times 100 = 15\%$. Similarly in the *K* = 7 situation the excess distance would be $[(3 - \sqrt{7})/\sqrt{7}] \times 100 = 13\%$, while in the *K* = 4 situation there is no excess distance.

In the primitive form of this theory, there will be just six routes out of any town. Examples of towns with just six major roads leading out are Baldock (Herts), Launceston (Cornwall), and Thirsk (Yorks). Overseas examples are Nancy (France), Dijon (France), Magdeburg (East Germany) and Regina (Saskatchewan).

Many small towns show this pattern, and it also occurs with railway routes as well. On the other hand many towns have developed far more routes than this. In these cases the centres are sufficiently important to make savings of the order of 15% worthwhile. In most cases, not all twelve routes have developed into main roads. Sheffield (discounting motorways) has twelve, while Madrid also has twelve or thirteen.

An attempt has been made on figure 21.9 to show how the pattern of major routes might develop on the Löschian system, although any such pattern is inevitably arbitrary. The twelve routes to the metropolis are assumed to have developed of which three are shown in the figure. The criteria for the other major routes are:

(a) they connect end points with a minimum of five central place functions.
(b) in the three primary directions with points one unit apart, solid lines indicate an average of four and pecked lines an average of three central place functions.
(c) in the three secondary directions with points $\sqrt{3}$ units apart, these are averages of $4\sqrt{3} = 6.93$ and $3\sqrt{3} = 5.20$ central place functions respectively.

These are not the same as Lösch's criteria which he does not state, but give similar results. Certainly the difference in transport route development powerfully emphasises the difference between rich and poor sectors. Also evident is the poor development of routes around the metropolis with the consequent traffic congestion within it.

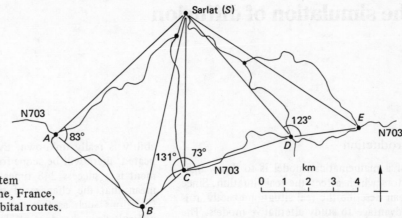

Figure 21.13. Road system
south of Sarlat, Dordogne, France,
illustrating radial and orbital routes.

21.8. Radial and orbital routes

Briggs, 1972, makes a useful distinction between radial and orbital routes for a central place. Between junctions, routes are treated as straight lines. Any route to the town centre is radial. Any route which does not end at the town centre has the angle between the line joining its outer and inner ends and the line joining its inner end to the central place measured. If this is over 120°, the route is classified as *radial*, otherwise it is classified as *orbital*.

Figure 21.13 illustrates this. It shows part of the French route nationale N703 along the valley of the Dordogne, and the connections to the small town of Sarlat to the north. Clearly the sections west of A and east of E are radial to Sarlat. Since $B\hat{A}S = 83°$ and $D\hat{C}S = 73°$, the sections AB and CD of the N703 are orbital. On the other hand $B\hat{C}S = 131°$ and $E\hat{D}S = 123°$, so that the sections BC and DE are radial. The latter is clearly a marginal case, and the direct route from E to Sarlat saves little in distance.

Exercises

1. Using paper with an equilateral triangle dot pattern, draw hexagons like those in figure 21.1 for some higher values of K.
2. Extend table 21.1 for higher values of p and q.
3. Show that in the solution to exercise 2 other duplicate values of K besides $K = 49$ are 91, 133, 147, 169, 196, 217, 247, 259, 273, 343, 361, 364, 399, 403, 427, 441, 507, and 553.
4. Draw on triangular dotted paper the equivalent figure to 21.5 and 21.6 for $K = 7$.
5. Draw some mixed K systems along the lines of figure 21.7.
6. Use square dotted paper to develop the square analogue of Christaller's and/or Lösch's systems. (The square system is rather simpler.)
7. Try to identify city-rich and city-poor sectors around some major cities.
8. Analyse the road system around a town into radial and orbital routes. Try to determine why orbital routes exist. In England many have developed from Roman roads. (Through routes which are orbital to a town for part of their route and radial for the rest are sometimes known as *tangential*.)

Further reading

Abler, Adams and Gould, 1972, pp. 364-84
Bradford and Kent, 1977, pp. 6-27
Briggs, 1972, pp. 30-4
Briggs, 1974, pp. 1-22
Christaller, 1966
Cole and King, 1968, pp. 485-91
Everson and Fitzgerald, 1969, pp. 101-11
Haggett, 1972, pp. 286-97, 332-5
Haggett and Chorley, 1969, pp. 118-26
Haggett, Cliff and Frey, 1977, pp. 60-3, 97-106, 142-53
Jordan, 1973, pp. 330-5
Ling, 1977, pp. 99-101
Lloyd and Dicken, 1977, pp. 23-33, 44-56, 90-5
Lösch, 1954, pp. 114-34
Meyer and Huggett, 1979, pp. 11-29
Tidswell, 1976, pp. 170-84
Wilson, 1973b, pp. 66-79

22 The simulation of diffusion

22.1. Introduction

One aim of a mathematical model is to throw light on the factors which affect the real situation. Since no model can describe the real situation exactly, it is often an advantage to study alternative models. The map, which is the most familiar model of reality the geographer possesses, suffers from one grave disadvantage: it is static. Even where attempts are made to show growth the results are often unsatisfactory. A map may show the boundaries of the built-up area of a city at ten-yearly intervals, but will fail to show the effects of urban renewal in the city centre. The flow diagram (see for example figure 29.7) does give some element of movement, but this in fact cloaks a careful rigidity of response at every point of choice.

In this chapter the simulation model will be studied. The idea owes much of its geographical development to the work of Hagerstrand, a Swedish post-war geographer. We shall show how geographers have used the idea of simulation to inject an element of dynamism into their studies, and to build models which change through time.

22.2. Probability

A key mathematical idea in the use of simulation is that of *probability*. It is not the intention in this book to become involved with the definition of probability. There are basic differences of approach which make this a difficult and dangerous area for the layman. Nevertheless, most people have some intuitive idea of what probability is, and of the meaning of the word *chance*, even though an attempt to pin them down to detail might only serve to confuse.

In simplistic terms, when we say that the probability of a successful outcome in a given situation is $\frac{1}{4}$, then we mean that if we repeat the situation many times in the same way, then we would be successful once every four times on average. The qualification 'on average' is important; we might have a run of many trials without success, or we might have three consecutive successes, but it is the situation in the long run which is important. In most such situations, the experiment cannot be repeated anyway, so our prob-

ability is really unknown. Even where it can be repeated, there will be scope for variation. If an experiment is a success 248 times out of 1000, does this mean that the chances of success are not 1 in 4? Questions such as this make statistics conceptually difficult once the stage of elementary definitions has been passed.

The mathematical theory of probability is vast, we shall only observe here that the probability of an event occurring is always between 0 and 1. The first number corresponds to impossibility and the second to certainty.

22.3. Examples of random models

One does not have to look far for examples of random models. Many popular commercial games involve random number simulations. Snakes and ladders is an obvious example, and another is ludo. In these, the random element is provided by a cubic die, and it is no accident that probability theory began with the mathematical study of gambling. Many adults as well as children enjoy games, and it is hardly surprising that teachers are making increasing use of games in their work. This is not just in subjects such as mathematics where they have a theoretical interest, but also in subjects such as history, geography and sociology where they can give the learner the excitement of involvement in a developing situation, thus bringing in the time factor which is so lacking in most types of mathematical model.

Some idea of the range of games which have been used in the teaching of geography can be obtained from the following list, which could easily be extended considerably.

(a) Spread of Neolithic civilisations across Europe (Oxford Geography Project, 1974b, pp. 16–19).
(b) Development of competitive railway systems (Watts, 1973).
(c) Random drainage patterns (Haggett and Chorley, 1969, pp. 285–302).
(d) Election campaigns (Smith and Cole, 1969).
(e) Locating a steel works (Dalton et al, 1972).

Not all such games are competitive (e.g. (c) above), and some are not even random (e.g. Conway's Game of Life, see Gardner, 1970, 1971, which is vaguely biological). Many commercial games have both random and competitive elements. Monopoly is a standard textbook example with a particularly interesting method of generating random numbers by throwing two dice and adding their scores, which range from 2 to 12 with 7 being the most probable.

22.4. Generating random numbers

We return to a more detailed examination of random numbers which were first met in section 10.2. By examining some of the ways in which they can be generated, we can learn to avoid some of the traps involved in using them.

(a) *Coins*. A coin gives probabilities of $\frac{1}{2}$ for heads and $\frac{1}{2}$ for tails, thus generating a binary system (see section 1.7). Tossing two coins gives probabilities $\frac{1}{4}, \frac{1}{2}, \frac{1}{4}$, since one head and one tail is twice as likely as two heads or two tails. Two different coins give four equal probabilities which is useful in deciding points of the compass.

(b) *Dice*. A cubic die generates random numbers from 1 to 6. By grouping pairs or triples of numbers the probabilities of $\frac{1}{3}, \frac{1}{2}$ and $\frac{2}{3}$ can also be obtained. Using two or more dice and addition or multiplication of their scores will give more complicated probabilities. Loaded dice are now commercially available, as well as four, eight, twelve and twenty sided dice in the shapes of tetrahedra, octahedra, dodecahedra and icosahedra. The last are usually numbered twice from 0 to 9 and are most useful as an alternative to random number tables, even being used for sampling in industrial contexts.

(c) *Playing cards*. These are frequently used in probabilistic examples as they give probabilities related to $\frac{1}{4}$ and $\frac{1}{13}$. However, once a card is withdrawn from the pack, the probabilities alter. Thus if cards are used to generate random numbers, the card drawn must be replaced in the pack and the whole thoroughly shuffled before drawing another card. This is tedious, and a single dog-eared card can upset the probabilities very easily, so they are best avoided.

(d) *Spinners*. Roulette-type spinners are sometimes used to generate random numbers. They are difficult to make accurately, and even commercially produced ones are sometimes badly biassed.

(e) *Random number tables*. These are tables containing the digits 0 to 9 selected by some random method. They can be found in most collections of statistical tables and at the backs of many statistics books. One can reproduce one's own by using the icosahedral die mentioned above or with a telephone directory. When using the latter, select a page of private subscribers and read down the next to last digit in each telephone number (multi-line subscribers tend to have numbers ending 1).

When using printed random number tables, start at any arbitrary point and work systematically in any way you please. If you need more than the digits 0 to 9, pick two or more numbers at a time. For ninety numbers, for example, use 01–90 and ignore 00 and 91–99 when they occur, simply moving on to the next choice. For forty numbers, it is more economical to use 01–80, subtracting 40 from 41–80, and ignoring the rest. By such means any given range of numbers can be easily reproduced.

(f) *Electronic calculators*. A few expensive electronic calculators have a pseudo-random number generating facility which may be used.

22.5. Diffusion models based on random numbers

Diffusion models are popular in geography because of the time element they introduce into a situation. They are usually used to simulate the development of point features, or less commonly line features, over an area of a map. The area is covered with a grid to reduce it to some semblance of order, and each cell of the grid replaces a point at its centre. Square grids are easier to use and to develop computer simulations from, but hexagonal grids like that in figure 11.3(b) where the points at the centres of the hexagons are in a triangular pattern are usually more satisfactory. These hexagons are often confusingly referred to as 'squares' in the jargon of simulation.

With the grid established, a method of moving about it must be developed. The neolithic civilisation game with the square grid uses a six-faced die. Figure 22.1 shows how migration is simulated from the shaded square to any one of the six numbered squares close to it, the asymmetry of the pattern carefully ensuring movement generally in a direction north of west. Play begins in the fertile crescent of the Middle East and each step simulates 50 years in lowland territory and 250 years in mountains. The time taken to reach Britain can be worked out, and when the game is played by several groups, the results can be compared.

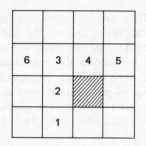

Figure 22.1. Random number pattern using one die for the neolithic civilisation game.

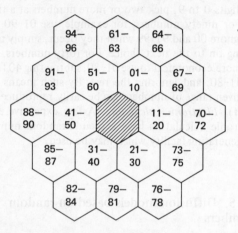

Figure 22.2. Diffusion pattern using two digit random numbers (Smith and Cole)

Smith and Cole, 1969, in the second game in their pamphlet use two digit random numbers to illustrate how a new idea will diffuse from village to village with a symmetrical pattern on a hexagonal grid (figure 22.2). Pairs of random numbers are drawn, in the first round for the starting village, then in the second round for both villages which have the idea and so on, giving a snowball effect. There is a probability of $\frac{1}{10}$ of diffusion to an adjoining 'square' (ten random numbers to each of six squares), and $\frac{3}{100}$ of diffusion to each square around these (three random numbers to each of twelve squares). For the other four random numbers the idea does not diffuse. Figure 22.3 shows an example of this diffusion. The starting point is labelled 0. In the first round the random number is 58, which leads to the diffusion to the square marked 1. In the second round the random numbers are 93 (diffusing from the square marked 1 to one of the squares marked 2) and 09 (diffusing to the other square marked 2). This is continued through consecutive rounds in a strict pre-determined order. Sometimes diffusion takes place onto a square where the idea is already established, and is then ineffectual.

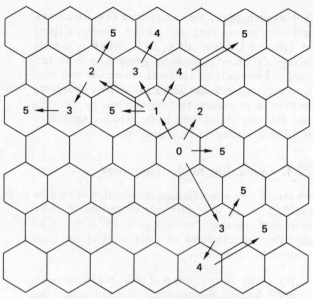

Figure 22.3. Example of Smith and Cole's diffusion pattern on a plain hexagonal grid.

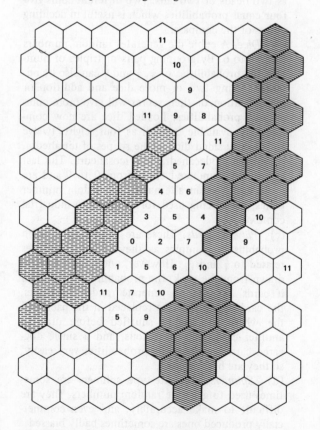

Figure 22.4. Simulation of the diffusion of an insect pest. The numbers indicate successive generations.

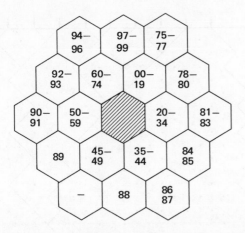

Figure 22.5. Asymmetric diffusion pattern with two digit random numbers used in figure 22.4.

Figure 22.3 simulates reality very well, in particular the asymmetrical development produced by the symmetrical pattern is most marked.

In practice, Smith and Cole's game does not take place on an unadorned grid such as that in figure 22.3, but in common with most effective diffusion games, embellishments are added. Various squares are designated mountain, marsh, forest or sea and the diffusion dies out on them. Also various lines between squares can be designated boundaries or rivers, across which the diffusion cannot take place. An easily accessible example of this is one by Gowing and Jones in Taylor and Walford, 1972. This simulates the urban growth of Bristol. Unfortunately the example is marred by poor explanation of the use of random numbers and errors in the squares marked as having zero potential for growth.

22.6. Example of a diffusion simulation

A typical example of a simulation game is illustrated in figure 22.4. Such games are not difficult to construct, and the reader is encouraged to develop his or her own examples. Like many diffusion games it is non-competitive and intended for a single player or a small group. Much benefit can be obtained if the game is played by several different groups and the results are compared. To play the game a quantity of hexagonal grids should be duplicated as shown in the figure, but without the numbers. The stippled area represents the sea, and the shaded area hills and the object of the simulation is to model the spread of an insect pest which is imported at the point labelled 0 in figure 22.4. The map represents approximately the area around Bristol in south-west England.

Hammond and McCullagh, 1974, give a similar example developed in a rather different manner.

The diffusion pattern itself in this case is asymmetrical, and is shown in figure 22.5. It is assumed that the spread of the insect will be affected by the prevailing south-westerly wind. Otherwise the simulation works as in figure 22.3, except that many possible infections are wasted by landing on unsuitably hilly country, on sea, or on already infected areas.

The whole simulation gives a good idea of how the spread of the pest might take place. Advances are intermittent, generation 5 shows more spread than generation 6. The simulation also shows the crucial points at which the pest might be contained, especially between the hills and the sea. Notice the jump over the hills in generation 9. A similar jump could also have occurred across the estuary. This suggests that measures to combat the pest should also include a 'flying squad' to take care of isolated outbreaks which might start new centres of infection.

It is essential to do a simulation in order to experience the sense of expectancy which it generates. This is all the more marked if the simulation has specific relevance and definite objectives in mind. Repetitions of the same simulation produce different results and yet have similarities which add considerably to the understanding of random processes.

Sadly, simulation games are less accurate in outcome than straight-forward predictions based on probability because of the random element. Some town expansion games available can be worked more accurately by ignoring the random element. In these, each square is assigned a set of random numbers proportional in quantity to its development potential. It is quicker simply to place the developments in the proportions chosen, the random element merely inserts a slight uncertainty into the simulation. In a good random simulation, the random element should be an essential part of the process of achieving the desired effect, not merely included as dressing up.

22.7. An alternative approach

An alternative approach to simulation uses personal decision making and is sometimes called an autocorrelation method. While not in itself mathematical it can lead to mathematical ideas such as nearest neighbour analysis (chapter 11) and correlation techniques. A plan is prepared of a situation where a choice has to be made (for example, the choice of a position on a beach, or a pitch on a camp site), and the members of a group have to choose their positions successively. Discussion can take place about

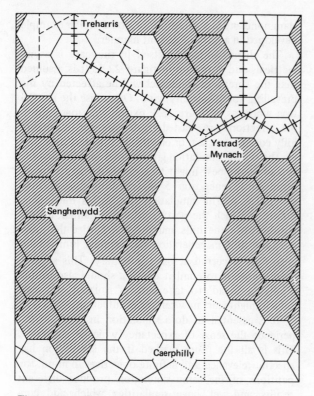

Figure 22.6. Part of one of Watts' games showing lines of competing railway companies produced in play.

criteria for the choice and these criteria compared with similar criteria for settlers in a new country. These criteria can be ranked and individual ranks correlated with the average. We shall use a similar idea in sections 25.2 to 25.4, but develop it slightly differently.

22.8. Diffusion on networks

We now turn to ideas of diffusion along networks and in the development of networks. Such games involving lines have been slower to develop than those involving points and squares (or hexagons) because of the problem of marking the playing surface. Games of this sort often have to rely on disposable playing surfaces which can be difficult to reproduce. From time to time games appear on the market involving travelling around existing road or rail networks, but these have not made a great deal of impact. Their value in teaching basic geographical facts should not, however, be neglected.

Where the objective of the game is to develop a new network, rather than use an established one, it is rather more difficult to know how to set about the

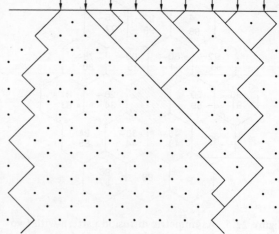

Figure 22.7. Simulation of stream system from a spring-line.

problem. Watts, 1973, illustrates the easiest way of doing this. His games illustrate the development of competing railway companies in the nineteenth century. The use of hexagons enables mountains and other barriers to be shown, and the networks themselves are in fact drawn between the centres of the hexagons which form a triangular dot lattice. Figure 22.6 shows part of the network resulting from a game showing the south Wales coalfield. Some of the competing companies formed by the players striving to carry coal to the various ports are shown. The construction of the lines is governed by the throw of a die which determines the money available for construction; mountain routes and duplicate lines costing extra. The importance of the valleys and gaps and the position of towns at route junctions, as well as the advantages of being first in the field are vividly illustrated. The last point is only easily illustrated by use of the simulation technique.

22.9. Simulating river systems

A successful example of non-competitive network simulations is the reproduction of river system patterns. Paper with square or triangular dot patterns is useful in this exercise. Suppose a line of springs emerges from a hillside above a plain which is slightly but evenly tilted. The emergent streams will tend to combine to produce rivers. Figure 22.7 illustrates one way of simulating this, the square pattern of dots is placed diagonally, the springs being in a straight line across the top of the figure at the points indicated by small arrows. A stream flows either south-west or south-east according as a tossed coin falls heads or

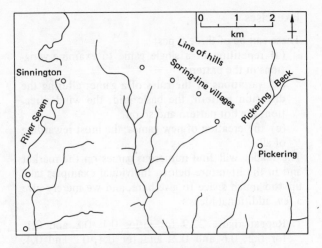

Figure 22.8. Spring-line stream system near Pickering, N. Yorks. (circles indicate village sites).

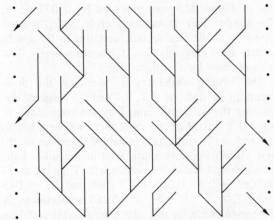

Figure 22.9. Simulation of stream system on a tilted plain (probabilities 0.255 south-west, 0.490 south, 0.255 south-east).

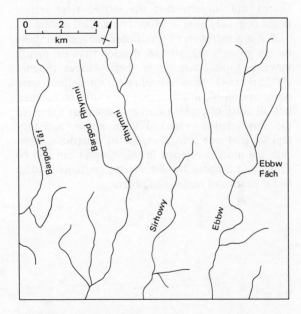

Figure 22.10. River pattern in part of north-west Gwent, Wales.

tails. The pattern is plotted systematically across the page from left to right and row by row; for example the initial row is generated by the sequence HTTTTHTHT where H stands for heads and T for tails. Already two pairs of streams have combined, and so two fewer tosses are required for the next row which is generated by HTHTTTH. By the bottom of the diagram the nine streams have become one stream and one river supplied by the remaining eight streams. A similar but more sophisticated example may be found in Sparks, 1972, p. 163.

The simulation is not accurate at the edges where other springs might feed in from outside the border, but nevertheless the pattern is not dissimilar to many geographical situations. Spring-line villages are common, a good example is the line of villages along the north side of the Vale of Pickering in North Yorkshire, part of which is shown in figure 22.8. It is often pointed out that villages above the spring-line will find water supply difficult, but rarely noticed that, below the spring-line, the inevitable junction of streams on purely random grounds alone produces large areas of country without any streams other than those generated by surface water after rain. Thus villages often tend to become further apart as the number of spring-fed streams becomes fewer.

The same method can be adapted to illustrate the streams generated on an inclined plane generated by direct rainfall. To illustrate this we use a slightly more complicated variation of the idea by placing the dot pattern of squares parallel to the edges of the paper, but assuming that streams will still flow southwards in general. The random element is provided (see figure 22.9) by random numbers; the numbers

0–2 indicate a flow to the south-west, 3–6 indicate a flow to the south, and 7–9 indicate a flow to the south-east. This time we allow every point to generate a stream, rather than just taking the initial points as in the earlier simulation. One problem which arises is that south-westerly and south-easterly flows from adjacent points can clash. We use a sub-routine to cope with this: we toss a coin and if it falls heads the south-westerly flow predominates, while if it falls tails the south-easterly flow predominates. The top row of figure 22.9 was generated by 0307716516. The number pair 71 causes a clash, which was resolved by a coin landing tails, resulting in the south-easterly flow predominating, the south-westerly flow being replaced by a southerly one.

The basic probabilities for deciding the three directions of flow are 0.3, 0.4 and 0.3 respectively. Ignoring the variations caused by the boundaries, in $0.3 \times 0.3 = 0.09$ of the cases there will be a south-east and south-west clash. In half of these, the south-west stream becomes south, and in the other half, the south-east stream becomes south. Thus the probabilities are $0.3 - 0.045$, $0.4 + 0.09$, and $0.3 - 0.045$ which give 0.255, 0.49 and 0.255 respectively. A more even plane, or one with a greater tilt could be simulated by varying the random numbers to give basic probabilities of 0.2, 0.6 and 0.2. Figure 22.9 may be compared with the river system in south Wales; figure 22.10 shows part of this in north-west Gwent and suggests that the incised river system might originally have developed on a tilted plateau.

Some geographers have criticised the method above on the grounds that streams develop from the mouth upwards rather than from their sources (Sparks, 1972, p. 164). More complicated simulations have been developed, mainly using computer techniques, but all sorts of problems arise of a similar nature to the flow clashes remarked upon above, and they rapidly lead one into complicated situations. However the ideas developed in this chapter can also be varied and adapted by altering the patterns of dots and the ratios of random numbers.

Exercises

These can be of three types:

(a) repetition of a single game to examine variations in the pattern.

(b) variations in the rules of a game: altering the diffusion pattern, the basic grid, the wind direction, the dot pattern and so on.

(c) the creation of new games; the most rewarding of all.

The reader will find numerous games on the market and in the literature below. Individual examples take up too much space to give here, and we merely give a few additional ideas.

1. Repeat figure 22.9 for ratios 0.1, 0.8 and 0.1; for 0.2, 0.6 and 0.2; and for 0.4, 0.2 and 0.4. Notice the variations in pattern.
2. (Mathematical) Calculate the modified probabilities for the above ratios as explained in section 22.9.
3. Repeat the simulation of figure 22.7 say twenty times and draw a histogram of the number of streams resulting at the end of the simulation.

Further reading

Abler, Adams and Gould, 1972, pp. 389–451

Bale, Graves and Walford, 1973, pp. 211–21

Bradford and Kent, 1977, pp. 128–42

Cole, 1969a

Cole and Beynon, 1968a, 1968b, 1972

Cole and King, 1968, pp. 469–79, 511–18

Dalton et al, 1972

Dinkele, Cotterell and Thorn, 1976a–1976e (various examples)

Everson and Fitzgerald, 1969, pp. 9–19

Haggett, 1972, pp. 348–64

Haggett and Chorley, 1969, pp. 285–302

Haggett, Cliff and Frey, 1977, pp. 231–58

Hammond and McCullagh, 1974, pp. 252–65

Ling, 1977, pp. 102–7

Lloyd and Dicken, 1977, pp. 56–66, 111–15

Meyer and Huggett, 1979, pp. 52–67

Oxford Geography Project, 1974a, 1974b, 1975 (various examples)

Selkirk, 1973–4

Smith and Cole, 1969

Sparks, 1972, pp. 163–4

Taylor and Walford, 1972

Tidswell, 1976, pp. 156–69

Watts, 1973

Wilson and Kirkby, 1975, pp. 228–39, 250–62

Wilson, 1973a, pp. 55–63

23 The geometry of movement

23.1. Transformations

In this chapter and the following ones we move towards a particular type of model involving operations on geographical space which preserve some, but not all, the physical properties of that space. Mathematicians use a variety of words to describe this including transformation, mapping and function. Unfortunately the texts are not always consistent about the definitions of these words, and to complicate matters further the mathematical meaning of the word mapping is somewhat different to the geographical one so that we shall avoid using the word in its mathematical sense in this book.

The idea of movement geometry, developed in Abler, Adams and Gould, 1972, pp. 238–55, allows a neat introduction to the idea of a transformation. Superficially, the idea is not very mathematical, but beneath the surface there is a great deal of geometrical pattern building involved, and it provides an interesting way of classifying all movements which take place in the real world. We shall see later, especially in chapter 24, that the idea of transformation is still wider than the ideas embraced in movement geometry, but many of the transformations we meet in practice are covered by it. Like the definition of the word probability in section 22.2, we shall allow the idea of a transformation to develop through examples rather than attempt a formal definition.

23.2. Movement geometry

Basically all movement takes place from one point to another. For instance a particular molecule in the valve of a bicycle tyre moves on a cycloidal path above the road surface as the rider travels on his journey. Such a trivial view of a bicycle ride is not, however, very productive because we are normally much more interested in the motion of the bicycle and rider as a whole than in what happens to an individual molecule. Alternatively we can think of the bicycle and rider as a three-dimensional object moving in three-dimensional space, initially occupying one volume and finally occupying another volume of much

the same shape. This attitude to motion is not very helpful either because it presents too detailed a view of the situation.

We need to adopt a simplification which is neither too trivial nor too detailed. It is far more productive to regard bicycle and rider as a single point moving from one position in space to another. This type of simplification enables us to classify movements by taking into account the scale of the situation; since the bicycle and rider are small compared to the length of the journey, it makes sense to regard both as a single point moving through space from start to finish of a journey.

When individual movements are grouped together, then we have a more complicated pattern to analyse. If we consider a postman's 'walk' when he delivers letters, then this is a point-to-point movement starting and finishing at the sorting office. If however we consider the letters the postman carries, then many individual point-to-point movements take place. Each letter moves from the sorting office to an individual house on the walk, and thus the letters as a whole move from a single point to a set of points located along the line of the walk. This line will not be a straight one, but we can identify the delivery points by distance or by house numbers, thus setting up a coordinate system as in chapter 2, only one coordinate being needed to identify the delivery point. The delivery of the letters can therefore be regarded as a point-to-line movement.

A similar, but slightly more complicated example is that of a farmer sowing a field with seed. The seed travels from a point (the seed bin) to an area (the surface of the field) which needs two coordinates to identify any particular delivery point. Each individual seed makes a point-to-point journey. The tractor path over the field makes a convoluted line and if the seeds were planted one at a time along this line rather than scattered, the movement could then be regarded as a point-to-line movement. It is more sensible to regard the line-path of the tractor as a convenient intermediate step in a point-to-area movement, and to regard the planning of this line path in the most economical way as an exercise in geometrical pattern.

	TO A POINT	TO A LINE	TO AN AREA	TO A VOLUME
FROM A POINT	1. Path of a man travelling to his place of work. 2. Selected route for a new bypass road 3. Paths of the weekly letter from a student to his parents.	1. Possible paths of rugby player scoring a try. 2. Passage of waste from a sink to a sewer. 3. Paths of a man going to fetch water from a river.	1. Pollution fall-out from a chimney. 2. Ripples from a stone thrown into a pond. 3. Soccer player scoring a penalty.	1. Radio waves leaving a transmitter. 2. Solution of a lump of sugar in a cup of tea. 3. Sewage disposal from an outlet pipe into the sea.
FROM A LINE	1. Collection of water from a trough by a moving steam locomotive. 2. Putting in a connection to new electricity supply. 3. Path of water from gutter to spout.	1. Joining points on two different lines as in producing envelopes by curve stitching. 2. Paths of vehicles on a flyover between motorways. 3. Possible paths of cross-channel steamers between two coastlines.	1. Knitting cloth from yarn to material. 2. Movement of cars queuing to enter a car park. 3. Path of a man mowing the lawn covering the area.	1. Fluorescent lighting strip lighting a room. 2. Winding a cable on a cylindrical drum. 3. Passage of food from intestine to body.
FROM AN AREA	1. Children travelling to school. 2. Surface water run off to the mouth of a river. 3. Villagers travelling to a spring to collect water.	1. Passage of water from a roof to a gutter. 2. Movement of farm crops to a road. 3. Deposit of floating debris by a flood.	1. Migration of a tribe from one country to another. 2. Collection of seaweed from shore to spread as fertilizer. 3. Movement of employees from workplace to seats in canteen.	1. A central heating panel heating a room. 2. Evaporation of water from sea into atmosphere. 3. Collection of hay from field to haystack.
FROM A VOLUME	1. Extractor fan – air from room to the fan outlet. 2. Cars leaving multi-storey car park. 3. Outlet tap on a tank of liquid.	1. Movement of grain from storage silo to animal feeding trough. 2. Water from a river flowing over a weir. 3. Steel from an ingot being rolled into a strip.	1. Pastry being rolled from a lump to a flat sheet. 2. Rain falling from a cloud to the ground. 3. Removal of lime from a quarry to spread on a field.	1. Re-organisation of books in a library. 2. Delivery of oil from a tanker to a storage tank. 3. Meteorological movement of air in the atmosphere.

Table 23.1. Examples of various types of movement.

The picking of an apple crop can be regarded in a variety of ways:

(a) from the orchard (a point) to the wholesaler's depot (a point). The company purchasing the crop might regard the movement in this way.

(b) from a tree in the orchard (two coordinates, hence an area) to the lorry collecting the apples (a point). The person collecting the trays of apples might see it like this.

(c) from a place in the tree (three coordinates, hence a volume) to the tray at the bottom of the tree (a point). The picker might see it like this.

Further views are possible, but each view is determined not only by the position of the movement in the chain, but also by the point of view of the observer.

In essence, then, source and destination points can be regarded as having no dimensions (a single defined point); one dimension defined by one coordinate and giving points distributed along a line; two dimensions defined by two coordinates and giving points distributed in an area; or three dimensions defined by three coordinates and giving points distributed throughout a volume. Since there are four starting states and four finishing states, movements can be analysed into sixteen types. Three examples of each are given in table 23.1. It will be noticed that movements starting at points and moving to lines, areas and volumes are essentially distribution movements, while the reverse situation gives rise to collection movements. While not all movements fit neatly into this system, with a little care a great many can be analysed in this way. Many movements, like the apple picking, go in chains. For example, rain in a cloud (volume), falls on a roof (area), runs into a gutter (line), down a drainpipe and out of a spout (point), into the sewer (line) and so on.

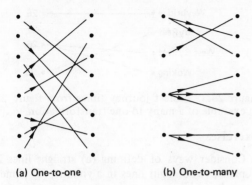

(a) One-to-one   (b) One-to-many   (c) Many-to-one   (d) Many-to-many

Figure 23.1. Types of transformation.

23.3. Movement geometry between areas

One of the commonest types of movement is that between two areas, or between two two-dimensional surfaces, and this is the type with which we shall be mainly concerned for the rest of this book. Since much of geography is the study of a two-dimensional surface, that of the earth, this particular movement is clearly of special importance. While locally there are extensions into three dimensions – cliffs, caves, houses, trees, and so on – geographical space is essentially the two-dimensional surface of the sphere as explained in chapter 2.

So far, as in table 23.1, we have restricted our examples of movement geometry to cases where movement actually takes place, but of course the movements may be only theoretical. A map is an example of such a movement where the points on the ground may be said to 'move' onto the corresponding points of the piece of paper which is the map.

Because the map is static, it shows only the end point of this 'movement'. We call this process a *transformation* and the map shows the end point of the transformation. Different types of map preserve different aspects of the situation, but essentially they place a one-to-one relationship between the points on the ground and the points on the piece of paper. Since the piece of paper is a plane and the ground is roughly the surface of a sphere, we must take approximations to achieve this. When the transformation is described by a mathematical formula it is called a map projection. Map projections are a highly mathematical branch of geography which have been sadly neglected in recent years; unfortunately their study is too involved to include in detail in this book.

In some cases we wish to emphasise the three-dimensional nature of the earth's surface, and so we use contours to draw a relief map. Here the movement

is essentially volume to area, the contour lines acting as substitutes for the lost third dimension (in mathematical terms the loss of a degree of freedom). In other cases we are only concerned with the order in which points are related to one another, and so obtain the stylised maps which are called topological maps. We are familiar with such maps of the underground railway systems of cities like London and Paris, and we shall return to this topic in chapter 25.

23.4. An alternative classification of transformations

Transformations can be classified in an alternative way to those which rely on the dimensions of the starting and finishing points. In most maps, each point on the ground is transformed into a single point on the map, and each point on the map represents a single point on the ground. Nearly all the transformations we shall meet will have this property, and such transformations are sometimes called one-to-one transformations. To be of interest, such transformations will, of course, have additional properties such as the preservation of length, area, angle, or even simply the order in which points occur.

Some transformations are not one-to-one, but may be one-to-many, many-to-one or many-to-many. Illustrations are given in arrow diagram form in figure 23.1; in each case the transformation is from the left-hand set to the right-hand set of points. In some map projections a few special points are excluded from the one-to-one property, for example in many maps the poles transform into a line. For virtually all maps, however, a single point on the map corresponds to a definite point on the earth, and the map-to-earth's surface transformation is a many-to-one transformation; indeed in most cases it is a one-to-

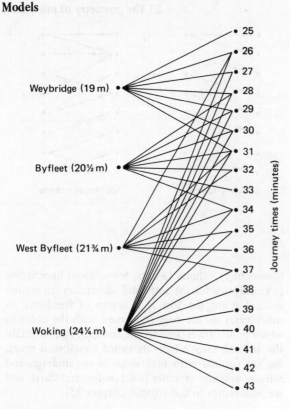

Figure 23.2. Train journey times from London (Waterloo) to four stations; an example of a many-to-many transformation.

one transformation. Mathematicians classify many-to-one and one-to-one transformations as *functions*. Essentially a function is rather like a mathematical machine into which we feed in any permitted input. Out of the function machine comes a unique *unambiguous* output; for every starting point there is a unique end point determined by the function.

Figure 23.2 shows an example of a many-to-many transformation. If the stations on a railway line are transformed into times of travel from the terminal, it can take the same time to reach two different stations, and two different times to reach the same station. The transformation is not a function because each input (station) does not have a single unambiguous output (time). If we consider only the fastest times to each station, then each input does have an unambiguous output (fastest time) as illustrated in figure 23.3. This is then a function. Continuity, however, is not preserved since the fastest train to Woking is quicker than the fastest train for the shorter distance to Byfleet, indicated by the crossing of the lines in the arrow diagram when both stations and times are in order.

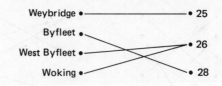

Figure 23.3. Fastest journey times from figure 23.2; an example of a many-to-one transformation.

Exercises

1. Consider ways of defining (a) straight lines in a plane, (b) straight lines in a volume, (c) planes in a volume.
2. Add other examples to table 23.1.
3. Consider the patterns of movements in table 23.1 rather than the sources and destinations. Try to classify them in some way, for example whether they take place along lines, in areas or in volumes (obviously they cannot take place in points since movement implies dimensionality).
4. Consider patterns of points filling area or space. You might find it helpful to think of points as circles or spheres respectively. Extend the regular patterns of points in a plane to consider packing of spheres in a volume. (See, for example, Nuffield Chemistry, 1967.)
5. (Mathematical) Consider the most efficient way to irrigate a field with sprinklers connected by pipes to a tap. How does efficiency vary with the relative cost of sprinklers and pipes? (You might wish to call the cost of a sprinkler £x, the cost of a pipe £y per metre, and the radius of the circle watered by a sprinkler r metres.)
6. Consider the problem of covering an area with strips as with a tractor ploughing a field. You can add arbitrary difficulties such as the minimum turning circle of the tractor. Reconsider the irrigation problem for a line source of water, e.g. holes all along a pipe.
7. Investigate the weaving patterns formed by two sets of perpendicular strips (threads). Consider one and two colours of threads.
8. Consider patterns of lines filling space, e.g. refrigerating a large cold store or control rods in a nuclear reactor.
9. Find practical examples of transformations which are not one-to-one.

Further reading

Abler, Adams and Gould, 1972, pp. 236–55
Cole and King, 1968, pp. 392–403
Haggett and Chorley, 1969, pp. 117–30
Nuffield Chemistry, 1967, pp. 122–86

24 Transformations in space

24.1. Introduction

The idea of a transformation introduced in the last chapter has become more familiar with the changes in the school mathematics syllabus which have taken place since about 1960. Rather surprisingly, there has been relatively little exploration of how these ideas can illuminate our view of geography. In this chapter we shall explore some simple ideas in an attempt to wean ourselves from our rather fixed view of the earth with north at the top and south at the bottom. While convenient for normal use, this convention can be restricting, a point which becomes clearer when we remember that even experienced map readers find it more difficult to follow a journey from north to south on a map rather than the other way round.

While removing preconceptions about shape is an important advantage, transformation can also be used to eliminate unimportant spatial aspects of a problem and so focus attention on the task in hand. This is of great value in situations where comparison is the objective. In sections 16.10 and 16.11 we saw how an example which had been transformed could be treated as a theoretical exercise because any likelihood of a preconceived idea was removed. In this chapter we shall concentrate more on the comparison aspects which can be achieved by transformations.

24.2. Comparing line distributions

The distribution of points along two lines may be simply compared by transforming the lines to straight parallel lines and placing them side by side, as illustrated for the exit points along the French autoroute A1 north of Paris and the British motorway M1 north of London in figure 24.1. The differing patterns are very clear, French planners clearly intended much more local traffic in the neighbourhood of the capital to use the new route than did British planners, and this is borne out by observations of traffic densities along the two routes. Further from the capital, the closer spacing of towns and main traffic routes in England is also reflected by the more frequent exits on the M1. This technique of laying out a route along a straight line while keeping distances in proportion

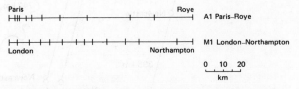

Figure 24.1. Exit points along French autoroute A1 and British motorway M1 compared.

is an old one dating from the road books popular in the eighteenth and early nineteenth centuries.

Figure 24.2 indicates five different ways of comparing the distances between two places. Newcastle is almost exactly the mid-point of the line joining London to Wick in northern Scotland. We can place these points in their relative positions on the map (a), but the idea of the distances being equal is emphasised by moving the line for Newcastle to Wick beside the line from London to Newcastle (b). Such a movement which does not involve any change of direction is called a *translation*.

If we now consider the rail routes connecting London with Newcastle and Newcastle with Wick, we can draw these end to end or we can enable the comparison to be made directly by drawing the routes side by side as in (c). The Newcastle–Wick route is very convoluted, and this can be made clearer by transforming each route to lie along straight lines as in (d) in exactly the same way as was used in figure 24.1. (In 1980, the route from Newcastle to Wick was via Edinburgh, Ladybank, Perth and Inverness.)

However a further transformation can illustrate the times between the towns for the fastest journey, and this is done in (e), showing that while the crow's flight distances are equal, the times of fastest travel differ by a factor of nearly four. We shall return to this idea in the next chapter, and to this example in section 28.2.

So far we have compared distances which lie in the same direction. Even more surprising can be the result of rotating one line to lie alongside the other. Figure 24.3(a) shows the relative positions of London, Muckle Flugga (the most northerly point of the British Isles) and Prague. When the two lines are placed side by side as in figure 24.3(b), the surprising fact is

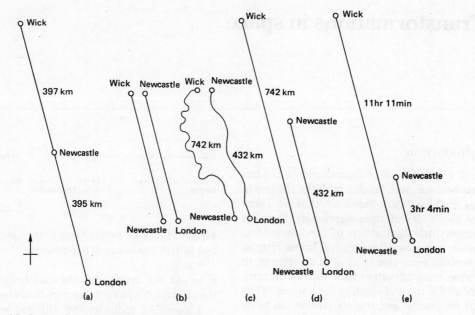

Figure 24.2. Methods of comparison of distances between towns.

realised that the habitants of one eastern European capital live closer to London than the inhabitants of the north of the Shetland Isles. A transformation which involves a turn of this sort without change of scale is called a *rotation*. (In fact a simple rotation about London would place the two lines on top of one another; for clarity one has been translated slightly to one side in figure 24.3(b).)

24.3. Introducing a third point. Reflection

While rotations and translations may be used in comparing the relative positions of two pairs of points, when a third point is introduced, in some circumstances the comparison cannot be made without introducing reflection, which is a different transformation. Reflection has already been met in chapter 17 in a rather different context.

Suppose we wish to comprehend the scale of distances involved in travelling about India. We select the three major towns of Bombay, Calcutta and Delhi shown in figure 24.4(a). For an American audience these might be compared with New Orleans, Washington and St Louis (b), and we can aid this comparison by rotating the second diagram slightly and translating it on top of (a) to produce (c).

For a European audience we might select Madrid, Glasgow and Berne, the distances between these towns being very close to those required (d). By rotation and translation, a comparison may be obtained as in (e), but it is not the best one possible. If we reverse the positions of Glasgow and Madrid, Berne lies

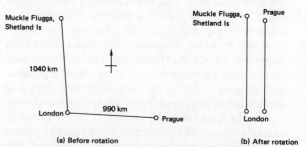

Figure 24.3. Comparison of two distances using rotation.

in the position shown by the dotted lines in part (f) of the figure. The position of Berne may now be reflected into that shown by the pecked lines and the two triangles now correspond very closely, but the Madrid–Glasgow–Berne triangle is now viewed from inside the earth by using the transformation of *reflection*.

24.4. Example

As a practical example we use the ideas above to compare the road crossings of three British estuaries; the Forth, the Severn and the Mersey. The maps of the three estuaries in figure 24.5 are drawn on the same scale and the lowest road crossings are placed vertically above one another as indicated by the line in the figure. The lowest traditional crossing is placed horizontally to the left of the vertical line (the three crossings are at Stirling, Gloucester and Warrington respect-

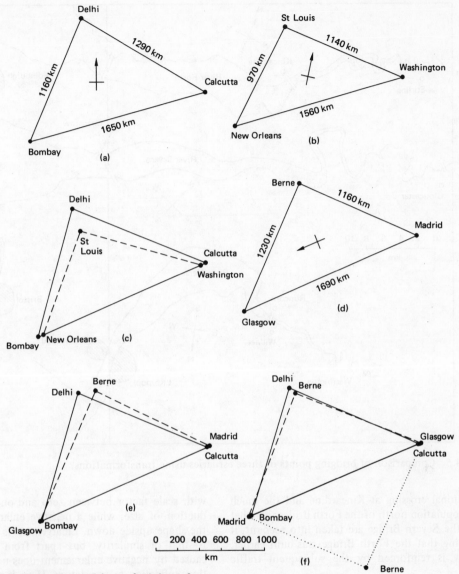

Figure 24.4. Comparing the positions of triplets of towns.

ively). More recent bridges at Kincardine and Widnes (constructed between the two World Wars) are also shown. The Mersey road tunnel has been duplicated, but this is not shown.

In the map of the Forth estuary there is little change. North is approximately in the usual position, and the shape is familiar. The shape of the Mersey estuary looks odd, but this is simply because it has been turned upside down. The Severn estuary does not have a particularly memorable shape and may not appear odd until the position of Bristol is noted. In fact it has been reflected so that east and west on the compass rose are reversed. This enables the re-

lative positions of the major towns of Edinburgh, Bristol and Liverpool to their river crossings to be compared. The relative 1971 populations of these cities are 454 000, 425 000 and 607 000 respectively. These differences and the closeness of Liverpool to the crossing explain why the Mersey road tunnel was built some thirty years before the bridges.

The Forth and Severn comparison is more interesting. Bristol is somewhat further from the Severn Bridge than Edinburgh from the Forth Bridge, but their positions are very similar, as are the traditional crossing points at Gloucester and Stirling. The two bridges are almost identical in size. However, when

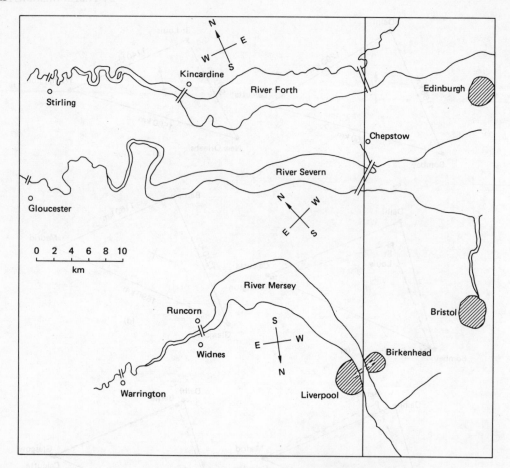

Figure 24.5. Comparison of bridging points of three estuaries using transformations.

the additional crossing at Kincardine and the much smaller population north of the Forth Bridge than that west of the Severn Bridge are taken into account, it is surprising that the Forth Bridge was built earlier. This view is reinforced by the subsequent traffic figures.

24.5. Comparison of areas. Enlargement

Essentially figure 24.5 compares lines (the lines of the estuaries) with the addition of a point outside (the large town). Actual areas can be compared in a similar way. This is sometimes done in quiz games when the shapes of countries have to be compared, and can be quite difficult when reflections as well as rotations and translations are allowed. Since the shapes may be of differing scales, the idea of *enlargement* can be included here. An example of the island of Iona is given in figure 24.6, the original map is shown solid, the enlargements are pecked. The *scale factors* of the enlargements are given, a fractional enlargement

with scale factor between zero and one entails a reduction of size, while a negative enlargement turns the shape upside down. Enlargement is a similar idea to that of similarity, but apart from the inversion caused by negative enlargement does not allow rotation, reflection or translation. There is always a point called the *centre of enlargement*, and it is the relative distances from this point which are altered by the scale factors. When comparing areas, however, the scale factors must be squared as suggested in section 4.3. Thus if the scale factor is 3, the new area is $3^2 = 9$ times the old, while if it is $\frac{1}{2}$ the new area is $(\frac{1}{2})^2 = \frac{1}{4}$ times the original.

24.6. Example

As an example we shall show how the areas of France and Italy together with the relative positions of their capitals Paris and Rome may be compared, thus taking up the ideas in chapter 12. First we draw maps of both countries, marking their capitals and then trans-

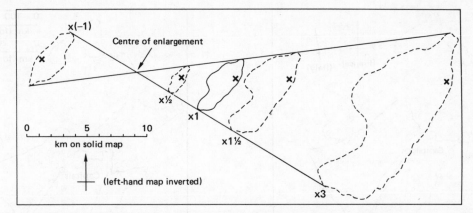

Figure 24.6. Enlargements of map of Iona, Scotland, Original solid. Scales of enlargement (from left to right x(-1), x$\frac{1}{2}$, x1, x1$\frac{1}{2}$, x3. The cathedral is marked with a cross. Note that the negative enlargement is inverted.

late the Italian map (without rotation) so that Rome and Paris occupy the same point. This is shown in figure 24.7 and enables the comparative positions of the two capitals to be related more easily. For example the relative remoteness of Corsica might help to explain unrest in that island – it is far more remote from Paris than Sicily is from Rome.

The comparison is still not at its best because much of the bulk of Italy is in the north, while that of France lies to the south of Paris. On figure 24.7 the two straight lines mark the directions of the most distant points from the capitals. We now rotate the map of Italy about Rome until these two lines coincide, obtaining figure 24.8. The greatest bulks of the two countries now coincide, although slight changes in the angle of rotation might improve this coincidence even more. A reflection could also be incorporated at this stage if it was felt to be helpful.

It can be argued, however, that this process is not altogether fair, since France is a larger country than Italy, and a larger country is bound to look more scattered than a small one. We can cope with this by an enlargement. The areas of France and Italy are approximately 551 000 km^2 and 301 000 km^2 respectively and thus the ratio of the areas is 551:301 = 1:0.55. Since the ratio of corresponding lengths is the square root of the ratio of the areas, the ratio of the lengths must be 1:$\sqrt{(0.55)}$ = 1:0.74. Figure 24.9 shows the result of reducing the scale of the French map in this ratio, leaving the scale of the Italian map unaltered and keeping the capitals coincident. The areas of the two countries *on the map* are now equal. The less compact shape of Italy is now even more obvious; despite the fact that Rome is very centrally placed as a capital compared with Paris, a much larger proportion of the country lies away from the capital

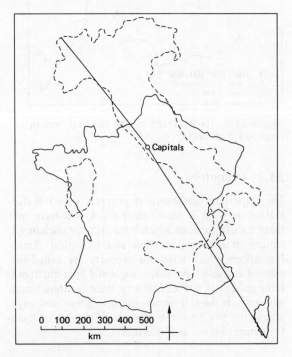

Figure 24.7. France and Italy with capitals superimposed (the lines join the capitals to the most distant points.)

than for France.

Whether this final enlargement is valid or not (it is a fractional enlargement since the size of France is reduced) depends on the nature of the comparison required. The change in scale does not affect the real life distances; the remote areas remain just as remote. In a comparative study however, it may be justifiable to change the scale to compensate for the difference in total areas which cannot be altered either.

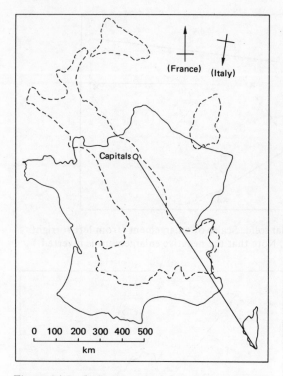

Figure 24.8. Italy rotated so that the two lines in figure 24.7 coincide.

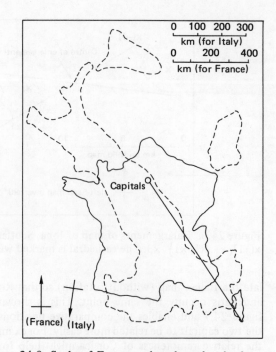

Figure 24.9. Scale of France reduced so that both countries have the same area on the map.

24.7. Isometries

The important mathematical property of a transformation is what it leaves unchanged. We have met three transformations which leave distance unchanged, namely translation, rotation and reflection. Transformations which have this property are called *isometries* and also leave shape, angle and area unaltered. Enlargement is not an isometry since it alters length and area. It does, however, preserve shape and angle and is for this reason a member of the set of transformations known as *similarities*.

Exercises

1. Compare other rail or road routes between towns which are:
   (a)   similar distances apart as the crow flies.
   (b)   similar distances apart by the usual routes.
2. Compare other bridging points in estuaries to those in figure 24.5. British examples are the Thames, the Humber, the Tay, the Clyde and the Tamar.
3. Consider which of the following British estuaries might most profitably be bridged: Wash, Dee (England/Wales border), Morecambe Bay and Solway Firth.
4. Using the towns of Edinburgh, Perth, Dundee and Aberdeen for the Forth Bridge, and Bristol, Newport, Cardiff and Swansea for the Severn Bridge, construct a gravity model (chapter 16) to compare theoretical traffic figures across the two bridges.
5. Compare the United Kingdom and Sweden (or some other pair of countries) by the method used in section 24.6.
6. In discussions over the siting of the third London Airport, the noise 'umbrella' from Heathrow has been superimposed on possible sites to assess the noise effects. Try this on some other airports. Comment on factors which would invalidate your results.
7. Compare the relative positions of Lima, Rio de Janeiro and Buenos Aires with three cities in the USA and with three cities in Europe using the method of figure 24.4.
8. Compare some routes through Alpine or other passes in relation to the major towns at either end of them (e.g. Turin–Grenoble, Turin–Lausanne and Milan–Berne).

Further reading

Cole and King, 1968, pp. 231–9
Oxford Geography Project, 1974b, pp. 114–6

25 New views of space

25.1. Introduction

In the last chapter some transformations of space were examined, but one or two essential properties were left unaltered, namely distance, or in the case of enlargement, shape. In this chapter we shall turn to more complicated transformations. The commonest illustration of how a quantity varies over the map is by the use of isograms, or lines on the map joining points with equal numerical values of the quantity. The best known example is the contour line, and another example occurs in figure 3.9. Before turning to more complex ideas involving transformations we shall explain how a figure built up in a manner similar to figure 18.8 can be used to illuminate our understanding of the world about us.

25.2. Perception space

Sociologists ·in particular are interested in our view of the world around us. Gould and White, 1974, have developed the idea of mapping the world as we see it. The mathematical sections of their work are highly technical, but most of their work is very readable. Here we shall massively simplify their analytical technique so that it becomes accessible at a much lower level of understanding. The aim of the work is to discover people's opinion of the world about them, and this has many implications for planning; for example, in tourism, housing, industrial location, and so on. Space will not permit a full coverage of all the problems involved which include such topics as the writing of questionnaires and statistical analysis, but the outline given should be sufficient to enable the reader to produce similar results. We give two examples, which are related to the author's opportunities and are thus local in nature – indeed the local application is at the very heart of the idea.

25.3. A national perception study

The first example is of a study of fifty post-graduate students on a one year Post-Graduate Certificate in Education course at Nottingham University. At the time these students were applying for teaching posts in England and Wales, and they were asked to rate the various local authority areas for their attractiveness to them as places to work on a six-point scale. The ratings were as follows:

6   I'd very much like to work for this authority.

5   A second choice authority; if a job turned up here I'd be very tempted to accept it.

4   I'd quite like to work for this authority if nothing better turns up.

3   Not very keen, but would work here if pushed for a job.

2   I'd only work for this authority if hard pressed and on a temporary basis.

1   I'd not work for this authority even if I was offered a post.

The selection of an even number of points was deliberate, and avoids neutral decisions. The rating from 6 to 1 is convenient since it means that favourable ratings give high scores. In many such questionnaires very high or very low scores are avoided by respondents, but in this case most used the whole range of scores, and those committed to looking for a post in a particular area frequently used only 1 and 6.

There are over one hundred local education authorities in England and Wales which was too many to include on a questionnaire, so some of the metropolitan boroughs were grouped to reduce the numbers to fifty-eight. In the event students were able to differentiate well between the fifty-eight areas except for those in south Wales, and many found it an interesting and helpful exercise in the process of job-hunting.

In contrast to Gould and White, the analysis done was very simple. The scores were averaged for all fifty replies for each area. These average scores were then pencilled onto a map showing the boundaries of the areas under consideration. The usual way of illustrating data such as this is to shade in the areas used according to scores, and this is done in figure 25.1. The final scores all lay between 2 and 5 and are shown by the shading indicated in the figure. One objection to this method of illustration is that rapid changes in perception are unlikely to occur over a short geographical distance; for example, for most prospective

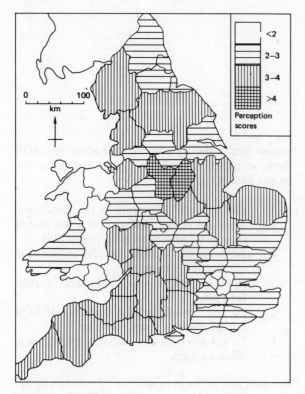

Figure 25.1. Perception scores of Nottingham students of English and Welsh local education authorities (LEAs) as places to work. Divided by LEAs.

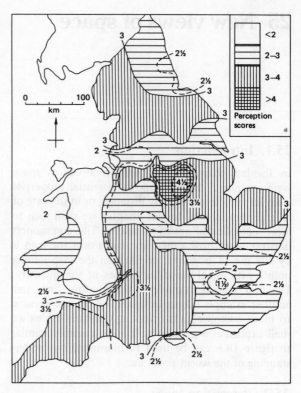

Figure 25.2. Perception scores of Nottingham students of English and Welsh LEAs as places to work. Isogram map.

teachers there will in reality be little difference between schools on either side of the Staffordshire–Derbyshire border even though scores differ by over one point. A way round this is to draw an isogram map to illustrate the situation. Where the boundaries, as in figure 25.1, divide areas of greatly differing perception, the iso-lines are pushed apart; the amount by which this is done is of course arbitrary. This allows the presentation of the map in the form of figure 25.2. This has the frequently under-valued advantage of greater visual impact, and the reduction in boundary detail allows isograms to be shown between those illustrated in figure 25.1, thus adding detail. Both illustrations are valuable and valid, and the choice is a matter for individual decision.

It is important to attempt some analysis of these and similar maps. If several different but related maps are available this is an added advantage. Certain features of Gould and White's maps appear in figure 25.2, confirming the validity of our highly simplified analysis. Among these features are a low perception of London and other large industrial

towns as places to live, and a high perception of the south and particularly of the south-west. An exception to the low perception of large cities is the Bristol area which is usually perceived very highly as a place to live. Another common feature is high perception of the local area, in this case Nottinghamshire and Derbyshire, and more widely the east Midlands. Interesting features of figure 25.2 are the high perception of mountainous areas (for mainly active young people), and the low perception of Wales, partly accounted for by the language problem. Gould and White produced their maps by questioning school-leavers; it seems probable that the older students questioned here would be more knowledgeable about the country and this would account for some differences in the results.

25.4. A local perception study

It is possible to examine perception of the local area in a similar way. This example was carried out as a class exercise with thirteen to fourteen year old pupils of moderate ability in a Nottingham comprehensive

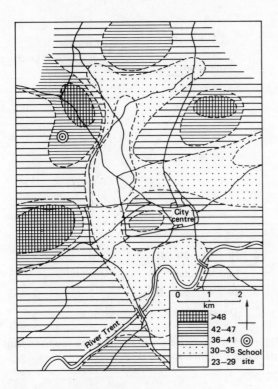

Figure 25.3. Perception scores of areas of Nottingham as a place to live by a class of school children. (Main roads in the city are also shown.)

school (I am grateful to the Headmaster of William Crane School, Aspley, for permission to publish the results). In this case the task was to answer on a four-point scale the question: 'If you had to move house how keen would you be on moving to each of the areas of Nottingham given?' On the questionnaire thirty-three areas of Nottingham were named and a map given showing the parts of Nottingham in which they were located. The questionnaire was to be taken home and answered as a family, not individually. From the sheets returned, the total scores were added for each suburb, and these scores were used to draw the map of figure 25.3. (It is only necessary to take averages if two or more maps are to be compared and when there is a different number of respondents in each group.) On the map the main road network of the city is shown, together with the site of the school 4 km north-west of the city centre. The map has some interesting features and shows some clear knowledge of the social structure of the city. The highly perceived areas are of two types; areas of well-to-do housing which may be beyond the means of many of the families involved, and areas which are one step up from the area around the school; precisely

those areas to which one would expect the more prosperous families to progress. The low spots are interesting as well, and again fall into two types. Those areas which are remote and to some extent unknown or would create difficulties for travel to work; and more noticeably those inner-city areas of decaying housing which are well known because they lie between the school and the city centre. Similar areas in other parts of the city did not have such low scores. Unlike the national map, the local area was not rated most highly, suggesting an aspiration for many families of moving out of the area. While a wider investigation would be needed to confirm these points, they also came out in class discussion, and this revealed considerable knowledge of the local area and social structure.

25.5. Time space

As was suggested in section 3.6, figures such as figure 3.9 can be adapted to show time isograms rather than distance isograms for journey times from a central point. This is illustrated in figure 25.4 by reproducing figure 14.10 and giving journey times from Worcester rather than the best motorway exits to use. The speeds used are those given in section 14.7. In a simpler situation the sets of circles can be given for alternative routes as in figure 14.8.

Another way in which the time dimension may be illustrated is by drawing the lengths of the lines to

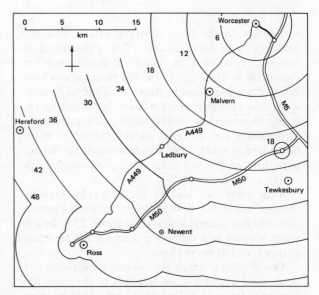

Figure 25.4. Time isograms for travel from Worcester (compare figure 14.10). The figures indicate time in minutes.

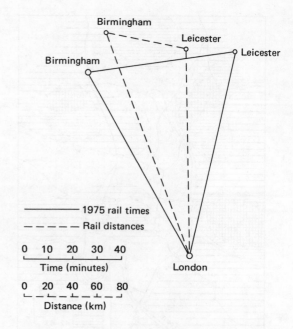

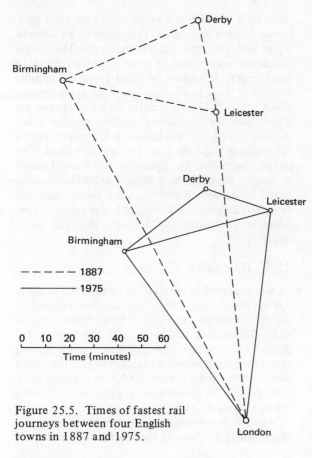

Figure 25.5. Times of fastest rail journeys between four English towns in 1887 and 1975.

Figure 25.6. Relative positions of three towns in time space and distance space.

correspond to the times of travel rather than the distances as in figure 24.2(e). This is illustrated in figure 25.5, which gives fastest rail travel times for four cities in 1887 and 1975. The figure shows how Birmingham has become closer to London in time space than Leicester, which is nearer in distance space. It also illustrates how cross-country journeys between Birmingham and Leicester have remained virtually unchanged in speed, a fact which accounts for the unpopularity of this and many other cross-country rail routes.

This point can also be illustrated by drawing distance space and time space in the same diagram with suitably chosen scales as in figure 25.6. In the scales adopted here distance and time scales are equal at speeds of 120 km per hour.

One difficulty which the process causes does not occur until a fourth town is added to the map. Returning to figure 25.5, Derby has been added by using times from Birmingham and Leicester. As it happens all trains from London to Derby stop at Leicester, and there is no other London–Derby service. If there

were, it would be impossible to insert it on the diagram because the distance from London to Derby is already fixed, and the framework of lines is 'rigid' for each of the two chosen dates. This limits the usefulness of the method to very simple situations.

25.6. Time space using a single centre

This difficulty does not occur when times are measured from a single centre. Figure 25.7 shows a map of south-east England with the railway lines which connect London with various coastal towns. The map is a familiar one to many, but for travellers from London it does not reveal everything. For example, although Rye is closer to London than Hastings it takes longer to reach. For a Londoner in search of a day at the seaside, this is an important consideration.

The situation can be clarified by drawing a time space map as in figure 25.8. Lines are drawn from central London in the correct directions for each town, but with lengths proportional to the fastest rail journey from London to that town. The relative times of travel to the towns from London are now much clearer though of course, the distances between the seaside towns bear little relationship to the times of travel between them.

The whole map can be made more graphic by sketching in a supposed coastline. This is shown in figure 25.8 and should be compared with that shown in

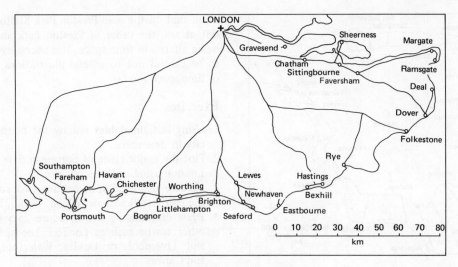

Figure 25.7. Rail routes from central London to south-east coast, 1975.

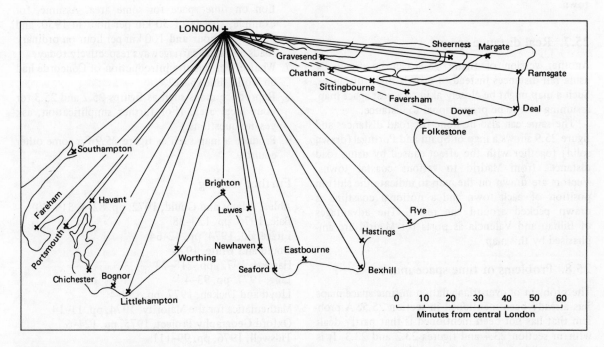

Figure 25.8. Seaside towns in south-east England in rail time space from central London, 1975. (80 km on the scale of figure 25.7 corresponds to 60 minutes on the scale of this figure.)

figure 25.7. The advantages of Folkestone, Brighton and Southampton are now clear, as they are all deeply embayed. In fact, of course, the intermediate stretches of coast are largely mythical; the times taken to reach most points on them from London being very much greater because no rail service is available to them at all. The visual impact of the map is considerable, however, and for further examples the reader is referred to the books quoted at the end of the chapter.

Figure 25.9. Spain and Portugal showing the expansion caused by considering road distance space. The vectors indicate the change in position of each town.

25.7. Real distance space

Another version of figure 25.8 can be drawn by using rail distances instead of crow's flight distances. Such a map might be closely akin to a cost space map, assuming cost to be proportional to distance.

The same can also be done for road distances and figure 25.9 shows a map of Spain and Portugal (drawn solid) together with the effect caused by using road distances from Madrid to various coastal towns. Vectors are drawn on the map to indicate the shift in position of each town and a notional coastline is drawn pecked around the result. The advantages of Bilbao and Valencia as ports for Madrid are emphasised by this map.

25.8. Problems of time space maps

The problem of over-triangulation in time space maps has already been mentioned in section 25.5. A problem that has not been mentioned is that partly dealt with in section 23.4 and figures 23.2 and 23.3. It is quite possible for two different places to plot onto the same point of the time space map. In the next chapter we shall meet topological transformations which leave the order of points along any line unchanged. The transformations of sections 25.5 and 25.6 are not topological and this can cause difficulties. For example in figure 25.8, Preston Park Station is the station north of Brighton on the way to London. The fastest train from London, however, takes longer than the fastest train to Brighton, and this would

mean that on the map Preston Park Station would be out at sea, the order of Preston Park and Brighton being altered in time space. It is necessary, therefore, to be careful not to extend illustrations of the idea of time space too far.

Exercises

1. Using bus timetables redraw the boundaries of a city in time space.
2. Plot the major cities of Europe in time space from London using air-line schedules.
3. Up-date figure 25.8, or redraw it for some time in the past (see Bradshaw, 1968a, 1968b, 1969).
4. Draw diagrams similar to figure 25.5 or 25.6 for other towns such as London, Leeds, Manchester and Liverpool, or Dublin, Waterford, Limerick and Galway.
5. Draw the rail-distance map equivalent to figure 25.8.
6. Try to assess the effect of post-war road construction on time space for some area. Assume, for example, speeds of 50 km per hour in 1950, and 60 km per hour and 100 km per hour on ordinary roads and dual carriageways respectively today.
7. What effect has the introduction of Concorde had on world time space?
8. Reproduce maps such as figures 25.2 and 25.3 for your local area. (For further simplification, ask yes–no questions.)
9. Produce a map such as figure 25.9 for some other country.

Further reading

Abler, Adams and Gould, 1972, pp. 82–4, 519–30
Bale, 1976, pp. 123–38
Fitzgerald, 1974, pp. 42–64
Gould and White, 1974
Haggett, 1972, pp. 218–24
Ling, 1977, pp. 93–4
Lloyd and Dicken, 1977, pp. 193–4
Mathematics for the Majority, 1974, pp. 11–14
Oxford Geography Project, 1975, pp. 124–6
Tidswell, 1976, pp. 99–111

26 Topological ideas

26.1. Topology

In this chapter we shall examine a type of transformation which lies between the two extreme types of the last two chapters. Unlike the transformations of the last chapter they are one-to-one as defined in section 23.4, but they do *not* preserve shape, distance or angle. They do, however, preserve the relative order of any two points in the original diagram. The branch of geometry which deals with such transformations is known as *topology*.

The idea of a topological transformation is often explained by imagining a rubber sheet on which the points are drawn and then stretching it in any way whatsoever without tearing. The beginnings of topology are very simple, and it is fortunate that it is mostly at this level that geographical applications are found.

26.2. Networks

Most topological transformations we shall examine will be on networks. The study of networks is part of another branch of mathematics known as *graph theory*, which has come into prominence in recent years. Networks play an important part in geography, particularly in transport applications where roads, railways, canals, pipelines, telephones, and electricity grid systems are all examples of networks. In this chapter we shall consider only some topological aspects of networks. While geographers have developed all the ideas used in this chapter, care must be taken not to use some of the indices mentioned for their own sake rather than for the light they throw on the geographical situation. One difficulty with the study of networks in geography is that of keeping their complexity within bounds without descending to triviality. For more complex networks the computer is a valuable aid.

26.3. Network terminology

We shall need to extend the network terminology which was first encountered in section 9.9. One problem is the variety of terms used. A *network* is a collection of points, some or all of which are connected by lines. A network is sometimes also called a *graph*, but we shall avoid using that word in this context. A network may be drawn on a two-dimensional surface such as a plane or sphere (we shall call these *planar* networks), or may be in three dimensions, and we must distinguish carefully between these two situations.

In this book we shall call the points *vertices* and the lines joining them *edges*, since these terms are used by at least some books in both mathematics and geography. Vertices are also known as nodes, points, junctions and intersections. We shall use the word node when we wish to describe the number of edges which meet at a vertex, for example if four edges meet at a vertex (such as happens at a crossroads) we shall call it a *four-node*. Edges also go by the titles of links, arcs, routes and branches.

Since our representation of non-planar networks will be on a sheet of paper, bridges will then be possible. These may be real as, for example, in a motorway or pipeline system, or imaginary as in an airline network. In the latter case the vertices, which are airports, are real, but the edges are imaginary in the sense that they have no physical existence. Most networks in this book are planar, and where the formulae are different for non-planar networks we shall indicate this. In a planar network, any intersection of two edges constitutes a vertex as in figure 26.1(a). If the network is non-planar, the bridge may be indicated by the conventional map symbol as in (b), or by emphasising the actual vertices, leaving the bridges unmarked as in (c).

Planar networks have a third important constituent. In such a network the edges divide the plane up into areas which are separated from one another. Mathematicians, who have in mind the surfaces of solid figures, tend to call these areas *faces*, while geographers will find the word *regions* more appropriate. We shall normally use the latter term, though the word faces will frequently be found in elementary mathematics books.

On a solid figure, the network of the edges divides the surface into regions (or faces) which are often

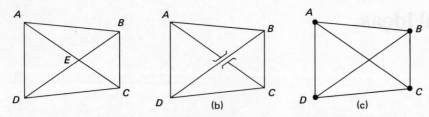

(a) Planar network with five vertices Alternative diagrams for a non-planar network with four vertices

Figure 26.1. Representation of planar and non-planar networks.

plane surfaces as in the cube, but may also be curved as in the sphere. The cube is illustrated in perspective in figure 26.2(a). If this is made of rubber and a small hole is made in the back, the rubber can (with a little imagination) be opened out until it lies flat as in figure 26.2(b). The back surface of the cube is now around the outside of the diagram. Such a diagram is called a *Schlegel diagram* after its originator, and provides a useful method of illustrating problems on solid surfaces. It also explains why, in the case of plane diagrams, the area outside the network is conventionally always counted as a region, and failure to remember this will lead to errors when using formulae. In figure 26.3, for example, the railway network of the Isle of Wight is shown at its maximum extent, There are two regions, one inside the closed loop bounded by Newport, Smallbrook Junction, Sandown and Merstone, and one outside it.

26.4. Euler's formula

Euler's formula, which is a simple relationship between the three components of a planar network, has already been quoted in section 9.9. It states that for a planar network

$$v + r = e + 2$$

where v is the number of vertices, r is the number of regions and e is the number of edges. In figure 26.2, the cube has 8 vertices, 12 edges and 6 regions; while in figure 26.3, there are 11 vertices (circled), 11 edges and 2 regions, thus verifying the formula. The reader who has not met the formula before should check it for a few other simple planar graphs, remembering to count terminal vertices with only a single edge, called one-nodes (such as Cowes in figure 26.3), among their vertices.

Many networks in geography are not connected; for example the railway system of Indonesia is in several unconnected pieces. These still constitute a network, but each separate piece is called a *sub-graph*. Technically an isolated vertex can count as a sub-graph; for example an airport which is only used in

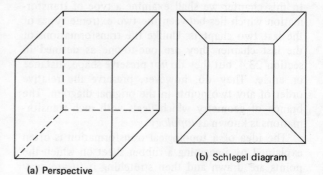

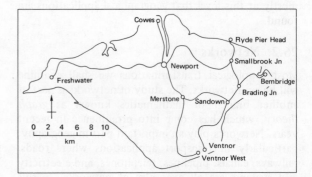

(a) Perspective

(b) Schlegel diagram

Figure 26.2. Two illustrations of the cube.

Figure 26.3. Rail network of Isle of Wight at maximum extent.

emergencies and does not form part of the airline network, or a town on an island without roads. We shall call such isolated vertices zero-nodes. The letter p will be used for the number of sub-graphs in a network, in most cases $p = 1$. We can then give a modified version of Euler's formula which takes the number of sub-graphs into account; this is

$$v + r = e + p + 1$$

26.5. Cyclomatic number, μ

Geographers have devised a number of indices which describe the properties of networks. In this chapter we shall consider only those which use the quantities

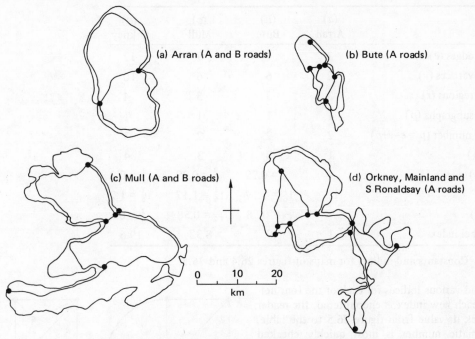

Figure 26.4. Road networks on four Scottish islands.

v, *r*, *e* and *p*, which are essentially topological properties, postponing consideration of further indices to chapters 27 and 28.

In geographical applications, the number of circuits is often of more interest than the number of regions. In figure 26.3, for example, the edges joining Newport, Smallbrook Junction, Sandown and Newport constitute a circuit which completely encloses a region. If any link in this circuit is broken, the network still remains connected. The number of circuits in a network is thus the same as the number of edges which can be cut without creating additional subgraphs. Since one region will always be left, the number of circuits is one less than the number of regions. It is called the cyclomatic number and denoted by the Greek letter *μ* (mu). Using the modified form of Euler's formula,

$$\mu = r-1 = e - v + p$$

However since this definition of *μ* is only in terms of *e*, *v* and *p* it can also be used with non-planar networks. Clearly it will always be a positive whole number or zero, and the more complex a network becomes, the higher the value of *μ* is likely to be.

The indices described in this chapter will be illustrated by referring to the road networks of four Scottish islands, shown in figure 26.4. For the purposes of this study it is easier to redraw these maps in a topologically equivalent form, and this is done in

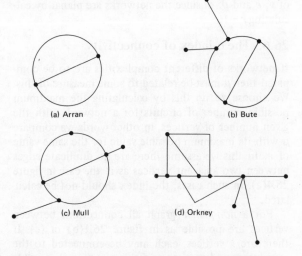

Figure 26.5. Topological maps of road networks of four Scottish islands in figure 26.4.

figure 26.5. Clearly geographical information is lost in this process because no account is taken, for example, of the lengths of the various sections of route. However such information will be lost anyway in the indices used in this chapter, and must be regarded as part of the nature of any use of indices to simplify data. Readers will be familiar with diagrams similar to those of figure 26.5 used to illustrate local transport networks. Table 26.1 gives the values

	(a) Arran	(b) Bute	(c) Mull	(d) Orkney
Number of edges (e)	3	7	7	12
Number of vertices (v)	2	6	6	10
Number of regions (r)	3	3	3	4
Number of subgraphs (p)	1	1	1	1
Cyclomatic number ($\mu = e-v+p$)	2	2	2	3
Diameter (δ)	1	3	3	4
$a = \mu/(2v-5)$	–	$\frac{2}{7} = 0.29$	$\frac{2}{7} = 0.29$	$\frac{1}{5} = 0.2$
$\beta = e/v$	1.5	$1\frac{1}{6} = 1.17$	$1\frac{1}{6} = 1.17$	$1\frac{1}{5} = 1.2$
$\gamma = e/3(v-2)$	–	$\frac{7}{12} = 0.58$	$\frac{7}{12} = 0.58$	$\frac{1}{2} = 0.5$
Mean Shimbel index	1	9	8.33	19.6

Table 26.1. Constants and indices for maps of figures 26.4 and 26.5.

of v, e, r and various indices for each of the four networks. As each new index is encountered, the reader should check its value from figure 26.5 to the table. The cyclomatic number is most quickly checked from the figure, but can be calculated from the values of v, e and p, or since the networks are planar by calculating $r - 1$.

26.6. The a-index of connectivity

If networks of different complexities are to be compared then μ must be related to some measure of this. We choose to do this by calculating the maximum possible number of circuits for a network with the given number of vertices, in other words we compare μ with its maximum possible value for the same value of v. In this we assume there are no duplicate edges between two adjacent vertices as is the case in figure 26.4(a). In such cases, the index should not be calculated.

For a *non-planar* graph all connections between vertices are possible as in figure 26.1(b) or (c). If there are v vertices, each may be connected to the remaining $v - 1$ vertices, and this counts each possible edge twice, once in each direction. Thus, if there are no duplicate edges, the maximum possible number is $\frac{1}{2}v(v-1)$. For twelve vertices, for example, there will be $\frac{1}{2} \times 12 \times 11 = 66$ possible edges. If the network is connected, $v-1$ edges will be needed to connect up the v vertices. Any additional edge after this will create a new circuit, so that there are $\frac{1}{2}v(v-1) - (v-1)$ circuits. For $v = 12$, there are thus $66 - 11 = 55$ possible circuits. The formula for the number of circuits simplifies to

$$\frac{1}{2}(v-1)(v-2)$$

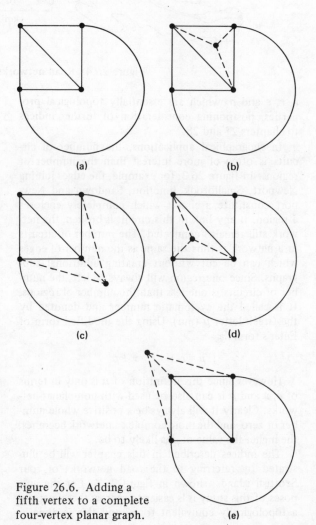

Figure 26.6. Adding a fifth vertex to a complete four-vertex planar graph.

For non-planar networks we define the a-index (alpha-index) by dividing μ by this giving

$$a = \mu/\tfrac{1}{2}(v-1)(v-2) \qquad \text{for } non\text{-}planar \text{ networks}$$

In this formula, v is greater than or equal to three, since for only two vertices, no circuits are possible.

Unfortunately, for *planar* graphs the situation is different. Figure 26.6 shows the various ways in which a complete planar four-vertex may have a fifth vertex introduced. In a complete planar network every region is surrounded by three edges, otherwise it would be possible to divide the region by joining two non-adjacent nodes around its edge. Even the 'outside' region only has three edges. If we insert an extra vertex in any region, it can be joined to all of the three vertices around that region (the figure shows all four possibilities when the fifth vertex is inserted). In every case one region is replaced by three, and two extra regions result. Thus for a complete planar four-node there are four regions, and for the five-node there are six regions. Arguing in this way, each new vertex adds two possible regions. For four vertices there are $(2 \times 4) - 4$ regions, for five vertices there are $(2 \times 5) - 4$ regions, and so on, so that for v vertices, there are $2v-4$ regions. When systematised, such a proof may be made watertight. It is called proof by induction and is a powerful mathematical tool.

Since in the planar graph the number of circuits is one less than the number of regions, the maximum number of circuits is $2v-5$, and this is the maximum value of μ. Thus

$$a = \mu/(2v-5) \qquad \text{for } planar \text{ networks}$$

Once again, v must be at least three, otherwise $2v-5$ becomes negative. For $v = 3$ and $v = 4$, there is no difference between planar and non-planar networks, and the reader should check that the two forms of the formula for a are equivalent.

26.7. Discussion of the a-index

In essence, the a-index gives a measure of the completeness of a network. It should not be used when there are duplicate links between adjacent vertices, for otherwise the calculations for the maximum values of μ are invalid. In addition, we must have $v > 3$ in all cases. One way of coping with such situations as that in figure 26.4(a) is by inserting additional two-nodes. Thus by inserting two-nodes on the north and south coast of Arran we have $v = 4$, $e = 5$ and $r = 3$. We can then write $\mu = 2$ as before, but since $2v-5 = 3$ we have $a = \tfrac{2}{3}$. However by inserting further two-nodes, the value of a can be made still smaller. This illustrates a problem of applying topological indices

to geographical situations, since it is often a difficult decision to know where to place any two-nodes. In any case, care must be taken when comparing different networks to use constant criteria. The effect of duplicate edges is less in larger networks, and occasional examples can then be ignored.

A useful feature of the a-index is that its value varies between zero and one. When it is zero, there are no circuits if the network is connected, while when it is one the network is complete. In practical networks, especially large ones, the value of a is usually, however, rather small. Sometimes the value of a is multiplied by 100 and expressed as a percentage.

As with other indices discussed in this chapter, a fails to distinguish between two networks having the same values of v, e and r, but which are not topologically equivalent, that is cannot be topologically transformed into one another. Figure 26.4(b) and (c) gives an example of this. It will, of course, fail to distinguish between any two networks with no circuits, since in these cases $\mu = 0$.

It is interesting to calculate values of a for the regular triangular, square and hexagonal grids which have been met with frequently in this book, for example in sections 9.9, 11.6 and 21.1, and which are illustrated in figure 9.5. Because these grids are infinite, a may not be calculated in the usual way, but figure 26.7 shows how we may proceed for the triangular grid. An extra vertex produces two extra regions and three extra edges, and this process can be repeated again and again to produce further vertices. For n extra vertices there are $3n$ extra edges and $2n$ extra regions, so that

$$\mu = e - v + p = 3n - n + 1 = 2n + 1$$

Thus
$$a = \mu/(2v-5) = (2n+1)/(2n-5)$$

For large values of n, this is close to one. We would expect this since it is not possible to create more

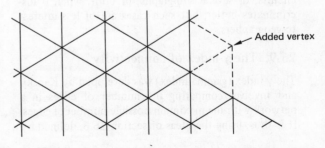

Figure 26.7. In an incomplete triangular net, one extra vertex adds three edges and two regions.

regions without duplicating edges; a must therefore have its maximum value.

For the square network, each vertex adds two edges and one region, giving $a = \frac{1}{2}$, which is a likely value for a road network in a city (see section 3.7). For the hexagonal case, each two extra vertices create three edges and one region, giving $a = \frac{1}{4}$.

26.8. The β-index of connectivity

While the a-index is in some ways the most obvious means of describing the completeness of a network since it is basically the proportion of possible circuits which occur, it is more complicated than the β-index (beta-index), which is defined for both planar and non-planar networks by $\beta = e/v$. Thus the higher the number of edges compared with the number of vertices, the more complete is the network. For connected networks, if there is just one circuit, β equals one; if there are no circuits, β is just under one, the exact value depending on the number of vertices. The reader should have no difficulty in verifying the figures given in table 26.1, and should note that the duplicate links in (a) inflate the value in that case. It is interesting to note that while in (c) a is greater than in (d), for β the reverse is the case. The two indices therefore do not measure the same thing, but it is not easy to see the difference between the two approaches.

For the infinite grids, figure 26.7 shows that in the triangular grid, each vertex adds three edges, giving $\beta = 3$ which is the maximum for a planar network. For a network consisting entirely of zero-nodes, $\beta = 0$, but if the network is connected, the lowest possible value is the case when $v = 2$, $e = 1$, giving $\beta = \frac{1}{2}$. For the complete square and hexagonal networks, $\beta = 2$ and $\beta = 1\frac{1}{2}$ respectively.

In most geographical examples β lies between 1 and $1\frac{1}{2}$, and despite (or perhaps because of) its simplicity, it does not seem to discriminate well between networks. It is much more useful where there are no circuits, or several sub-graphs, or both, when it discriminates better, but such cases are of less interest to geographers.

26.9. The γ-index of connectivity

The γ-index (gamma-index) was developed by Kansky and involves comparing the number of edges in a network with the maximum possible number of edges. It is thus, using the ideas of section 26.6, defined by

$$\gamma = e/\tfrac{1}{2}v(v-1) \quad \text{for } non\text{-}planar \text{ networks } (v > 2)$$

$$\gamma = e/3(v-2) \quad \text{for } planar \text{ networks } (v > 3)$$

These formulae give the same result for $v = 3$ and $v = 4$. Like a, γ lies between zero and one and is often expressed as a percentage.

There is little difficulty in calculating γ, but it is not so popular in geographical uses, and there is little point in a multiplicity of indices when it is not easy to distinguish between the slightly different concepts they measure. The reciprocal of γ (i.e. $3(v-2)/e$ for planar networks) called the *degree of circuity* can also be encountered, and varies from one to infinity. The reader would probably do best to use a.

The chief use of the a, β and γ indices has been in the study of simple road and rail networks, particularly in developing countries, and of their correlation with measures of economic activity such as gross national product, and with population.

Before we can develop another topological aspect of networks, that of accessibility, we need to introduce the idea of a matrix, which is dealt with in the next chapter. Meanwhile, this is a convenient point to examine the network concept of duality, followed by the use of topological ideas with areas.

26.10. Duality in networks

The idea of duality was hinted at in section 22.8 where networks were simulated by joining the centres of hexagons. The idea of duality depends on a relationship between the vertices and regions of a network which allows them to be interchanged in a surprising way. Consider the square grid shown by the solid lines in figure 26.8(a). Inside each square mark a point which is conveniently, but not necessarily, at its centre. If these points, shown as small circles in the figure, are joined by pecked lines, so that one pecked line crosses each edge of the original grid, we produce a second pecked network, which in this case is identical to the original. The same process is shown for the hexagonal grid in figure 26.8(b), but this time a different triangular grid is produced. Clearly the process is reversible, starting with the pecked grids, the solid ones are obtained. Such pairs of networks are called *dual*, so that the hexagonal and triangular grids are duals of one another. The square grid is said to be *self-dual*.

Figure 26.9 suggests how this idea can be applied in a geographical situation. The original network consists of the boundaries of the nations in South America, together with the coast (the boundaries are shown pecked except for that between Colombia and Panama which is to be regarded as the edge of the area under consideration). The points inside the regions are the capital cities of each nation, and the

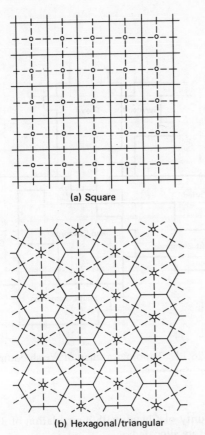

(a) Square

(b) Hexagonal/triangular

Figure 26.8. The regular tesselations and their duals.

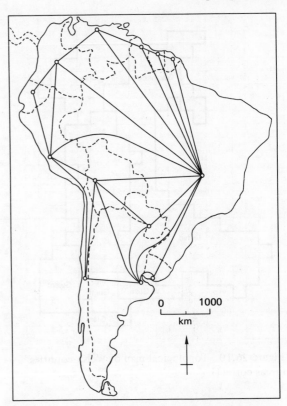

Figure 26.9. A dual pair of networks based on the boundaries and capitals of the nations of South America.

dual network of lines is a network joining the capital cities of adjacent nations in such a way that each edge crosses one and only one international boundary. The dual network (shown solid) consists only of regions with three edges, that is distorted triangles.

An interesting feature of the pairs of dual networks is that the number of edges is the same in each, while the number of vertices and regions interchanges. This is still true in figure 26.9, even though the 'outside' region is ignored, except that the coastlines of each nation should not be counted in the number of edges. The number of regions (countries) is, however, clearly equal to the number of vertices (capitals) in the dual networks, while the number of boundary segments is equal to the number of lines joining capitals, and the number of points at which three nations meet is equal to the number of capital city triangles. The main advantage of the idea of duality is that it becomes possible to see that two different networks are merely two different views of the same configuration.

This is a convenient point to mention one of the most famous conjectures of topology known as the four-colour theorem. (A computer-based proof of this has recently been published, but no simple proof is known.) It states that any planar map may be coloured so that no two adjacent regions have the same colour by using at most four colours. Geographers should note that the sea is not a special case; for example in the map of Europe, Luxembourg must have the same colour as the sea. A dual statement of the four-colour theorem is that in any planar network not more than four letters are needed to label the vertices in such a way that no edge has the same letter at each end.

26.11. Topological maps using areas

Topological maps may also be used to illustrate variables connected with regions in a very vivid way by transforming the areas of the regions on the map to be proportional to the size of the variable concerned. There is no real reason why this transformation should be topological and preserve the boundaries between the regions under consideration except that this makes the topological map easier to identify and

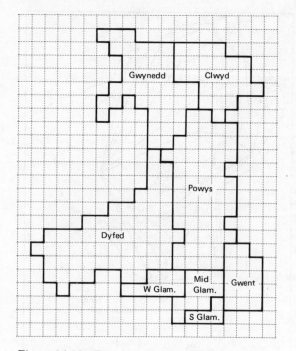

Figure 26.10. Topological map of Welsh counties (areas correct).

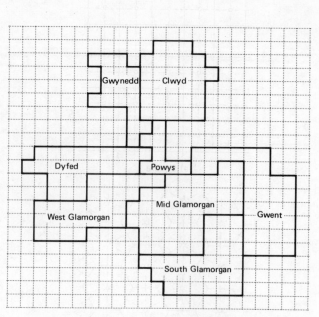

Figure 26.11. Topological map of Welsh counties (populations correct).

interpret. Indeed the aim in drawing such topological maps is to distort the geographical boundaries as little as possible to preserve recognition. This requires care to produce the most effective results.

We illustrate the idea by drawing the Welsh counties in such a way that their areas are proportional to their populations. It is very helpful to begin by simplifying the county map as in figure 26.10. We allocate one square unit to each 100 square kilometres of the area of the country. By using a 1:625 000 map of Great Britain on which 10 km grid squares are marked, and drawing the map on squared paper, the shapes of the counties may be reduced to the nearest whole squares as far as possible, and the areas of each county remain correct. At the same time, segments of boundary between adjacent counties should be preserved.

The preparation of the population map in figure 26.11 requires more care. Figure 26.10 has 211 squares, so that the whole population of Wales, which in mid 1974 was estimated to be 2 759 000, is divided by 211, giving approximately 13 000 to each square.

The county of Clwyd, with a population of 373 000, is therefore allocated

$$373\ 000 \div 13\ 000 = 29 \text{ squares}$$

A similar calculation is made for each of the remaining counties, and figure 26.11 is drawn as similar as possible to figure 26.10, but with the new number of squares for each county, and preserving all the boundary segments. The results are by no means unique, but the new figure displays how the counties are more even in population than in area, and in particular the sparse population in mid-Wales.

This method can be used to display a wide variety of statistics. An example which relates it to the ideas of perception space in chapter 25 is of making the areas in the map proportional to mentions in a local newspaper (see Holt and Marjoram, 1973, p. 227). Similar maps have been used to illustrate parliamentary constituencies, production of crops and gross national product.

Exercises

1. Analyse some more island road systems such as those in figure 26.4.
2. Analyse the main road systems for towns of similar size and function (roads leading out of the towns will have one-nodes at their ends). Suitable towns are Bedford, Carlisle, Chester and Guildford.
3. Analyse some simple theoretical networks. For example start with a hexagon with six two-nodes, add another vertex in the centre and join to the other six vertices one at a time, observing the changes in the values of a, β and γ.
4. (Mathematical) Complete the calculations of a, β and γ for infinite square, hexagonal and triangular networks begun in section 26.7 to 26.9.
5. (Mathematical) Draw a graph showing the maximum number of edges for planar and nonplanar networks for values of v from 3 to 10. Repeat for the maximum number of circuits.
6. (Mathematical) Show that γ is greater than a for planar networks when v is greater than 3.
7. Repeat figure 26.10 and 26.11 for the pre-1974 counties of Wales.
8. Produce topological maps for the rateable values of the counties of Wales. (Data may be found in *Rates and Rateable Values in England and Wales*, HMSO, published annually.)
9. Draw topological maps to illustrate data for other areas: regions of England, the EEC countries etc.
10. Devise a regional division of England using local authority boundaries, and illustrate your answer by topological maps showing area and population. Which regions might need special aid from central government because of low population or low density of population?

Further reading

Berry and Marble, 1968, pp. 78–9
Bradford and Kent, 1977, pp. 93–105
Briggs, 1972, pp. 9–17
Cole and King, 1968, pp. 218–25, 538–70
Commission of European Communities, 1974, sheet 13
Continuing Mathematics Project, 1977c, pp. 1–12
Dalton et al, 1973, pp. 7–20
Davis, 1974, pp. 37–44
Fitzgerald, 1974, pp. 42–80
Haggett and Chorley, 1969, pp. 31–5, 261–72
Hammond and McCullagh, 1974, pp. 50–2
Hay, 1973, pp. 46–55
Holt and Marjoram, 1973, pp. 221–36
Hurst, 1974, pp. 53–128
Kansky, 1963, pp. 5–19
Ling, 1977, pp. 94–7
Oxford Geography Project, 1975, pp. 66–78
Smith, 1975, pp. 279–85
Tidswell, 1976, pp. 259–70
Tolley, 1978
Walker, 1973b, pp. 4, 5, 10, 11, 221–36

27 Matrices and networks

27.1. The associated number of a vertex

In this chapter we move from the connectivity of a network to examine the related but different idea of accessibility. This is more readily developed through the idea of a matrix. We begin by examining accessibility as a property of a single vertex of a network, developing as an example the Isle of Wight network of figure 26.3, of which a topologically equivalent form is shown in figure 27.1. First we draw up table 27.1, which gives the least number of edges between any two vertices of the figure. Such a rectangular array of numbers is known mathematically as a *matrix*, though usually the key (shown abbreviated) is omitted. This particular matrix has the same labels horizontally and vertically in the same order. It is therefore a *square matrix* with the property that, since the least number of edges between any vertex and itself is zero, all the entries on the *principal diagonal* (between top left-hand and bottom right-hand corners) are zero. Further, since all routes may be traced in either direction, the matrix is *symmetrical* about this principal diagonal. These last two terms may only be applied to square matrices.

	Be	Br	C	F	M	N	R	S	SJ	V	VW
Be	0	1	4	4	3	3	2	2	2	3	4
Br	1	0	3	3	3	2	2	1	1	2	3
C	4	3	0	2	2	1	3	3	2	4	3
F	4	3	2	0	2	1	3	3	2	4	3
M	3	3	2	2	0	1	3	1	2	2	1
N	3	2	1	1	1	0	2	2	1	3	2
R	2	2	3	3	3	2	0	3	1	4	4
S	2	1	3	3	1	2	3	0	2	1	2
SJ	2	1	2	2	2	1	1	2	0	3	3
V	3	2	4	4	2	3	4	1	3	0	3
VW	4	3	3	3	1	2	4	2	3	3	0

Table 27.1. Least number of edges between any two vertices of figure 27.1.

For any vertex, the largest number in the corresponding row or column of table 27.1 is called its *associated number* or *König number*. These are shown in parentheses ( ) in figure 27.1. Newport, for example, has associated number 3, since every other vertex can be reached by traversing at most three edges. Average associated numbers for a network can be calculated; that for figure 27.1 is

$$(4+4+3+3+4+4+3+3+3+4+4) \div 11 = 3.55$$

Briggs, 1972, also suggests that isograms can be drawn around a network rather in the manner of figure 18.8. For many uses, however, the varying lengths of the edges make this unhelpful; several vertices close together will increase the associated number, thus reducing the accessibility measures of these vertices.

27.2. Diameter

The highest associated number of a network is called its *diameter* and denoted by δ (delta). Like the associated number it is only meaningful if the network is connected. Thus δ is the maximum number of edges which need to be traversed between any two vertices. While difficult to describe it is really a simple concept, and one rarely needs to draw up the actual matrix such as that in table 27.1 to calculate either δ or the associated numbers. The diameter δ is simply, therefore, the maximum 'topological distance' across the network. It is a crude measure, but we shall need it again in section 28.9. Both δ and the associated number can be considerably affected by the introduction of two-nodes (e.g. extra stations) into the network. Diameters for the networks of figures 26.4 and 26.5 are given in table 26.1 and will serve as additional examples.

27.3. Shimbel index

The associated number has the disadvantage that it concentrates on the least accessible point from each vertex. We can avoid this by using table 27.1 to calculate the total number of edges traversed to reach all the other vertices. Thus for Sandown (*S*), the calculation is the total of the path lengths to the other

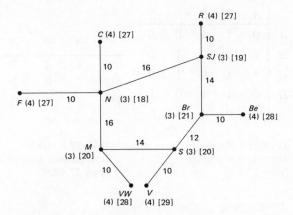

Figure 27.1. Topological equivalent of figure 26.3. showing associated number of each vertex in parentheses ( ), Shimbel index of each vertex in brackets [ ], and frequency of use of each edge.

ten vertices and is simply the appropriate row or column sum of the table which is 2+1+3+3+1+2+3+ 2+1+2 = 20. This quantity is called the Shimbel index of the vertex and is shown in brackets [ ] in figure 27.1 for each vertex. It is now immediately apparent from the figure that Newport and Ventnor with Shimbel indices 18 and 29 respectively are the most and least accessible vertices in the network.

The sum of all the Shimbel indices for a network is called its *index of dispersion* and its value for our example, which may easily be checked by addition on figure 27.1 is 264. The *mean Shimbel index* is this value averaged over the vertices, in our example 264 ÷ 11 = 24. This is a measure of the overall accessibility of a network. Further examples are given for figures 26.4 and 26.5 in table 26.1. It is interesting to note that the networks for Bute and Mull, which are indistinguishable on indices of connectivity, are different on this index. Such comparisons should not, however, be made between networks with different numbers of vertices.

In comparing networks of different sizes, the average associated number of the vertices might seem an obvious measure. It is odd that no attempt seems to have been made to use this.

27.4. Flow-line graphs

Another aspect of networks is the relative importance of the edges. In practice this depends largely upon factors outside our present concern (such as the population at the vertices and the length of the edges as in the gravity model of chapter 16), but we can make some progress on purely topological criteria. If a complete planar network has v vertices, we showed in section 26.6 that it would have $\frac{1}{2}(v-1)(v-2)$ edges. This is the same as the total possible journeys between vertices for a planar network, providing we do not distinguish between the two directions for each possible journey. Thus in the network of figure 27.1 with eleven vertices there are $\frac{1}{2} \times 10 \times 9 = 45$ possible journeys. If we trace out all these journeys by the smallest possible number of edges, and count the number of times each edge is used, we obtain the frequencies given on the edges of figure 27.1. The least used edges serve the one-nodes, while the most used are M to N and N to SJ. This type of diagram can be helpful when some contraction in the network is envisaged; the links which are least necessary can be pinpointed. It can also help in deciding which links are overloaded and might need duplicating, improving or relieving by the insertion of new links. While it is unlikely that this would be done solely on topological grounds, the diagram can be a useful first step. It is interesting to note that the sum of the frequencies must be equal to half the index of dispersion, for example in figure 27.1,

$$10+10+16+10+14+10+12+10+14+10+16 = 132$$
$$= \frac{1}{2} \times 264$$

The half arises because we have counted journeys between vertices in one direction only in determining the frequencies. This calculation forms a useful check on the results.

Such frequency networks, usually known as *flow-line graphs*, are often drawn with the thickness of their edges proportional to their frequency of use. Figure 27.2 shows an example of this for the network illustrated in figure 26.5(d). While this type of illustration can be effective, it is difficult to draw the widths of the lines accurately. This figure is also misleading because the actual routes used by traffic between C and F are via D and E. The direct loop be-

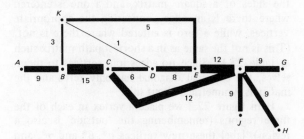

Figure 27.2. Figure 26.5(d) redrawn showing the main traffic routes in Orkney with edges proportional to their topological use.

Models

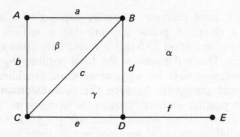

Figure 27.3 A simple hypothetical network with vertices, edges and regions labelled.

Table 27.2. Matrix description of edges of figure 27.3.

	A	B	C	D	E
A	0	1	1	0	0
B	1	0	1	1	0
C	1	1	0	1	0
D	0	1	1	0	1
E	0	0	0	1	0

Table 27.3. Matrix description of edges of figure 27.4(b)

	a*	β*	γ*
a*	2	2	2
β*	2	0	1
γ*	2	1	0

tween C and F does however illustrate the effect of building a bypass around D and E; if it were eliminated, E to F would be the busiest link in the system. There are also alternative two-link routes between C and E and between C and K. In these cases we have chosen the shortest route on the ground, thus using a non-topological criterion.

27.5. Matrix descriptions of networks

We now turn to examine briefly how mathematicians use matrices to describe networks. The non-mathematical reader need pursue this no further than he or she wishes, but the ideas are worth including for they give an excellent demonstration of an application of the multiplication of matrices. The value of the matrix is its ability to store a great deal of information in a compact space; this makes it very suitable for use in computer applications.

It will be convenient to show how a matrix can describe a network by using the simple example illustrated in figure 27.3, which shows a network with five vertices (A, B, C, D, E), six edges (a, b, c, d, e, f) and three regions (a, β, γ). The most obvious description of this network is given in table 27.2, where the vertices are arranged in order along the top and down the sides of a square matrix, and a one is entered where there is an edge connecting the appropriate vertices, while a zero is entered where there is not. (This is not the same as in a shortest path matrix such as table 27.1). Since no edges join vertices to themselves, the principal diagonal has only zeros and the matrix is symmetrical about this.

If in figure 27.3 we place a vertex in each of the three regions (remembering the 'outside' is also a region), label these new vertices a^*, β^* and γ^*, and then draw pecked lines across each of the edges between these as shown in figure 27.4(a), we obtain the dual network illustrated separately in figure 27.4(b).

(See also section 26.10.) This can be described by the matrix shown in table 27.3 which has two new features. Firstly we now have twos appearing since there are two edges joining a^* and β^* as well as a^* and γ^*, and this matrix can therefore display the presence of alternative routes like those in figure 26.4(a). Secondly a two appears in the principal diagonal because we have a loop at a^* which results from the single node at E in figure 27.3. Since this can be traversed in either direction, just like all the other edges it must be counted twice.

Table 27.3 can also be obtained directly as a region table for figure 27.3 in which case the asterisks are deleted, and tells us that there is one edge with region a on both sides (counted twice since all other edges are counted twice), two edges with region a on one side and region β on the other and so on. Similarly table 27.2. with the addition of asterisks is a region matrix for figure 27.4(b).

27.6. Describing one-way flows by matrices

Because every edge (apart from loops) appears in the matrix on either side of the principal diagonal, we can use this to distinguish in which directions the flows take place. As an example we consider the Wirral lines of the Merseyside underground railway which have the unusual feature that services operate only one way round the circuit shown in figure 27.5. Thus there is an edge linking James Street (D) with Moorfields (E), but not the reverse. This is described by using the letters down the side of the matrix to represent the source of the edge and across the top to represent its destination. This conventional arrangement is shown in table 27.4, and the idea can be developed by using the methods in the following sections. We shall not however pursue it here, but leave it as an exercise for the reader.

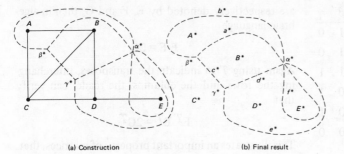

(a) Construction   (b) Final result

Figure 27.4. Obtaining the dual network to that of figure 27.3.

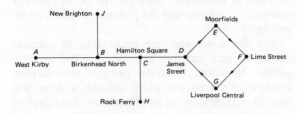

Figure 27.5. The Wirral lines of the Merseyside underground railway.

Table 27.4. Matrix description of figure 27.5 with one-way links.

to		A	B	C	D	E	F	G	H	J
from	A	0	1	0	0	0	0	0	0	0
	B	1	0	1	0	0	0	0	0	1
	C	0	1	0	1	0	0	0	1	0
	D	0	0	1	0	1	0	0	0	0
	E	0	0	0	0	0	1	0	0	0
	F	0	0	0	0	0	0	1	0	0
	G	0	0	0	1	0	0	0	0	0
	H	0	0	1	0	0	0	0	0	0
	J	0	1	0	0	0	0	0	0	0

27.7. Matrices describing edge properties of networks

There are two types of table describing edges of networks, illustrated for figure 27.3 by tables 27.5 and 27.6. These show edges which have a common vertex and edges which have a common region as boundaries respectively. Notice that in the second the two sides of edge f must both be counted. The reader should verify that for the dual network of figure 27.4(b) these matrices reverse their rôles.

Table 27.5. Matrix of edges with a common vertex.

	a	b	c	d	e	f
a	0	1	1	1	0	0
b	1	0	1	0	1	0
c	1	1	0	1	1	0
d	1	0	1	0	1	1
e	0	1	1	1	0	1
f	0	0	0	1	1	0

Table 27.6. Matrix of edges which are boundaries of a common region

	a	b	c	d	e	f
a	0	1	1	1	1	2
b	1	0	1	1	1	2
c	1	1	0	1	1	0
d	1	1	1	0	1	2
e	1	1	1	1	0	2
f	2	2	0	2	2	2

27.8. Matrices describing two properties of a network

Matrices which connect two properties of a network can easily be drawn up, although they will no longer normally be square, and the principal diagonal will have no special significance. The three types are shown for the network of figure 27.3 in tables 27.7 to 27.9. The reader should be able to work out the applications of these to the network and its dual for himself. There is no reason why rows and columns should not be interchanged, in which case the *transposed* matrix is obtained.

27.9. Relationships between different pairs of matrices describing a network

(This section and the next one involve multiplication of matrices and the reader who has not met this process will probably prefer to omit them.)

The multiplication of matrices is a little complicated and even those who have met it before might need to refresh their memories. When two matrices are to be multiplied the number of columns in the first must equal the number of rows in the second. If the first matrix has p rows and q columns and the second has q rows and r columns, the resulting matrix

Models

	a	b	c	d	e	f
A	1	1	0	0	0	0
B	1	0	1	1	0	0
C	0	1	1	0	1	0
D	0	0	0	1	1	1
E	0	0	0	0	0	1

Table 27.7. Vertex–edge matrix for figure 27.3.

	a	β	γ
a	1	1	0
b	1	1	0
c	0	1	1
d	1	0	1
e	1	0	1
f	2	0	0

Table 27.8. Region–edge matrix for figure 27.3.

	a	β	γ
A	1	1	0
B	1	1	1
C	1	1	1
D	2	0	1
E	1	0	0

Table 27.9. Vertex–region matrix for figure 27.3.

has p rows and r columns. The element in the i th row and j th column of the resulting matrix is obtained from the elements in the i th row of the first matrix (say $a, b, c, \ldots, q$) and the j th column of the second (say $a', b', c', \ldots, q'$) by calculating the sum of the individual products of pairs thus:

$$aa' + bb' + cc' + \ldots + qq'$$

Take the matrices of tables 27.7 and 27.8. When these are multiplied, the calculation is written thus:

$$\begin{pmatrix} 1 & 1 & 0 & 0 & 0 & 0 \\ 1 & 0 & 1 & 1 & 0 & 0 \\ 0 & 1 & 1 & 0 & 1 & 0 \\ 0 & 0 & 0 & 1 & 1 & 1 \\ 0 & 0 & 0 & 0 & 0 & 1 \end{pmatrix} \begin{pmatrix} 1 & 1 & 0 \\ 1 & 1 & 0 \\ 0 & 1 & 1 \\ 1 & 0 & 1 \\ 1 & 0 & 1 \\ 2 & 0 & 0 \end{pmatrix} = \begin{pmatrix} 2 & 2 & 0 \\ 2 & 2 & 2 \\ 2 & 2 & 2 \\ 4 & 0 & 2 \\ 2 & 0 & 0 \end{pmatrix}$$

For example the 4 in the fourth row and first column of the product is obtained from the fourth row of the first matrix (0 0 0 1 1 1) and the first column of the second $(1\ 1\ 0\ 1\ 1\ 2)^T$. (The T merely indicates that the column has been transposed or written as a row for convenience.) The 4 in question then arises from

$$(0 \times 1) + (0 \times 1) + (0 \times 0) + (1 \times 1) + (1 \times 1) + (1 \times 2) = 4$$

The resulting matrix is that of table 27.9 except that all the terms are doubled. If tables 27.7, 27.8 and 27.9

are respectively denoted by **E**, **F** and **G**, then in algebraic language

$$\mathbf{E}\,\mathbf{F} = 2\mathbf{G}$$

Again using T to indicate the transposes, interchanging the rows and the columns, the reader can verify that

$$\mathbf{F}^T\,\mathbf{E}^T = 2\mathbf{G}^T$$

This illustrates an important property of matrices, that

$$(\mathbf{E}\,\mathbf{F})^T = \mathbf{F}^T\,\mathbf{E}^T$$

(The order in which the matrices are placed in multiplication is important; since we choose to multiply row-wise by column-wise the process is basically asymmetrical.)

For the geographer the importance of matrices lies in the fact that they are easily handled by computers. Networks illustrate perhaps the simplest example of the ways in which this can be done, and thus have great value as an illustration of the type of process which can be undertaken.

27.10. Squaring matrices

In this section we shall use a simplified version of figure 27.1 which reduces the number of one-nodes and also saves space. This is shown in figure 27.6 and its connectivity matrix in table 27.10. The interpretation of row and column sums of this matrix should now be clear, and the grand total of these is twice the number of edges in the network. If this matrix is denoted by **A**, then $\mathbf{A}\,\mathbf{A} = \mathbf{A}^2$ may be calculated as

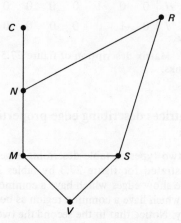

Figure 27.6. Simplified version of figure 27.1 for use in section 27.10.

174

	C	M	N	R	S	V
C	0	0	1	0	0	0
M	0	0	1	0	1	1
N	1	1	0	1	0	0
R	0	0	1	0	1	0
S	0	1	0	1	0	1
V	0	1	0	0	1	0

Table 27.10. Connectivity matrix **A** for figure 27.6.

	C	M	N	R	S	V
C	1	1	0	1	0	0
M	1	3	0	2	1	1
N	0	0	3	0	2	1
R	1	2	0	2	0	1
S	0	1	2	0	3	1
V	0	1	1	1	1	2

Table 27.11. The matrix $\mathbf{A}^2$.

	C	M	N	R	S	V
C	0	–	7	–	–	–
M	–	0	6	–	8	11
N	7	6	0	15	–	–
R	–	–	15	0	10	–
S	–	8	–	10	0	10
V	–	11	–	–	10	0

Table 27.12. Matrix showing lengths of paths in figure 27.6 in km.

explained in section 27.9 giving the matrix shown in table 27.11. This gives all the possible two-edge routes in figure 27.6. For example, from M to R there are two two-stage routes via N and via S. The diagonal terms give the two-stage routes back to the starting point, and since there are no duplicate edges give the number of edges from each vertex. In this way a computer can easily determine the edge structure of a network. In the same way, $\mathbf{A}^3$ and $\mathbf{A}^4$ can be found, and it is possible to avoid journeys of this type which use the same edge twice, thus finding all the useful three- and four- stage journeys.

By adding the corresponding terms in tables 27.10 and 27.11, we obtain the matrix $\mathbf{A} + \mathbf{A}^2$. This has only four zero entries, namely those connecting C to S and V, and vice versa. These are thus the only journeys which cannot be made in two stages. If $\mathbf{A}^3$ is added as well, there are no zero entries, showing that the diameter of the network is three. The use of matrices for analysing networks by computer has received some criticism, which can be overcome (see, for example, Hay, 1973, pp. 56-9).

27.11. The matrix as an information store

Table 27.12 gives an example of how a set of non-topological data can be stored in a matrix, and any other convenient statistic could be stored in a similar way. Care should be taken, however, to distinguish between zeros and non-entries, which are shown by dashes. In a computer this is sometimes done by entering an impossibly large number, e.g. 1 000 000, for non-entries.

Exercises

1. Work out associated numbers, average associated numbers, diameters, Shimbel indices and mean Shimbel indices for some of the networks in figure 26.5. (Some of these may be checked in table 26.1.)
2. Work out the various matrix descriptions of a simple network with about six vertices and check the relationships between them.
3. Determine the meanings of the various row and column sums of tables 27.2 to 27.9, and the sum of the terms of the principal diagonal in tables 27.2, 27.3, 27.5 and 27.6.
4. (Mathematical) Show that in section 27.10, the matrix giving two-stage journeys without duplicated edges is the matrix $\mathbf{A}^2$ with zeros substituted in its principal diagonal.
5. Verify that the ideas of sections 27.9 and 27.10 also apply to networks with one-way flows such as that in figure 27.5.
6. Check that tables 27.5 and 27.6 can also be applied to the dual network.
7. (Mathematical) Check that in section 27.9,

$$\mathbf{F}^T \mathbf{E}^T = 2\mathbf{G}^T.$$

Further reading

Abler, Adams and Gould, 1972, pp. 236–55
Briggs, 1972, pp. 18–25
Cole and King, 1968, pp. 589–96
Continuing Mathematics Project, 1977c, pp. 12–21
Dalton et al, 1973, pp. 21–2
Davis, 1974, pp. 44–54, 84–97
Haggett and Chorley, 1969, pp. 35–47, 199–204
Hay, 1973, pp. 56–60
Hurst, 1974, pp. 53–128
March and Steadman, 1974, pp. 285–302
Mathematics for the Majority, 1974, pp. 31–7
Tolley, 1978
Wilson and Kirkby, 1975, pp. 104–28

28 Non-topological ideas in networks

28.1. Introduction

In the next two chapters we shall examine networks from a non-topological standpoint. We shall not simply be concerned with vertices, edges and regions, but with attaching quantities to these; chiefly we shall attach the idea of distance to the edges. While the ideas in these two chapters may seem more immediately practical than those in the last one, they are generally more mathematically advanced, not in the sense that they are harder, but in the sense that they involve additional properties.

28.2. Detour index

The detour index is a measurement based upon the lengths of the edges of a network and defined by

$$\text{detour index} = \frac{\text{actual distance along route between two points}}{\text{straight line distance between those points}} \times 100$$

It is expressed as a percentage and is always greater than 100. From a mathematical point of view, it would be more sensible to use its reciprocal, ignoring the 100 and defining

$$\text{directness coefficient} = \frac{\text{straight line distance between two points}}{\text{actual distance along route between those points}}$$

This would have the value one for a straight line and decrease to zero as the routes were more circuitous. However it is probably too late to change the established usage.

As an example consider the rail routes between London and Newcastle and between Newcastle and Wick illustrated in figure 24. 2. The direct distances are 395 km and 397 km respectively, and the rail distances are 432 km and 742 km respectively. The detour indices are:

$$(432 \times 100) \div 395 = 109.4\%$$

and

$$(742 \times 100) \div 397 = 186.9\%$$

The directness coefficients are 0.91 and 0.54 respectively. These figures indicate the approximate ranges of these statistics which are likely to be encountered in practice.

Care must be taken where the detour index is used for individual edges of a network. For example, when considering the effect of the Severn Bridge, the detour indices between Cardiff and Bristol are 173% and 359% with and without the Bridge. This is a reasonable use of the index. However between Chepstow and Aust immediately on the other side of the Bridge, the figures are 117% and 1500% respectively. By placing the vertices close to the ends of the Bridge, the detour index avoiding the Bridge can be made very large.

The detour index is also sometimes used slightly differently as the ratio of the distances between two routes (not using the crow's flight distance). This is the same as the ratio of the old and new detour indices expressed as a percentage, for Cardiff–Bristol above it is therefore

$$(359 \times 100) \div 173 = 207\%$$

It is a useful measure, but the use of the same title for something essentially different is confusing.

28.3. Detour indices for a complete network

There is less likelihood of difficulties such as those above when the detour index is used for a complete network. To illustrate this we choose two areas of France which have seven towns distributed roughly at the centre and vertices of a hexagon, and the twelve lengths of road connecting them. The Compiègne area (figure 28.1) is north-east of Paris and has a low relief, the only barriers to roads being two rivers and some forest areas. The Gorges du Tarn area (figure 28.2) in central southern France is an area of high limestone plateaux intersected by deep river gorges. The distances in kilometres for these areas are readily obtained from tourist maps. Table 28.1 gives the data for the calculation of the individual detour indices and the indices themselves for the various possible routes in the Compiègne area. The direct distances are given for the Gorges du Tarn

	Bl	Ch	Com	Cou	LM	N	S
Blérancourt	–	14	31	15	19	14	23
Chauny	14	–	41	15	33	17	32
Compiègne	31	41	–	46	14	24	38
Coucy-le-Château	15	15	46	–	34	29	17
La Motte	19	33	14	34	–	33	24
Noyon	14	17	24	29	33	–	37
Soissons	23	32	38	17	24	37	–
Total	116	152	194	156	157	154	171

(a) Road distances (km)

	Bl	Ch	Com	Cou	LM	N	S
Blérancourt	–	12	26	12	16	13	20
Chauny	12	–	36	12	28	16	27
Compiègne	26	36	–	37	13	22	37
Coucy-le-Château	12	12	37	–	26	24	16
La Motte	16	28	13	26	–	20	24
Noyon	13	16	22	24	20	–	34
Soissons	20	27	37	16	24	34	–
Total	99	131	165	127	127	129	158

(b) Direct distances (km)

	Bl	Ch	Com	Cou	LM	N	S
Blérancourt	–	117	119	125	119	108	115
Chauny	117	–	114	125	118	106	119
Compiègne	119	114	–	124	108	109	103
Coucy-le-Château	125	125	124	–	131	121	106
La Motte	119	118	108	131	–	165	100
Noyon	108	106	109	121	165	–	109
Soissons	115	119	103	106	100	109	–

(c) Individual detour indices

Table 28.1. Calculation of detour indices for journeys of figure 28.1.

	B	C	F	LM	M	LR	SE
Balsièges	–	9	21	30	34	38	14
Chanac	9	–	26	23	34	33	13
Florac	21	26	–	33	21	34	15
Le Massegros	30	23	33	–	25	13	20
Meyrueis	34	34	21	25	–	18	21
Le Rozier	38	33	34	13	18	–	25
St Enimie	14	13	15	20	21	25	–

Table 28.2. Direct distances between towns in figure 28.2 (km).

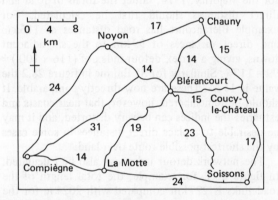

Figure 28.1. Road network east of Compiègne, France (distances in km).

Figure 28.2. Road network in the Gorges du Tarn, France (distances in km).

area in table 28.2; the road distances may be determined from the map and the calculations are left as an exercise for the reader. With one exception the road distances in the Compiègne area are in the range 100-131, while in the Gorges du Tarn they lie in the range 117-194. In addition bends and steep hills in the Gorges du Tarn area will reduce average speeds, thus impeding communications in that area still more.

In the calculation of the detour indices for all routes from a given vertex (the vertex detour index), all routes out of the town to adjacent towns should be taken so that results for several towns are comparable. It is mathematically incorrect to average the indices for each route as suggested in Mathematics for the Majority, 1974; rather the totals of road and direct distances should first be calculated. For example Blérancourt has road distances of 116 km and direct distances of 99 km to the six adjacent towns, giving a vertex detour index of $(116 \times 100) \div 99 = 117\%$. Similarly for St Enimie in figure 28.2 the value is 157%. These are now directly comparable. It should be remembered, however, that near coasts and estuaries the indices can be very distorted, and it may be desirable to replace direct distances in some cases by the shortest possible route over land.

The network detour index can also be calculated. In figure 28.1, for example, the total length of the road links is 227 km compared with 202 km for the direct lengths, giving a network detour index of 112%. For figure 28.2, the value is 151%. If, however, it is desired to focus attention on all possible journeys, thus counting some edges several times, then the total distances in table 28.1(a) and (b) can be used, giving slightly different results; for the Compiègne area its value is then 118%.

28.4. Some theoretical detour indices

It is instructive to compare the total network detour indices obtained above with those for the geometrical net shown in figure 28.3. If in that case the length of each edge is one unit, there are twenty-one possible routes in the network. Of these twelve are direct one-unit routes and three are direct two-unit routes. The other six routes are two units along edges, but $\sqrt{3}$ units direct. Thus the total route length is thirty units, and the total direct length is $18 + 6\sqrt{3} = 28.39$ giving the detour index as

$$(30 \times 100) \div 28.39 = 106\%$$

Since in the Compiègne area the value of the network

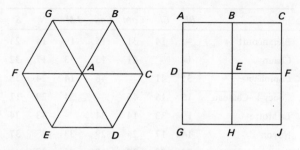

Figure 28.3. Theoretical triangular network.

Figure 28.4. Theoretical square network.

detour index for all possible routes is 118% for a topologically equivalent net, about one-third of the detour in that area is due to the mathematical configuration of the network, the other 12% agreeing with the detour index of 112% for sum of the road distances.

Since many urban road systems are basically a square net, it is also interesting to note the detour index for the nine vertices of the network in figure 28.4, which is 122%. The calculation is left as an exercise for the reader, but this is a higher value than occurs for road systems in many areas of low relief and this lends weight to the theory expressed in chapter 21 that the natural communication systems are hexagonally rather than square based. In both these theoretical examples, however, the exact values of the detour indices will depend on size of the network investigated.

28.5. Sinuosity index and relief index

Applied to rivers, the detour index is called the *sinuosity index*. In using this the problem mentioned in section 3.5 should be remembered. In the example of that section, the measured length of the stretch of the River Usk on the largest scale map is 11.49 km, while the direct distance is 8.85 km, giving a sinuosity index of 130%. The longer the stretch of river investigated, the larger the index will tend to be, particularly for rivers with a marked change in general direction such as the Usk or the Rhine (see also Chorley, 1969).

A similar index is the *relief index,* defined to be the true distance along a route divided by the horizontal distance, thus giving a measure of the relief along the route. Unfortunately, it is difficult to determine and will have values only slightly over 100% in most cases. (See Dinkele, Cotterell and Thorn, 1976d, p. 28.)

28.6. Accessibility

We shall now examine more briefly some of the other quantities which measure various network concepts. If we have a distance matrix such as that in table 28.3 for the six largest towns in France, we can easily determine the total distance from any one town to all the others. It is clear that Lyons, which has the least distance, is the most accessible of the six towns, while Lille is the least. This is a simple but effective way of making such comparisons within a single table; in this example Paris is less accessible than Lyons. In a similar chart giving rail journey times however, this would probably be reversed.

	Lille	Lyons	Marseille	Nice	Paris	Toulouse
Lille	–	676	992	1152	219	902
Lyons	676	–	316	476	461	549
Marseille	992	316	–	190	777	414
Nice	1152	476	190	–	937	579
Paris	219	461	777	937	–	679
Toulouse	902	549	414	579	679	–
Total	3941	2478	2689	3334	3073	3123

Table 28.3. Comparative accessibility of six major French cities.

28.7. Circuity

It we subtract the sets of figures in tables 28.1(a) and (b), we have the extra road distances for each link over the direct route. If these are squared and averaged we have the *circuity* for each town measured in square kilometres. For example for Blérancourt the circuity is

$$(2^2 + 5^2 + 3^2 + 3^2 + 1^2 + 3^2) \div 6 = 57 \div 6 = 9.5 \, \text{km}^2$$

Usually the central town in the network has the lowest circuity because it has the highest accessibility, but in this case the more important town of Soissons has the lower figure of 7.5 km^2.

Since it is permissible to average averages when the original averages have been calculated from the same number of items, the overall average circuity can be calculated by averaging those for the individual towns. For the towns in figure 28.1 this gives a value of 23.7 km^2.

It is not at all clear why circuity should use distances squared except by the statistical analogy of the calculation of variance. The effect of the squaring is to intensify the effect of the bigger detours. Circuity is a different concept to that of the detour index; the latter measures wasted distance in proportion to direct distance, while the former is a square quantity with no proportional aspect. Doubling the size of a network, for example, quadruples the circuity. Kansky also points out that by defining additional vertices on the network (e.g. an extra town along one edge), the value of the circuity is altered both for individual towns and for the whole network.

28.8. The η-index of edge length

The η-index (eta-index) is simply another name for the average edge length of a network. For the example in figure 28.1, it is simply

$$(24 + 17 + 14 + 14 + 15 + 31 + 15 + 19 + 23 + 17 + \\ + 24 + 14) \div 12 = 227 \div 12 = 18.9 \, \text{km}$$

28.9. The π-index

The π-index (pi-index) is defined to be the total length of the network divided by the length of the longest diameter. The diameter δ is defined in section 27.2. In figure 28.1, $\delta = 2$, and the longest necessary journey is Compiègne-Blérancourt-Coucy which is 46 km. Thus $\pi = 227 \div 46 = 4.9$.

This index is subject to occasional anomalies. For example, the road net of Orkney in figure 26.4(d) and 26.5(d), repeated with distances in figure 28.5, has $\delta = 4$ for journeys from A to E, G, H and J, and the longest of these is the 63 km from A to H. Since the total length of the network is 161 km, $\pi = 161/63 = 2.6$. However the same journey from A to H is only 57 km via a six-edge route, and yet a longer 75 km journey is possible by a three-edge route. There is a case for replacing the denominator in the definition of π by the greatest distance it is necessary to travel between any two vertices.

The lowest possible value of π is one in the case of a linear network connecting all the points (it is meaningless with a non-connected network). The more complete the network, the higher its value is, as is illustrated in the two examples above. Unlike accessibility, circuity and the η-index, it is a ratio and does not depend on the scales used in measurement, so that it can be used to compare networks, though this should only be done when they are not too dissimilar in size. Its name is due to the well-known ratio π which is the circumference of a circle divided by its

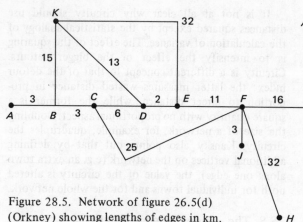

Figure 28.5. Network of figure 26.5(d) (Orkney) showing lengths of edges in km.

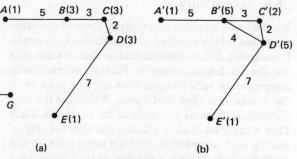

Figure 28.6. Two theoretical networks for the calculation of the ι-index. The distances are in km, and the weights given to each node are in brackets.

diameter. Dalton *et al*, 1973, suggest that the π-index can be most easily applied to networks when the total length is known, for example by reference to the statistics in the *Oxford Economic Atlas of the World*.

28.10. The θ-index of vertex density

If instead of dividing the total length of the network by the number of edges, as for the η-index, we use the number of vertices, then we have the θ-index (theta-index). For figure 28.1 this is $227 \div 7 = 32.4$ km. This quantity is the average length of network per vertex. Instead of length, other quantities can be used such as total volume of traffic.

28.11. The ι-index of vertex density

Kansky, 1963, suggests that the θ-index can be improved by emphasising the more important central vertices, it is then called the ι-index (iota-index). Inevitably the weighting of the vertices is somewhat arbitrary unless there is an objective criterion. As an illustration we give the two networks of figure 28.6. In that figure, vertex A has only one function, that of shipping goods to and from B. Vertex B has three functions, shipping goods to and from A and C, and trans-shipment between A and C. In addition to functions similar to those for B, vertex B' has in addition shipment to and from D', and trans-shipment between A' and D', totalling five functions. The various weightings are shown in brackets in the figure. Using the distances also marked,

for (*a*) $\iota = (5 + 3 + 2 + 7) \div (1 + 3 + 3 + 3 + 1)$
$= 1.55$ km
for (*b*) $\iota = (5 + 3 + 2 + 7 + 4) \div (1 + 5 + 2 + 5 + 1)$
$= 1.5$ km

The validity of this weighting procedure is rather questionable, and it is not completely clear what concept ι describes, so that it is probably best left to advanced workers. However the weighting suggested in table 18.1 could also be applied, and the sum of the weights of the road junctions in each 10km x 10 km grid square could also be used directly as a measure of network vertex density.

28.12. Network density

As well as using vertex density as a substitute for network density, it is sometimes possible to calculate network density directly. Thus Haggett and Chorley, 1969, p. 85, estimate the average densities of road networks in 126 countries as 10.3 km per 100 km^2.

Geomorphologists are also concerned with drainage density, and the length of stream per unit area of drainage basin can be calculated. The calculations are tedious, if of no great difficulty. For example the length of all the streams marked on the 1:25 000 map of the Rush Gill – Aira Beck basin used as an example in section 5.8 is 41.6 km and the area of the basin as calculated in section 5.11 is 13.64 km^2. Thus the drainage density is $41.6 \div 13.64 = 3.05$ km per km^2. Judging by figures quoted in Haggett and Chorley, 1969, p.75, this is a fairly high value as might be expected in an area such as the Lake District.

Care should be taken in comparing the units of this quantity with similar quantities calculated in imperial units. An equivalent calculation in miles to the above is

$$\frac{41.6 \times 0.621}{13.64 \times 0.621^2} = 4.91 \text{ miles per square mile}$$

Exercises

1. Complete the analysis of the Gorges du Tarn area of figure 28.2.
2. Repeat the detour index calculations for road networks in two other contrasting areas of a different country.
3. Analyse some detour indices for a major bridge crossing such as the Humber Bridge and compare them with those for the Severn Bridge.
4. Repeat the analysis of section 28.4 for figure 28.4, and for some other simple theoretical networks.
5. Find the lengths of some well-known rivers in a gazetteer and work out the sinuosity indices for their whole lengths. Comment on your results.
6. Analyse the accessibility of the six or eight largest towns as in section 28.6 for another country. Discuss reasons why population is an important factor which accessibility does not take into account.
7. Compare the accessibility of Goole and Hull for a selection of towns in south and west Yorkshire. What are the disadvantages of Goole as a port?
8. Complete the calculations of circuitry for the network of figure 28.1, and work out similar figures for figure 28.2. Compare your two results.
9. Calculate the π-index for some theoretical networks (e.g. regular triangles, squares with and without diagonals, hexagons with some diagonals).
10. Add further links to the networks of figure 28.6 one at a time, and re-calculate the ι-index in each case.

Further reading

Briggs, 1972, pp. 18-25, 35-42
Chorley, 1969, pp. 419-30
Cole and King, 1968, pp. 560-6
Dalton et al, 1973, pp. 23-35
Davis, 1974, pp. 44-9
Dinkele, Cotterell and Thorn, 1976d, pp. 28-9
Haggett, 1972, pp. 335-9
Haggett and Chorley, 1969, pp. 57-70, 74-90
Hammond and McCullagh, 1974 , pp. 46-50
Hay, 1973, pp. 38-9
Kansky, 1963, pp. 18-25
Mathematics for the Majority, 1974, pp. 8-11
Tidswell, 1976, pp. 284-90
Tolley, 1978
Wilson, 1973a, pp. 40-51
Wilson, 1973b, pp. 48-51

29 Routes in networks

29.1. Introduction

In this chapter we shall examine some of the problems connected with choosing routes through a network. There are various criteria for selecting routes through a network, and the difficulty of solving them varies greatly for apparently quite similar problems. Most path problems involve visiting the vertices of a network, but some require edges to be traversed, and since these are easier to solve, we shall begin with them.

29.2. The road-gritting network

We first consider a problem which a highway authority might face, that of gritting roads on nights when frost is expected. Lorries gritting roads effectively grit only their own side of the road so that every stretch must be covered in both directions. Figure 29.1 is an example of a typical network of roads to be gritted by lorries operating from a depot at D. While the figure is topological, distances are given in kilometres.

Suppose that a single lorry load is sufficient to grit all the roads. The solution is then remarkably simple and no waste mileage is involved. One possible route is *DPQRQ PDNUY ZYUVW XWYWV UNSTQ TWTSV SPSND*. This is illustrated in figure 29.2 and would be particularly suitable if N is a town centre and the routes out of it were R, Z, X and T in order of importance, connecting roads only being filled in at the latest possible moment. This is an example of the additional constraints likely to be placed on such a solution. For example, the reader might try to cover the work with four separate journeys with a maximum gritting distance of 50 km each and attempting to minimise wasted mileage.

29.3. Covering each edge of a network once only

If each edge has to be covered once only, we have a version of the Königsberg Bridges problem, which like the four-colour theorem is too well known to give full details here. The problem involves walking across a system of seven bridges connecting the banks and islands of a river so that each bridge is crossed once and once only. The arrangement of bridges is in fact

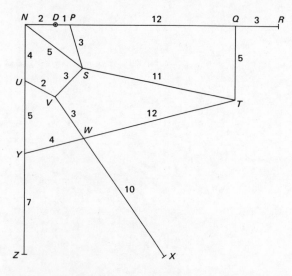

Figure 29.1. Theoretical network for the road-gritting problem.

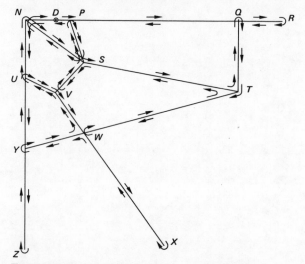

Figure 29.2. One solution to the road-gritting problem (n.b. driving is shown on the left of the road as in Britain).

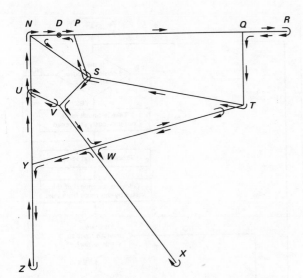

Figure 29.3. Optimal solution to the problem of covering each edge of the network of figure 29.1 at least once.

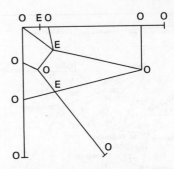

Figure 29.4. Network of figure 29.1 showing parity of vertices (O – odd, E – even).

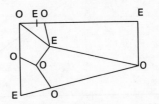

Figure 29.5. Network of figure 29.4 with one-nodes removed and parity adjusted.

such that no solution is possible, and this is true of any attempt to traverse the network of figure 29.1 in this way also. Thus redundant journeys are involved if no uncovered edges are to be left. In the figure *YZ*, *WX* and *QR* must unavoidably be covered twice since they are 'dead-ends' (unless other routes not shown in the figure can be utilised). A possible route is *DPQRQ TSPDN SVWTW XWYZY UVUND*. This is illustrated in figure 29.3, and it is not possible to improve on this solution. The redundant journeys not already mentioned are along *TW*, *UV* and *NP*.

The proof that this is the best solution uses the idea of odd and even vertices, that is vertices with odd and even numbers of routes leading from them, and from this can be developed a general method of attacking the problem. Since every journey must arrive at and leave a vertex, an even vertex can be served by through journeys completely, while an odd vertex requires a redundant journey. Figure 29.4 shows the odd and even vertices of the network, and this property of a vertex is called its *parity*, marked *O* for odd and *E* for even in the figure. There are only three even vertices, two four-nodes and one two-node (*D*). The odd vertices (of which there must be an even number) must be linked together in pairs along edges so that the duplicate journeys along them turn all the odd vertices effectively into even ones. (We could leave two odd vertices if we were allowed to start at one end and finish at the other; if we have to start and finish at the same point we cannot do this.) Before we

search for the most advantageous way of joining the odd vertices, the figure can be simplified by removing all edges ending in one-nodes since these must be covered twice, and adjusting the parity of the inner ends. This is done in figure 29.5. It is now an easy matter to group the six odd vertices in figure 29.5 together in pairs to give the smallest total distance. *T* must be joined to *W*, *U* to *V* and *N* to *P* (via *D*). The sum of the lengths of these edges is 12 + 2 + 3 = 17 km and added to the lengths of the edges ending in one-nodes this gives a total redundant distance of 37 km, which is the best which can be obtained. It is common to find problems of this type which do not contain actual distances in puzzle books. The addition of the need to minimise the wasted distances immediately makes the problems more meaningful, as well as more interesting, and it is a pity it is not done more often.

29.4. Planning a route through a network

The problem of choosing the best path between two given points in a network is a practical problem which faces a traveller who plans a journey through unfamiliar territory where there is no clear direct route. Figure 29.6 shows the network of main roads which faces a driver who wants to travel from Newcastle to Edinburgh, with the distances marked in kilometres. How does the driver set about planning a route through this network, remembering that the map does not

Models

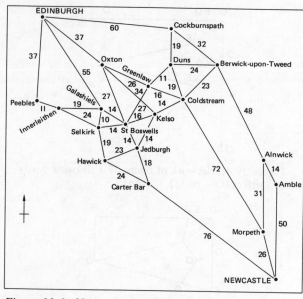

Figure 29.6. Network of main roads between Newcastle and Edinburgh (distances in km).

show all the bends and bottlenecks in the road, nor the hills which lie across some of the routes (see section 28.3)? There have in fact been three routes which at one time or another have been regarded as the main route between the two cities, those via Carter Bar and Oxton, via Coldstream and Oxton and via Morpeth and Berwick, so the choice in the past has been by no means easy and has depended on the means of transport and the prevailing weather. Our analysis will, however, be based only on the distance by each route.

Usually such problems are solved by eye; resulting errors are likely to be small. For a fool-proof solution a rule of procedure is needed, and an obvious way of presenting this is by a flow chart. These will not be dealt with in detail in this book, but this is a convenient place to point out that flow charts have an important part to play in the application of computing techniques to geography. A flow chart which solves our problem is given in figure 29.7, and highlights the intrinsic difficulty of our task, since it involves no less than six diamond-shaped decision boxes. It will probably be helpful to follow through part of the chart on figure 29.6.

The starting point is Newcastle, and there is a choice of three routes. We begin by choosing the left-hand one. (In a general context, this is ambiguous, but it should cause no difficulty here, and in any case it does not really matter which route we start with so long as we try all possible routes.) The initial move is to Carter Bar ($D = 76$). Here there has been no previous

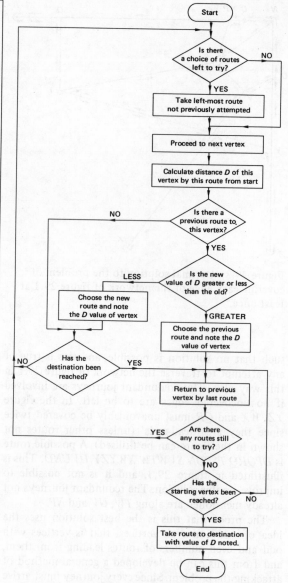

Figure 29.7. Flow chart showing how to obtain the shortest path between two given points on a network.

visit, and since we have not reached the destination, we choose the left-most route to Hawick ($D = 100$) and so on to Selkirk ($D = 119$), Innerleithen ($D = 143$) and Peebles ($D = 154$) where there is no choice but to proceed to Edinburgh ($D = 191$). We then return to Peebles and Innerleithen, where we try the route via Galashiels ($D = 162$) to Edinburgh ($D = 217$). We then explore a large number of fruitless routes through St Boswells which are clearly of no use, before trying the Selkirk road back from Galashiels. This completes a loop giving a higher D value than the previous visit to

Selkirk and can thus be immediately rejected and we can return all the way round this loop to try paths which take the Selkirk–Galashiels road in the opposite direction. While the brain makes many complex decisions to reject unlikely looking routes without bothering to try them out, the computer cannot do this. Clearly, however, a flow chart such as this could only be used effectively as the basis of a computer program.

A more practical procedure might be to work through the network writing against each vertex its distance from the start and amending it as better routes were found. While some routes might be missed by this method, they are unlikely to be practicable ones, and the possibility of error is compensated by speed of decision. One eventuality is not in fact covered by either system, and that is two routes having the same length.

The shortest route is in fact via Carter Bar and Oxton (172 km). That via Coldstream and Oxton (177 km) avoids the worse of the two climbs in the former route, while the route through Morpeth, Alnwick and Berwick (197 km) has always been important, especially in bad weather. The quantities in figure 29.6 need not be distances; they could equally well be times, or cost of travel. Other problems related to this one involve maximum flows through a network when the total flow exceeds the capacity of the most favourable route, see for example Lighthill, 1978, pp. 281–325.

29.5. Spanning trees

When a network has no circuits, but every vertex is connected, then every journey will be possible by one and only one route. Such a network is called a *spanning tree*, a tree being a network with no circuits. A spanning tree is of particular interest when it is necessary to connect all vertices on a network, but only one connection is needed for each vertex. An obvious problem is then to find the minimum spanning tree. We shall assume here that this refers to the one

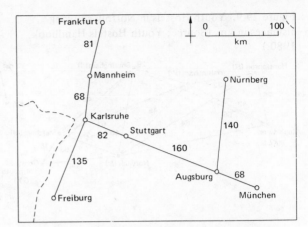

Figure 29.8. Minimum spanning tree for eight cities in south Germany.

with the least total length, but it could also refer to the one with the least cost of construction or operation. Some problems of this type were met in chapter 17, but here we shall assume that the only points at which edges meet are at the vertices.

As an example we shall find the minimum spanning tree for eight cities in south Germany. Table 29.1 gives the distances between them and figure 29.8 shows the minimum spanning tree. To determine this the shortest distance in the table is found. There are two routes of 68 km, so that Karlsruhe to Mannheim and Augsburg to München can be drawn in. The next longest link is the 81 km from Frankfurt to Mannheim, then the 82 km from Karlsruhe to Stuttgart. The next longest link is 133 km from Stuttgart to Mannheim which creates a circuit, so this is not built. Following this process in the table until all the vertices are joined will produce a minimum spanning tree, though a choice may be needed in the case of two routes of equal length.

An intuitive proof that this method works is easy; since no edge of the tree can be replaced by a shorter one, the only shorter ones than any constructed have already been rejected in favour of ones still

	Augsburg	Mannheim	Frankfurt	München	Freiburg	Nürnberg	Karlsruhe	Stuttgart
Augsburg	–							
Frankfurt	360	–						
Freiburg	353	271	–					
Karlsruhe	220	141	135	–				
Mannheim	287	81	198	68	–			
München	68	393	411	287	345	–		
Nürnberg	140	222	387	294	284	166	–	
Stuttgart	160	207	206	82	133	218	188	–

Table 29.1 Distances between eight cities in southern Germany (km).

Models

Figure 29.9. Youth Hostels in Norfolk showing distances in km. (Source: Youth Hostels Handbook, 1980.)

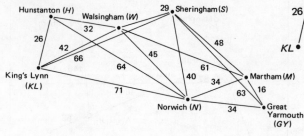

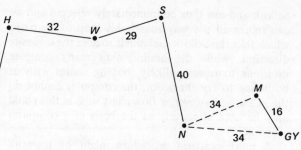

Figure 29.10. Solution to travelling salesman problem for figure 29.9 (start and finish at different vertices).

shorter. A more formal proof may be found in Wilson, 1972. The basic autobahn system of southern Germany is very similar to figure 29.8 except that there is a link between Frankfurt and Nürnberg avoiding a circuitous journey, and Nürnberg is connected to München rather than Augsburg, the former being much larger in size. The network shown might, however, be particularly effective as a telephone network where the time of travel is effectively zero.

29.6. The travelling salesman problem

If a traveller has to make a series of calls in no set order, then the minimum distance problem, although it bears a superficial resemblance to that above, is much more difficult. Indeed there is no general algorithm or rule by which a complete solution may be obtained. Small networks can be solved by trial and error, but for larger ones various simplifying assumptions must be made, see for example Haggett, Cliff and Frey, 1977.

As a simple illustration, suppose a youth hosteller wishes to visit all the hostels in Norfolk; these are shown with distances between them in figure 29.9, except for some of the longer distances. The problem assumes two slightly different forms depending on whether the start and finish are the same point or not. The former results in a closed loop, the latter in a spanning tree, though not necessarily in a minimum spanning tree.

In the case of the closed loop, a start can be made at any of the seven hostels. For the second hostel there is a choice of six, then successively five, four, three, two and one. Since any loop can be traversed in either direction, this halves the number of possibilities giving

$$\tfrac{1}{2} \times 6 \times 5 \times 4 \times 3 \times 2 \times 1 = 360$$

loops for seven vertices. If a closed loop is not needed,

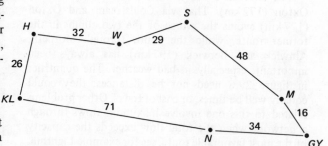

Figure 29.11. Solution to travelling salesman problem for figure 29.9 (start and finish at the same vertex).

then each starting point gives a different path and the number of solutions is

$$\tfrac{1}{2} \times 7 \times 6 \times 5 \times 4 \times 3 \times 2 \times 1 = 2520$$

While these numbers are too large to try all alternatives, a few subjective decisions make minimum length solutions possible in this case.

An initial trial solution is made by coupling the ideas of section 29.5 with the idea of nearest neighbour (chapter 11). In figure 29.10 each hostel is joined to its nearest neighbour (Norwich has two equal ones), and on adding the next two shortest distances in figure 29.9 we have a tree. Since there are no shorter distances than those actually used, we can be sure that figure 29.10 gives the minimum distance of 177 km for the second problem, and common sense would suggest Great Yarmouth as a more accessible end point than Martham, although distances are equal from Norwich.

The closed loop solution is given in figure 29.11 and has length 256 km. Although there are fewer alternatives it is not so easy to be sure this is a minimum solution; fortunately the placing of the hostels in a ring makes this a comparatively simple case.

29.7. Problems at vertices

One problem of networks which is often neglected is that of traffic at the vertices, and the reader will be familiar with some of the ways in which conflicting movements are avoided at motorway intersections. It is an interesting exercise to examine how the high cost of bridging at intersections can be reduced without the use of too much land, and avoiding stretches of route which are too sharply curved. The simple three-way intersections which occur in the hexagonal net of figure 9.5 are particularly attractive, especially if one-way traffic flow is allowed (see Buchanan, 1964, p. 62).

Figure 29.12 illustrates the conflicting flows at three- and four-way junctions (assuming driving on the left of the road). There are three and sixteen conflicting movements respectively. In the second case there are additional conflicts which we have not counted when vehicles approaching from opposite directions and wishing to turn to the offside adopt the correct manoeuvre of crossing each others' paths twice. The roundabout is a particularly attractive solution which avoids bridging and reduces conflicting traffic movement, but it is difficult to make it large enough to allow weaving of parallel streams of traffic.

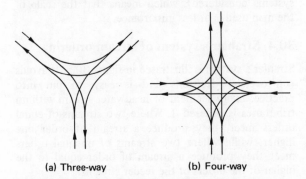

(a) Three-way   (b) Four-way

Figure 29.12. Conflicting traffic movements at road junctions. (Driving on left-hand side of road is assumed.)

Exercises

1. Investigate further examples of the road-gritting problem and the related problem when each edge needs to be traversed only once. Devise your own constraints.
2. Use a road map to plan an unfamiliar journey. How certain are you that you have chosen the shortest route?
3. Determine the minimum spanning tree for figures 29.9 and 29.6.
4. Investigate the minimum spanning tree problem for a larger network using a table of road distances between towns. Consider the relationship of your solution to the clustering problems of chapter 20.
5. Investigate the two versions of the travelling salesman problem for the towns shown in figure 29.8 and table 29.1.
6. Devise and solve your own travelling salesman problem. (Ten vertices will be as many as you can handle.)
7. Investigate conflicting traffic movements at a five way intersection, and (mathematical) devise a general formula for the number of conflicts at an n-way intersection.
8. Devise improved traffic systems for some busy intersection which you know well. Consider the relative costs of various solutions.
9. Examine how conflicting traffic movements are avoided at any multi-level traffic interchange you know well. Many modern junctions remove only some of the conflicts; how are others dealt with (roundabouts, weaving, traffic lights, give-way signs and banned turns)? Relate the use of these devices to the frequency with which the traffic uses that path.

Further reading

Abler, Adams and Gould, 1972, pp. 276-83
Buchanan, 1964
Haggett and Chorley, 1969, pp. 193-211
Haggett, Cliff and Frey, 1977, pp. 73-85
Hurst, 1974
Lighthill, 1978, pp. 281-325
Mathematics for the Majority, 1974, pp. 28-31, 37-8
Wilson, 1972 (mathematical)

30 Network trees and river systems

30.1. Introduction

In some of this chapter a slightly higher level of mathematical sophistication will be required than in the rest of the book. We show how an idea used in research by geomorphologists may be related to some basic axioms in algebra, and this provides a little known and interesting application of what is usually regarded as pure mathematics.

In section 29.5 a connected network with no circuits was called a spanning tree, often abbreviated to tree. An example of a tree is shown in figure 30.1 which shows the chain of beacons lit as part of the Royal Wedding celebrations. A similar example is the 'best route' charts from particular towns provided by motoring organisations. Such trees are typical of hierarchic structures from the chain of command of a battleship to the biological classification of flora and fauna.

Often the idea of a tree is linked with the idea of dichotomising sets in chapter 1, and an example using various types of number encountered in algebra is given in figure 30.2.

30.2. Stream networks as trees

In spite of the biological absurdity, stream networks form one of the most interesting geographical examples of trees. A river system usually contains no appreciable islands and can be regarded mathematically as a tree with the river mouth acting as a trunk. The normal view of a tree starts with the trunk, and this is sometimes a useful idea to transfer to a river system, beginning at the mouth rather than the headwaters. We shall examine the various ways geographers have tried to classify the components of a river system through a mathematician's eyes, discovering that in their independent way geographers have been moving towards an axiomatic mathematical system.

30.3. Gravelius' system of stream ordering

Haggett and Chorley, 1969, pp. 8-16, give six different systems of stream ordering which have been used by geographers; we shall illustrate the systems by using the example of the small River Glaven near Holt in Norfolk, England. The network as given on a 1:63 360 map is shown in figure 30.3, and comparison with other networks should only be made using maps of the same scale and style.

Figure 30.4, which is topologically equivalent to figure 30.3, shows Gravelius' system. He numbered every segment of the main stream 1, so that starting from the mouth, at each junction a decision is made about which is the main river. When this is finished up to the source, every other tributary debouching onto the main stream is numbered 2 up to its source and so on until all the streams in the system have been numbered.

There are a number of disadvantages to this method. Subjective decisions must be made at each junction, and these are not always easy, especially for minor streams where decisions may have to be quite arbitrary. Geographically a disadvantage is that a stream of order 1 may be anything from a tiny rivulet to a large river. On the other hand the main rivers of the system are clearer than in other ordering methods. Another advantage is that the process begins at the mouth of the river (unlike all the other systems considered), which means that the scale of the map used is of less importance.

30.4. Strahler's system of stream ordering

Strahler's system is illustrated in figure 30.5. It avoids controversial decisions and is easy to put into practice. Every segment of headwater stream with no tributaries is ordered 1. Where two streams of equal orders meet, they produce a stream of order one higher, while where two streams of unequal orders meet they produce a stream of order equal to the higher of the orders of the feeder streams.

This method of combination can be conveniently expressed mathematically as

$$a * b = a \quad (a > b)$$
$$a * b = b \quad (a < b)$$
$$a * a = a + 1$$

where feeder streams of orders a and b are combined with the operation $*$. Because of its simplicity, Strahler's system is the one most commonly used by geographers.

Beacon Sites

1 London
2 Windsor
3 Hog's Back
4 Hindhead
5 Butser Hill
6 Portsmouth
7 St Catherine's
8 Alderney
9 Sark
10 Herm
11 Guernsey
12 Jersey
13 Chantry Hill
14 Ditchling Beacon
15 Firle Beacon
16 Beachy Head
17 Fairlight
18 Lydd
19 Dover
20 Highclere
21 Inkpen Beacon
22 Beacon Hill (Bulford)
23 Westbury Down
24 Pen Hill
25 Bagborough
26 Dunkery Beacon
27 North Molton
28 Hendon Moor
29 Trevose Head
30 St Agnes Beacon
31 Carn Brea
32 Chapel Carn Brea
33 Land's End
34 St Mary's
35 Cardiff
36 Cefn Bryn
37 Pendine
38 Goetty Mountain
39 Dunstable Downs
40 Muswell Hill
41 White Horse Hill
42 Cleeve Hill
43 Malvern
44 Walton Hill
45 The Wrekin
46 Mow Cop Castle
47 Raw Head
48 Moel Fammau
49 Moelfre Isaf
50 Snowdon
51 Caernarvon
52 Rivington
53 Barnacre
54 Black Combe
55 Snaefell
56 Skiddaw
57 Criffell
58 Repentance Hill

59 Cairnsmore of Fleet
60 Cairn Pat
61 Knocknagh
62 Althorp
63 Leicester
64 Alport Heights
65 Harland South
66 Rotherham
67 Horkstow

68 Normanby le Wold
69 Boston
70 Sandringham
71 Chevin
72 Northallerton
73 Scotch Corner
74 Cleveland
75 Horseshoe Hill
76 Moat Law
77 Deadwater Fell
78 Birkscairn Hill
79 Scald Law
80 Dumyat
81 Duntilland
82 Dunrod Hill
83 Rothesay
84 Edinburgh
85 East Lomond
86 Craigowl
87 Cairn o' Mount
88 Lochnagar
89 Ben Nevis
90 Beinn na Cille
91 Seil Island

92 Rhum
93 Hecla
94 St Kilda
95 Balmoral
96 Ben Rinnes
97 Morven
98 Wideford Hill
99 Fair Isle
100 Bressay
101 Saxa Vord

Figure 30.1. Network tree showing chain of beacons lit to celebrate the marriage of Prince Charles and Lady Diana (*Radio Times*/Richard Draper, 1981).

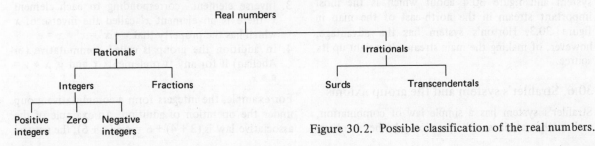

Figure 30.2. Possible classification of the real numbers.

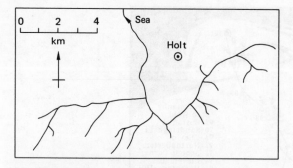

Figure 30.3. River system of the Glaven, Holt, Norfolk, England.

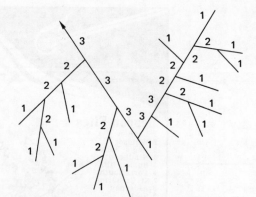

Figure 30.5. Strahler's system of classification for R. Glaven.

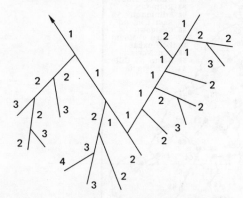

Figure 30.4. Gravelius' system of classification for R. Glaven.

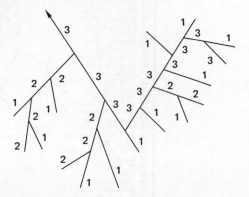

Figure 30.6. Horton's system of classification for R. Glaven.

30.5. Horton's system of stream ordering

Horton's system (Horton, 1932) starts with Strahler's system, and then re-orders streams from the mouth. At each junction where two streams of equal orders meet, the higher order is carried upwards from below the junction along the more important stream, which is taken to be the one most nearly in line with the trunk stream, or in the case of equal angles, the longer of the two. This involves some awkward topographical criteria and there is a difference of opinion between figure 30.6 which illustrates this system and figure 30.4 about which is the most important stream in the north-east of the map in figure 30.3. Horton's system has the advantage, however, of making the main stream clear right up its source.

30.6. Strahler's system and the group axioms

Strahler's system has a simple law of combination, and mathematicians will question whether it obeys the group axioms. These are:

A set of elements S forms a group if, to any two elements x and y of S taken in a particular order, there is a unique third element of S under an operation $*$ denoted by $x * y$ which satisfies the following laws:

1. Associative law – for any three elements x, y and z,

$$(x * y) * z = x * (y * z)$$

2. Neutral element – there is an element called the neutral element denoted by e which has the property that $x * e = e * x = x$ for all elements x.
3. Inverse element – corresponding to each element x there is an element x' called the inverse of x which has the property that $x * x' = x' * x = e$.
4. In addition the group is called commutative (or Abelian) if for any two elements x and y, $x * y = y * x$.

For example, the integers form a commutative group under the operation of addition. An example of the associative law is $(3 + 4) + 6 = 3 + (4 + 6)$; the neutral element is 0 since, for example, $4 + 0 = 0 + 4 = 4$; the inverse of 5 is -5 since $5 + (-5) = (-5) + 5 = 0$; and an example of commutativity is $3 + 4 = 4 + 3$. (An example of a non-commutative group is that of non-singular matrices with two rows and two columns under multiplication.)

Strahler's system is clearly commutative, since the order in which we consider streams at a junction is unimportant. The associative law involves not only the various possible equalities of three stream orders a, b and c, but also cases where they differ by a value of one. We shall assume a is greater than or equal to b, which is in turn greater than or equal to c. The symbol $\gg$ will be used to mean 'is more than one greater than'. The various cases are then:

(i) $a = b = c$ (vi) $a = b + 1 \gg c + 1$
(ii) $a = b + 1 = c + 1$ (vii) $a \gg b = c$
(iii) $a = b = c + 1$ (viii) $a \gg b = c + 1$
(iv) $a = b + 1 = c + 2$ (ix) $a \gg b \gg c$
(v) $a = b \gg c$

One case for which the associative law breaks down is (ii) since in that case

$(a * b) * c = \overline{(c + 1} * c) * c = \overline{c + 1} * c = c + 1$ and
$a * (b * c) = \overline{c + 1} * (\overline{c + 1} * c) = \overline{c + 1} * \overline{c + 1} = c + 2$

It is left to the reader to determine for which other cases the associative law does not apply. The result of this is that under this system the order in which three streams combine affects the outcome. For example if a third and a second order stream combine and then another second order stream joins, the result is a third order stream. If, however, the two second order streams join before the third order stream is added, the result is a fourth order stream. Dalton et al, 1973, pp. 50-1 illustrate an example of this and it is clearly a weakness of the system. In addition, there is no neutral element. The element 1 works except in the case $1 * 1 = 2$, in all other cases $a * 1 = 1 * a = a$. Unless we consider streams separating as well as joining, we cannot introduce an inverse element either.

30.7. Scheidegger's postulates for a consistent system

Haggett and Chorley give Scheidegger's four postulates for a consistent stream ordering system. These are:

(A) $a * a = a + 1$ (cf. Strahler)
(B) $[a * (a - 1)] * (a - 1) = a * [(a - 1) * (a - 1)]$
      (a particular case of the distributive law)
(C) $a * b = b * a$ (the commutative law)
(D) $a * (a - 1) * (a - 1) = a + 1$

This fourth postulate is redundant since

$$\begin{aligned} a * (a - 1) * (a - 1) &= a * [(a - 1) * (a - 1)] & \text{by B} \\ &= a * a & \text{by A} \\ &= a + 1 & \text{by A} \end{aligned}$$

Strahler's system obeys only A and C; if we want a system in which B works, we must abandon the parts of the law of combination which use $a * b = a$ for $a > b$ and $a * b = b$ for $b > a$.

The clue as to how this can be done lies in the postulate $a * a = a + 1$, and we must cast about for a mathematical rule which mirrors this. It turns out that a suitable rule is provided by the sequence

$$2^1 + 2^1 = 2^2$$
$$2^2 + 2^2 = 2^3$$
$$2^3 + 2^3 = 2^4$$
$$\cdots\cdots\cdots$$

The general form of this is $2^a + 2^a = 2^{a+1}$, which we can re-express as

$$a * a = \log_2 (2^a + 2^a) = \log_2 (2^{a+1}) = a + 1$$

(noting that the logarithms are to the unusual base 2), and extend it to cover two different elements a and b:

$$a * b = \log_2 (2^a + 2^b)$$

This obeys commutatitve and associative laws, but there is no neutral element and hence no inverse elements (a neutral element would have to be minus infinity).

Combinations can now be worked out as follows:

$$1 * 2 = \log_2 (2^1 + 2^2) = \log_2 6 = \log_{10} 6 \div \log_{10} 2$$
$$= 0.7782 \div 0.3010 = 2.585$$

	1	2	2.58	3	3.32	3.58	3.81	4
1	2	2.58	3	3.32	3.58	3.81	4	4.17
2	2.58	3	3.32	3.58	3.81	4	4.17	4.32
2.58	3	3.32	3.58	3.81	4	4.17	4.32	4.46
3	3.32	3.58	3.81	4	4.17	4.32	4.46	4.58
3.32	3.58	3.81	4	4.17	4.32	4.46	4.58	4.70
3.58	3.81	4	4.17	4.32	4.46	4.58	4.70	4.81
3.81	4	4.17	4.32	4.46	4.58	4.70	4.81	4.91
4	4.17	4.32	4.46	4.58	4.70	4.81	4.91	5

Table 30.1. Combination table for Scheidegger's system of stream classification (values of tributary streams up to 4 only).

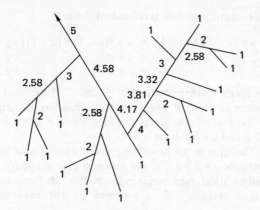

Figure 30.7. Scheidegger's system of classification for R. Glaven.

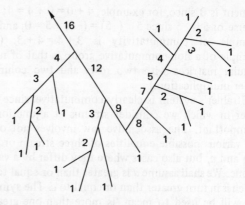

Figure 30.8. Shreve's system of classification for R. Glaven.

If every head-stream has unit value, only certain numbers can be obtained, and combinations of these up to the value 4 are shown in table 30.1, the numbers in this table are in fact logarithms to base 2 of even numbers. We have now evolved Scheidegger's system which is illustrated in figure 30.7. While this is mathematically satisfying, geographically it is cumbersome; the essential simplicity of Strahler's system is lost.

30.8. Shreve's system of stream ordering

The decimals in Scheidegger's system can be avoided by numbering each head stream one and adding at the junctions. This is Shreve's system illustrated in figure 30.8. While simple, this results in quite small streams having high orders, a situation from which there is no escape without approximation. If the numbers in Shreve's system are doubled, and then logarithms to base 2 taken, then Scheidegger's system is obtained.

30.9. Bifurcation ratio

Using Strahler's system of ordering, the bifurcation ratio is defined to be the number of streams of one order divided by the number of streams of the next higher order. In our example there are 16 first order streams, 4 second order streams and 1 third order stream (consecutive stretches of the same order are counted only once each). This gives bifurcation ratios of $16 \div 4 = 4$ and $4 \div 1 = 4$, which happen to be equal in this case. When they are unequal it is usual to average them to find a value for the system.

Figure 30.9 illustrates this using the basin of Griswold Creek, California, which has 58 first order,

12 second order, 2 third order and 1 fourth order streams. The bifurcation ratio is

$$\frac{1}{3}\left(\frac{58}{12} + \frac{12}{2} + \frac{2}{1}\right) = \frac{1}{3}(4.83 + 6 + 2) = 4.28$$

The process of averaging ratios is questionable on mathematical grounds, but has some geographical justification as it lends equal weights to both the small number of larger streams and the many smaller streams.

It is interesting to note that if the geometric mean were used, as would be mathematically correct, then the formula would be

$$\sqrt[3]{\left(\frac{58}{12} \times \frac{12}{2} \times \frac{2}{1}\right)} = \sqrt[3]{58} = 3.87$$

This is very simply determined; if n is the highest order stream, then it is the $(n-1)$th root of the number of first order streams.

When using the arithmetic mean, the bifurcation ratio cannot be less than two, and a high value is seven. High values tend to indicate a liability to flood since feeders discharge into a relatively short length of main stream.

30.10. Woldenberg's system of stream ordering

The final system of ordering is based on Shreve's system and is due to Woldenberg. If M is the order on Shreve's system, the order on Woldenberg's system is given by

$$W = \frac{\log_{10}M}{\log_{10}R_b} + 1$$

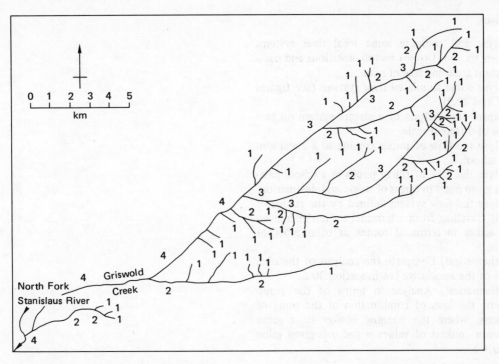

Figure 30.9. Strahler's system for basin of Griswold Creek, Tolumne County, ESE of Sacramento, California.

where R_b is the bifurcation ratio. This quantity W is, of course, not a whole number. The orders of streams in the Glaven system are shown in figure 30.10. For the Griswold Creek system, the order of the lowest stretch of the Creek on Shreve's system is 58 (i.e. the number of first order streams). On Woldenberg's system the order is

$$\frac{\log_{10} 58}{\log_{10} 4.28} + 1 = \frac{1.76}{0.63} + 1 = 2.79 + 1 = 3.79$$

The orders of streams on Woldenberg's system are, in fact, approximated to by the orders on Strahler's system; and tend to be related closely to the amount of discharge observed in practice. Geographers, however, have favoured Strahler's system because of its simplicity.

30.11. Conclusion

While the ordering systems described above do not constitute mathematical groups, they illustrate some properties of group structure. The ideas could be extended if sinks as well as sources occurred in the system. For example, stream ordering systems could be applied to roads feeding an important bridge, the distributary roads beyond the bridge being regarded

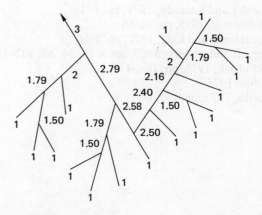

Figure 30.10. Woldenberg's system of classification for R. Glaven.

as sinks. The actual number of cars using any stretch would be its order on Shreve's system. The analysis of stream systems can be developed further as in section 5.11. Other quantities which can be used are the lengths of various orders of stream and the density of streams as discussed in section 28.12. For further details, consult the references below.

Models

Exercises

1. Analyse and compare some local river systems known to you. Do not be too ambitious and use a constant scale and size of map.
2. Analyse some simulated river systems (see figures 22.7 and 22.9).
3. Compare the analysis of a stream system on two maps of different scale.
4. Analyse the flow of pupils coming to a classroom in a school.
5. Analyse the flow of thirty pupils in a school passing a given point in terms of origin and destination.
6. Analyse the flow system defined by the routes of trains travelling from a terminal station on a given day either in terms of routes or of number of trains.
7. (Mathematical) Complete the analysis of the nine cases of the associative law in section 30.6.
8. (Mathematical) Analyse in terms of the group axioms the laws of combination of the game of conkers, where the winning conker of a game between conkers of values p and q is given value $p + q + 1$.

Further reading

Chorley, 1969, pp. 78–85
Chorley and Kennedy, 1971, pp. 1–4
Dalton et al, 1973, pp. 36–56
Doornkamp and King, 1971, pp. 3–16
Haggett and Chorley, 1969, pp. 8–25, 74–82, 302–12
McCullagh, 1978, pp. 16–34
Robin, 1976
Sparks, 1972, pp. 157–60

Bibliography

Abler, R., Adams, J.S. and Gould, P. *Spatial Organisation,* London: Prentice Hall, 1972.

Bale, J. *The Location of Manufacturing Industry.* Edinburgh: Oliver and Boyd, 1976.

Bale, J., Graves, N. and Walford, R. (Eds.) *Perspectives in Geographical Education.* Edinburgh: Oliver and Boyd, 1973.

Berry, B.J.L. and Marble, D.F. (Eds.) *Spatial Analysis, a Reader in Statistical Geography.* Englewood Cliffs, New Jersey: Prentice Hall, 1968.

Bilham, E.G. *The Climate of the British Isles.* London: Macmillan, 1938.

Birch, T.W. *Maps.* London: Oxford University Press, 1949.

Blair, D.J. and Biss, T.H. The measurement of shape in geography: an appraisal of methods and techniques. *Bulletin of Quantitative Data for Geographers.* September 1967.

Bradford, M.G. and Kent, W.A. *Human Geography – Theories and their Applications,* Science in Geography 5. London: Oxford University Press, 1977.

Bradshaw. *Bradshaw's August 1887 Railway Guide,* new edition. Newton Abbot: David and Charles, 1968a.

Bradshaw. *Bradshaw's July 1938 Railway Guide,* new edition. Newton Abbot: David and Charles, 1968b.

Bradshaw. *Bradshaw's April 1910 Railway Guide,* new edition. Newton Abbot: David and Charles, 1969.

Briggs, K. *Introducing Transportation Networks.* London: University of London Press, 1972.

Briggs, K. *Introducing Towns and Cities.* London: University of London Press, 1974.

Buchanan, C. *Traffic in Towns,* a shortened edition of the Buchanan Report. Harmondsworth: Penguin, 1964.

Chapallaz, D.P., Davis, P.F., Fitzgerald, B.P., Grenyer, N., Rolfe, J. and Walker, D.R.F. *Hypothesis Testing in Field Studies,* Teaching Geography no. 11. Sheffield: Geographical Association, 1970.

Chorley, R.J. (Ed.) *Water, Earth and Man.* London: Methuen, 1969.

Chorley, R.J. and Haggett, P. (Eds.) *Models in Geography,* the Madingley Lectures for 1965. London: Methuen, 1967.

Chorley, R.J. and Kennedy, B.A. *Physical Geography: A Systems Approach.* Englewood Cliffs, New Jersey: Prentice Hall, 1971.

Christaller, W. *Central Places in Southern Germany.* Englewood Cliffs, New Jersey: Prentice Hall, 1966.

Clark, P.J. and Evans, F.C. Distance to nearest neighbour as a measure of spatial relationships in populations. *Ecology* 35, pp.445-53, 1954.

Cole, J.P. The diffusion business, *Ideas in Geography* 23, Nottingham University, 1969a.

Cole, J.P. Mathematics and Geography. *Geography* 54, part 2, pp.152-64, April 1969 (reprinted in Bale et al, 1973, pp.222-38), 1969b.

Cole, J.P. and Beynon, N.J. *New Ways in Geography, Vol. 1.* Oxford: Basil Blackwell, 1968a.

Cole, J.P. and Beynon, N.J. *New Ways in Geography, Vol. 2.* Oxford: Basil Blackwell, 1968b.

Cole, J.P. and Beynon, N.J. *New Ways in Geography, Vol. 3.* Oxford: Basil Blackwell, 1972.

Cole, J.P. and King, C.A.M. *Quantitative Geography.* London: Wiley, 1968.

Commission of European Communities. *The European Community in Maps.* Brussels: the Commission, 1974.

Continuing Mathematics Project. *Nearest Neighbour Analysis.* York: Longman for the Schools Council, 1977a.

Continuing Mathematics Project. *The Rank Size Rule.* York: Longman for the Schools Council, 1977b.

Continuing Mathematics Project. *Network Analysis.* York: Longman for the Schools Council, 1977c.

Continuing Mathematics Project. *The Gravity Model.* York: Longman for the School Council, 1977d.

Cook, I. Unbiased dartboards and biased calculators. *Mathematical Gazette* 61, pp.187-91, 1977.

Coulson, C.A. Presidential address: Mathematics and the real world. *Institute of Mathematics and its Applications Bulletin* 9, pp.2-7, 1973.

Courant, R. and Robbins, H. *What is Mathematics?* London: Oxford University Press, 1941.

Coxeter, H.S.M. *Introduction to Geometry.* New York: Wiley, 1961.

Dacey, M.F. The spacing of river towns. *Annals of the Association of American Geographers* 50, pp.59-61, 1960.

Dalton, R., Garlick, J., Minshull, R. and Robinson, A. *Networks in Geography.* London: Geo. Philip and Son, 1973.

Dalton, R., Minshull, R., Robinson, A. and Garlick, J. *Simulation Games in Geography.* Basingstoke: Macmillan Education, 1972.

Daugherty, R. *Data Collection,* Science in Geography 2, London: Oxford University Press, 1974.

Davis, P. *Data Description and Presentation,* Science in Geography 3. London: Oxford University Press, 1974.

Dawson, A.H. Are geographers engaging in a landscape lottery? *Area* 7, pp.42-5, 1975.

Debenham, F. *Map Making,* 3rd edn. London: Blackie, 1954.

Bibliography

Department of Transport/Scottish Development Department/ Welsh Office. *Transport Statistics for Great Britain 1966-76.* London: HMSO, 1978.

Dickinson, G.C. *Statistical Mapping and the Presentation of Statistics.* London: Edw. Arnold, 1973.

Dinkele, G., Cotterell, S. and Thorn, I. *Introduction to Reformed Geography,* London: Harrap, 1976a.

Dinkele, G., Cotterell, S. and Thorn, I. *Farming.* London: Harrap, 1976b.

Dinkele, G., Cotterell, S. and Thorn, I. *Manufacturing.* London: Harrap, 1976c.

Dinkele, G., Cotterell, S. and Thorn, I. *Transport.* London: Harrap, 1976d.

Dinkele, G., Cotterell, S. and Thorn, I. *Settlement and Services.* London: Harrap, 1976e.

Doornkamp, J.C. and King, C.A.M. *Numerical Analysis in Geomorphology.* London: Edw. Arnold, 1971.

Dudley, B.A.C. *Mathematical and Biological Interrelations.* Chichester: John Wiley, 1977.

Durell, C.V. *A New Geometry for Schools.* London: Bell, 1939.

Everson, J.A. and Fitzgerald, B.P. *Settlement Patterns.* London: Longman, 1969.

Fitzgerald, B.P. *Developments in Geographical Method,* Science in Geography 1. London: Oxford University Press, 1974.

Gardner, M. Mathematical games. *Scientific American* 223, no. 4, pp.120-23, October 1970.

Gardner, M. Mathematical games. *Scientific American* 224, no. 2, pp.112-17, February 1971.

Gibbs, J.P. (Ed.) *Urban Research Methods.* Princeton, New Jersey: Van Nostrand, 1961.

Gould, P. and White, R. *Mental Maps.* Harmondsworth: Penguin, 1974.

Graves, N.J. and Talbot White, J. *Geography of the British Isles,* 3rd edn. London: Heinemann Educational, 1974.

Gregory, S. *Statistical Methods and the Geographer,* 3rd edn. London: Longman, 1975.

Guest, A. *Advanced Practical Geography,* 4th edn. London: Heinemann, 1975.

Haggett, P. *Geography: A Modern Synthesis.* New York: Harper and Row, 1972.

Haggett, P. and Chorley, R.J. *Network Analysis in Geography.* London: Edw. Arnold, 1969.

Haggett, P., Cliff, A.D. and Frey, A. *Locational Analysis in Human Geography,* 2nd edn. London: Edw. Arnold, 1977.

Hammond, R. and McCullagh, P.S. *Quantitative Techniques in Geography.* London: Oxford University Press, 1974.

Hanwell, J. and Newson, M. *Techniques in Physical Geography.* London: Macmillan, 1973.

Harley, J.B. *Ordnance Survey Maps: A Descriptive Manual.* Southampton: Ordnance Surrey, 1975.

Hay, A. *Transport for the Space Economy,* London: Macmillan, 1973.

Holt, M. and Marjoram, D.T.E. *Mathematics in a Changing World.* London: Heinemann Educational, 1973.

Horton, R.E. Drainage basin characteristics. *Transactions of the American Geophysical Union* 13, pp.350-61, 1932.

Howling, P.H. and Hunter, L.A. *Mapping Skills and Techniques: A Quantitative Approach.* Edinburgh: Oliver and Boyd, 1975.

Huff, D. *How to Lie with Statistics,* revised issue, Harmondsworth: Penguin, 1973.

Hurst, M.E.L. (Ed.) *Transportation Geography.* New York: McGraw-Hill, 1974.

Institut National de la Statistique et des Etudes Economique. *Annuaire Statistique de la France.* Paris: the Institut, 1977.

Jordan, T.G. *The European Culture Area.* New York: Harper and Row, 1973.

Kansky, K.J. *Structure of Transportation Networks.* Chicago: Chicago University Press, 1963.

Kent, W.A. and Moore, K.R. *An Approach to Fieldwork in Geomorphology, the Example of North Norfolk,* Teaching Geography no. 20. Sheffield: Geographical Association, 1974.

King, C.A.M. Mathematics in geography. *International Journal of Mathematics in Education, Science and Technology* 1, pp.185-205, 1970.

King, L.J. *Statistical Analysis in Geography.* Englewood Cliffs, New Jersey: Prentice Hall, 1969.

Krause, E.F. *Taxi-cab Geometry.* Reading, Massachusetts: Addison-Wesley, 1975

Lighthill, J. (Ed.) *Newer Uses of Mathematics.* Harmondsworth: Penguin, 1978.

Ling, J. *Mathematics Across the Curriculum.* Glasgow: Blackie, 1977.

Lloyd, P.E. and Dicken, P. *Location in Space: A Theoretical Approach to Economic Geography,* 2nd edn. New York: Harper and Row, 1977.

Lösch, A. *The Economics of Location.* New Haven: Yale University Press, 1954.

McCullagh, P. *Data Use and Interpretation,* Science in Geography 4. London: Oxford University Press, 1974.

McCullagh, P. *Modern Concepts in Geomorphology,* Science in Geography 6. London: Oxford University Press, 1978.

March, L. and Steadman, P. *The Geometry of the Environment.* London: Methuen, 1974.

Mathematics for the Majority. *Crossing Subject Boundaries.* London: Chatto and Windus Educational for the Schools Council, 1974.

Meyer, I.R. and Huggett, R.J. *Settlements,* Geography: Theory in Practice 1. London: Harper and Row, 1979.

Miller, V.C. A quantitative geomorphic study of drainage basin shape characteristics in the Clinch Mountain area, Virginia and Tennessee. *Department of Geology Technical Report,* no. 3. New York: Columbia University, 1953.

Monkhouse, F.J. and Wilkinson, H.R. *Maps and Diagrams,* 3rd edn. London: Methuen, 1971.

Nuffield Chemistry. *Handbook for Teachers.* London/Harmondsworth: Longman/Penguin for the Schools Council, 1967.

Oxford Geography Project (Kent, A. et al). *1. The Local Framework.* London: Oxford University Press, 1974a.

Oxford Geography Project (Rowe, C. et al). *2. European Patterns.* London: Oxford University Press, 1974b.

Oxford Geography Project (Grenyer, N. et al). *3. Contrasts in Development*. London: Oxford University Press, 1975.

Pearson, E.S. Comparison of tests for randomness of points on a line. *Biometrika* 50, pp.315–23, 1963.

Pinder, D.A. and Witherick, M.E. The principles, practice and pitfalls of nearest neighbour analysis. *Geography* 57, pp. 277–88, 1972.

Pinder, D.A. and Witherick, M.E. Correction to above. *Geography* 58, p.174, 1973.

Pinder, D.A. and Witherick, M.E. A modification of nearest neighbour analysis for use in linear situations. *Geography* 60, pp.16–23, 1975.

Poole, J. Mapping the political power lines. *Sunday Times*, London, 5 December 1976.

Prescott, J.R.V. *The Geography of Frontiers and Boundaries*. London: Hutchinson, 1965.

Reader's Digest Complete Atlas of the British Isles, London: Reader's Digest Association, no date.

Reichmann, W.J. *The Use and Abuse of Statistics*. London: Methuen, 1961.

Robin, A.C. The shortest distance between two points. *Mathematics Teaching* 75, pp.27–9, June 1976.

School Mathematics Project. *Book 1*. London: Cambridge University Press, 1965.

Schools Council Geography Committee. *Understanding Maps: A Guide to Initial Learning*. London: Schools Council, 1979.

Schumm, S.A. The evolution of drainage systems and slopes in badlands at Perth Amboy, New Jersey. *Bulletin of the Geological Society of America* 67, pp.597–646, 1956.

Selkirk, K.E. Random models in the classroom. Parts 1–3. *Mathematics in School*, 2:6, 3:1, 3:2, 1973–4.

Selkirk, K.E. Re-designing the dartboard. *Mathematical Gazette* 60, pp.171–8, 1976a.

Selkirk, K.E. A mathematician looks at geography. *Profile* 9, no. 25, pp.7–14, November 1976b.

Sherlock, A. and Brand, T. Venn diagrams must go? Parts 1 and 2. *Mathematics Teaching* 60, 61; September 1972, December 1972.

Smith, D.M. *Patterns in Human Geography*. Newton Abbot: David and Charles, 1975.

Smith, G.A. and Cole, J.P., Geographical games. *Bulletin of Quantitative Data for Geographers*, 7, 1969.

Sparks, B.W. *Geomorphology*, 2nd edn. London: Longman, 1972.

Sumner, G.N. *Mathematics for Physical Geographers*. London: Edw. Arnold, 1978.

Taylor, J.L. and Walford, R. *Simulation in the Classroom*. Harmondsworth: Penguin Education, 1972.

Theakstone, W.H. and Harrison, C. *The Analysis of Geographical Data*. London: Heinemann Educational, 1970.

Thom, A. *Megalithic Sites in Britain*. London: Oxford University Press, 1967.

Tidswell, V. *Pattern and Process in Human Geography*. London: University Tutorial Press, 1976.

Tolley, H. (Ed.) *Transport Networks, Teacher's Notes*, Schools Council Geography 14–18 Project. Basingstoke: Macmillan Education for the Schools Council, 1978.

Truran, H.C. *A Practical Guide to Statistical Maps and Diagrams*. London: Heinemann Educational, 1975.

Walker, E.A. *Location and Links, Book 1*. Oxford: Basil Blackwell, 1972.

Walker, M.J. *Location and Links, Book 2, Farming*. Oxford: Basil Blackwell, 1973a.

Walker, M.J. *Location and Links, Book 5, Environmental Problems*. Oxford: Basil Blackwell, 1973b.

Watts, D.G. *Railway Rivals*. Milford Haven: D.G. Watts, 32 Eastleigh Drive, 1973.

Wilson, A.G. and Kirkby, M.J. *Mathematics for Geographers and Planners*. Oxford: Clarendon Press, 1975.

Wilson, R.J. *Introduction to Graph Theory*. Edinburgh: Oliver and Boyd, 1972.

Wilson, T. *Location and Links, Book 3, Industry and Communications*. Oxford: Basil Blackwell, 1973a.

Wilson, T. *Location and Links, Book 4, Settlement*. Oxford: Basil Blackwell, 1973b.

Index

Index

Index